ANCIENT STRATEGIES

Lessons for the Modern Leader

ANCIENT STRATEGIES

Lessons for the Modern Leader

Brigadier Nick Sawyer

PENTAGON PRESS LLP

First published in 2024 by
PENTAGON PRESS LLP
206, Peacock Lane, Shahpur Jat
New Delhi-110049, India
Contact: 011-64706243

Typeset in New Times Roman, 11.5 Point
Printed by Aegean Offset Printers, Greater Noida

ISBN 978-81

Disclaimer: The views and opinions expressed in the book is the individual assertion of the Author. The Publisher does not take any responsibility for the same in any manner whatsoever. The same shall solely be the responsibility of the Author.

www.pentagonpress.in

Contents

Introduction

Strategy seeks to gain exploitable windows of competitive advantage in an adversarial, complex, changing, confusing and contradictory environment on a journey to protect critical interests or seek a specific outcome. In this regard, strategy is no different today than it was thousands of years ago. Furthermore, the human brain is the same today as it was in ancient times and is subject to the same emotions, cognitive errors, bias, and prejudice as our ancestors. However, the ancients did not have to concern themselves with technology, social media, the Westphalian system, or international law. The strategies they adopted were focussed on people and could be considered a 'pure' approach to complex problems. Strategy and complex problems are always ultimately about people, so this pure approach articulated by historical figures is worthy of deep analysis. The bottom line is that ancient philosophies and not only remain pertinent today, but also offer a deeper insight into the human aspects of strategy than perhaps some more contemporary works.

Unfortunately, the ancient texts make difficult reading even when translated and contextualised from their original languages. There also seems to be a view that simply skimming the texts or memorising clever quotes will somehow bestow deep knowledge upon the reader. No doubt, for a small number of natural geniuses out there this is the case, but, for the majority of us, an intermediate step is required that creates a pragmatic and useable doctrine from the ancient texts. This intermediate step has been missing for thousands of years. The aim of this book is therefore to address this shortfall and provide a series of strategic guides, handrails, toolsets, and methodologies for the modern world but based on ancient wisdom.

Good strategy requires three key elements. First and foremost is a leader with a strategic mindset. Strategic mindsets need to be created and nurtured, they are not something we are born with. Creating and developing a strategic mindset is therefore of critical importance and it should come as no surprise that many ancient philosophers and strategists concentrated on this aspect in their works.

Once a leader has developed a strategic mindset, then a strategic approach must be adopted when in a position of authority and attendant legitimacy. A strategic approach sits above individual strategies and provides the underlying 'tradecraft' that allows a leadership team to develop and implement effective strategies to address specific issues.

Even with the right mindset and approach, strategic toolsets are still essential for developing and implementing a strategy to tackle a specific complex problem. Each of these three areas (mindset, approach, and toolsets) requires a different learning and development methodology.

Part 1 of this book is about creating a strategic mindset and is based on the works of Miyamoto Musashi from Japan and the Indian epic, the *Mahabharata*. Musashi was a ronin warrior from 17th Century Japan who was known for his expertise in duels. He wrote the *Book of Five Rings* to record his philosophy on how to create a strategic mindset. His underlying message was that 'strategy' is a way of life and one cannot simply switch it on and off. The *Mahabharata* is an Indian book of political and military events portrayed from different perspectives and is strong on Indian historical traditions. Like Musashi's *Book of Five Rings*, it offers thoughts concerning a strategic outlook on life.

Part 2 looks at adopting a strategic approach within statecraft and explores how to introduce this at the very highest leadership levels within a government or organisation. The sources are Kautilya's *Arthashastra* and the Tamil Sangam *Purananuru* poems. Kautilya (also known as Chanakya) was an ancient Indian philosopher and strategist who lived around 1500 BCE and whose work on statecraft is today reawakening cultural discussion on the subcontinent about alternatives to the Western systems of diplomacy. The Tamil Sangam poems are far more obscure and poorly studied but have some unique insights into strategic approaches that are worth exploring.

Part 3 is about developing and implementing strategy via toolsets. It uses Sun Tzu's *Art of War* and Julius Caesar's *Commentaries on the Gallic War* as source documents. Sun Tzu needs no introduction as his works are regarded as one of the most important publications on strategy even today. Julius Caesar's records from the Gallic War offer a slightly different approach to strategy that contrasts with Sun Tzu in certain areas.

The astute reader will pick up common themes from all six of the ancient sources and these form the basis of the conclusion where some universal fundamentals are identified and discussed. Finally, there is a quick reference guide on these fundamentals of strategy that the reader can utilise as a 'check list' when faced with a complex problem.

Please note that this book is not a literal translation of the original works. Nor is it a regurgitation of previous interpretations. I have applied my own experiences and knowledge of strategy gleaned over 30 years as a military officer and diplomat and tried to contextualise the ancient lessons into a format and style that is useable today by modern leaders. This book is not an academic study either. There are no footnotes or references, it is simply my personal reflections on what I have learnt from reading the ancient texts.

This work can be read cover-to-cover or utilised as a guide wherein, the reader dips in an out of relevant sections. However, a word of warning! The ancient texts can be quite hard going with multiple rules and directives. This is in sharp contrast to modern strategy and management gurus who adopt a much more simplified approach. There is also a lot or repetition in the individual texts and across the book as a whole. This is actually reassuring as it means there are common themes and points from across the ages.

I would also like to highlight that strategic leadership is the 'golden thread' that weaves through the entire book and underpins mindset, approach and toolsets. Strategic leadership is a wide topic in its own right and not covered in detail within this book, but key leadership themes are clear throughout the ancient texts and are inseparable from the art of strategy.

Finally, it is worth explaining why I omitted certain other famous texts from the analysis. I have tried to utilise texts from before the industrial revolution and before technology significantly impacted statecraft, warfare and conflict. This, I believe, gives a pure human view of strategy. I have also chosen texts that have not been influenced by the modern Westphalian system of nations, states, territories and boundaries. Again, this provides a more human-centric view. There are of course a great many ancient texts that would still be applicable, but I have chosen six that I believe give wide-ranging views and differing perspectives. My four years as a diplomat in India have also perhaps given me an unconscious bias towards ancient texts from the subcontinent. Unconscious bias, as many of the ancient masters highlight, is a leadership weakness that must be addressed, and for this I apologise!

For those eager to get to the heart of the matter, my research has shown that across the ancient texts there are just twelve fundamental core aspects of strategy that stretch across mindset, approach and toolsets. These transcend race, religion, location, historical period and language. They are in essence the soul of strategy. Modern leaders would do well to ensure that any strategy they develop covers each of these critical elements. For ease of reference the twelve vital elements highlighted by the ancients are:

1. Adaptability, flexibility and continual learning.
2. Leadership.
3. Preparation and planning.
4. Deception and psychology.
5. Knowledge.
6. Logistics.
7. Ethics, values and standards.
8. Decisive action, courage and bravery.
9. Diplomacy, partnerships and alliances.
10. Understanding risk.
11. Self-awareness.
12. Innovation and creativity.

However, as the ancient texts articulate in greater detail, there are a myriad of different principles, techniques, rules and guidelines that underpin these fundamentals while the art and science of applying the fundamentals is where the true challenge lies. I hope the presented work provides some guidance and food-for-thought.

Brigadier Nick Sawyer

PART 1

CREATING A STRATEGIC MINDSET

The first essential requirement for successful strategy is for the senior leader to have a strategic mindset. Before any analysis, planning or process can be applied to a complex problem, the strategic leader must be in the right frame of mind. This can take a lifetime to develop as experience counts for a lot. Fortunately, there are two ancient texts that provide frameworks and handrails for creating a strategic mindset that can greatly reduce the time to develop the necessary wisdom and experience to be an expert strategist. In this section we will look at the works of Miyamoto Musashi (Chapter 1) and the Indian epic The *Mahabharata* (Chapter 2). Both can be used to help create the strategic mindset for senior leaders that is so critical for tackling complex problems in the 21st Century.

Chapter One

Miyamoto Musashi

"The path that leads to truth is littered with the bodies of the ignorant."

—Miyamoto Musashi

IN THIS CHAPTER

- A Short Biography of Musashi.
- Musashi's 'Way of Strategy'.
- The Nine Principles.
- The Eleven Techniques.
- Musashi's Strategic Concepts.
- The Five Rings.
- Creating a Strategic Mindset - Musashi's Guide for the Modern Strategist.
- Musashi – A Summary

A Short Biography of Musashi

Miyamoto Musashi was a Japanese warrior and strategist who lived during the early 17th century. He is considered to be one of the greatest swordsmen in Japanese history and is renowned for his martial prowess, strategic insights, and the development of his own distinctive style of combat utilising two swords. He was born in 1584 in Harima Province, Japan. Little is known about his early life, but it is believed that he initiated training in the martial arts as a toddler. Musashi became a skilled samurai (actually a ronin as he did not serve a single lord) and engaged in numerous duels. He is said to have fought over 60 duels (his first at the age of 13) killing 17 men without a single loss, earning him a reputation as an invincible swordsman.

Musashi was not only a swordsman but also a prolific writer. He authored "Gorin no Sho" (*The Book of Five Rings*), a classic treatise on strategy, tactics, and philosophy. The tome encompasses Musashi's insights into martial arts, strategy, and the way of the warrior. His teachings on strategy and philosophy have influenced not only martial artists but also individuals in various fields, including business, leadership, and personal development. He also wrote the *Dokkodo* (The Way of Walking Alone) the week before he died and there are many lessons in this work as well. Miyamoto Musashi remains an iconic figure in Japanese history, celebrated for his martial achievements, strategic insights, and the timeless wisdom found in his writings.

Musashi's *The Book of Five Rings* and *The Way of Walking Alone* are classics that offer profound insights into strategy and the mindset and outlook required for success. His key overarching strategic concept is that one cannot simply switch a strategic mindset on or off. It must be an outlook and state of mind that is all pervading. In essence, he offers a guide to a way of life that embraces strategic thinking, adaptability, and a deep understanding of the fundamentals. It encourages a practitioner to integrate these principles into their daily existence, fostering wisdom in decision-making. The strategic mind, according to Musashi, should be adaptable and able to navigate any situation. Before we look in detail at Musashi's Five Rings, it is necessary to understand his principles, techniques, and concepts, or what he describes as "The Way of Strategy."

Musashi's "Way of Strategy"

Although Musashi is most well-known for describing five rings that he named Earth (*Chi*), Water (*Sui*), Fire (*Ka*), Wind (*Fu*), and Void (*Ku*), he based these on certain foundation principles, techniques, and concepts. Musashi articulated the successful achievement of his teachings as the 'Way of Strategy' with the Five Rings as the method of application. Before we look at the Five Rings that are necessary to achieve a strategic mindset, it is first pertinent to look at his underlying thoughts. Ultimately, Musashi said strategy is about 'overcoming people' and therefore the Way of Strategy and its foundational principles, techniques, and concepts are largely focussed on the mind of the warrior and their adversaries.

Musashi's Nine Principles

In his writing, Musashi elaborates upon nine distinct principles that are essential for 'The Way of Strategy'. This is a literal translation from the original Japanese of the day, but in modern terms it simply means thinking strategically or having a strategic mindset. The original order of the nine principles was a little odd in my view, so I have rearranged them to place them in a more logical manner for anyone attempting to adopt Musashi's teachings. There are also multiple different and often conflicting translations, but I have mainly used those provided by the Samurai Museum, Kyoto and contextualised them for the strategist of today. The nine principles, as I understand them, from a strategic point of view are:

1. **Be Self Aware**. For Musashi, being self-aware involves understanding one's own strengths, weaknesses, and abilities, as well as one's own mindset and emotions. It also includes having an awareness of how one is perceived by others and how one's actions can influence the outcome of a situation. Staying true to one's personal values, and displaying honesty and integrity are important as well. One of Musashi's greatest quotes is:

"Truth is not what you want it to be; it is what it is..."

Here are some brief aspects of what Musashi meant by being self-aware:

- **Understanding oneself.** Musashi believed in the importance of knowing oneself, including one's capabilities and limitations. This understanding allows a person to make strategic decisions that play to their strengths and mitigate their weaknesses. Brutally honest self-reflection is a necessity.

- **Controlling emotions.** Musashi stressed the need to maintain control over one's emotions during combat and decision-making. Being aware of one's emotional state can prevent impulsive or reckless actions. It is essential that strategists understand their emotions, what causes them to change, and what effect this has on their mental state and decision-making. Most importantly, strategists need to develop coping mechanisms for dealing with emotional trigger events.
- **Being mindful of one's surroundings.** Self-awareness also involves being conscious of the environment, the opponent, colleagues, and the situation at hand. This situational awareness allows for better decision-making and adaptability. Strategists must have empathy and be able to put themselves in the shoes of others.
- **Continual self-improvement.** Musashi stressed the importance of continuous learning and growth. By being self-aware, individuals can identify areas for improvement and strive to refine their skills and knowledge. Strategists must learn quickly and adapt. This requires humility and an open mind.
- **Remaining calm and composed.** Self-awareness sustains a clear mind in stressful situations, enabling individuals to think rationally and respond effectively.

Overall, Musashi's concept of being self-aware encompasses understanding oneself, the adversary, one's environment, one's own team, and one's impact on the world around them. This awareness is crucial for achieving mastery in any discipline, not just the martial arts.

2. **Never Stop Developing and Improving your Strategic Mindset**. Musashi's second principle was the necessity of being a life-long learner. It is simply not possible to achieve a perfect strategic mindset, and one must continually seek to develop and improve.

When Miyamoto Musashi said "never stop developing and improving," he was emphasising and stressing the importance of continuous learning and self-improvement in both martial arts and life in general. This principle is foundational to his philosophy of mastery and excellence. Here are some key aspects of what Musashi meant by never stopping development and improvement:

- **Pursuing lifelong learning.** Musashi believed that learning should be an ongoing process throughout one's life. He encouraged individuals to constantly seek new knowledge, skills, and experiences that contribute to personal and professional growth.
- **Reflecting on experiences.** Continuous improvement involves reflecting on one's successes and failures, learning from them, and applying those lessons to future endeavours. This process helps individuals refine their skills and strategies.
- **Embracing humility.** Musashi's teaching implies an attitude of humility and openness to growth. By acknowledging that there is always room for improvement, individuals can stay motivated to continue learning and refining their abilities.
- **Challenging oneself.** Musashi encouraged pushing oneself beyond one's comfort zone and striving for excellence. This involves taking on new challenges and opportunities for growth.
- **Adapting to change.** The world is constantly changing, and Musashi believed in adapting to new circumstances and evolving with the times. Being open to change and innovation is key to continuous improvement.
- **Staying curious and inquisitive.** Musashi's teaching encourages a curious and inquisitive mindset, constantly seeking to learn from different sources and experiences.
- **Applying lessons across disciplines.** Musashi believed in drawing lessons from a wide range of realms and applying them to one's own discipline. This cross-disciplinary approach can lead to new insights and advancements.

Musashi's principle of never stopping development and improvement encourages individuals to pursue continuous growth and self-betterment. By embracing lifelong learning and constantly striving for excellence, individuals can achieve mastery and fulfilment in their chosen paths.

3. **Adopt a Strategic Mindset at all Times**. Perhaps Musashi's most philosophical principle was his perception that a strategic mindset cannot simply be switched on and off. One has to live with a strategic mindset at all times and use it in all pursuits. When Miyamoto Musashi said to "adopt a strategic mindset at all times," he was emphasising the importance of approaching every situation with a focus on strategy and long-term objectives. This principle extends beyond just combat or duels and applies to all aspects of life. It involves thinking ahead, assessing risks and opportunities, and making decisions that contribute to overall goals. Musashi advocated for his students to study other arts and to be able to 'create beauty' in order to adopt a strategic mindset at all times. Here are some key aspects of what Musashi meant:

- **Thinking ahead.** Musashi believed in planning and considering the future consequences of actions. This involves anticipating potential outcomes and making decisions that align with one's goals. This should apply to all aspects of one's life and not just professional careers.
- **Evaluating risks and opportunities.** A strategic mindset involves weighing the potential risks and benefits of a given course of action. By doing so, individuals can make informed decisions that optimise their chances of success.
- **Adapting to changing circumstances.** A strategic mindset includes the ability to adapt to new information and changing circumstances. Musashi believed in being flexible and open to adjusting plans as needed.
- **Using deception and misdirection.** In combat and other areas, strategic thinking often involves the use of deception or misdirection to confuse or outmanoeuvre opponents. Musashi was skilled at using such tactics to gain an advantage.
- **Focusing on long-term objectives.** Musashi focused on long-term goals rather than just immediate outcomes. This perspective helps guide decision-making in a way that aligns with one's overall vision.
- **Learning from experience.** Adopting a strategic mindset means continuously learning from one's experiences and refining strategies

over time. This process of reflection and improvement is key to achieving mastery.

- **Being patient and disciplined.** Strategic thinking requires patience and discipline, as it may involve waiting for the right moment to act or avoiding impulsive decisions.
- **Understanding the opponent and environment.** Musashi pinpointed the importance of knowing one's opponent and the environment in order to make strategic decisions that exploit weaknesses and capitalise on strengths.

Musashi's recommendation to adopt a strategic mindset at all times encourages individuals to approach every situation with thoughtful planning, patience, and adaptability. By focusing on long-term goals and evaluating risks and opportunities, individuals can make decisions that lead to greater success and mastery in any field. He also strongly advised strategists to study other arts so strategy could be practiced in many different settings.

4. **Know a Lot about Many Things**. Put simply, Musashi advocated for reading widely about many topics. He was strongly of the view that it was essential to understand and know 'the way of all professions'. That was of course a little easier in ancient Japan as it was pre-industrial, but this principle is very much valid today. Strategists must have a wide knowledge base so they can transfer skills and experience from 'out of sector' as this have proven to be essential for good strategy. Similarly, historical studies allow the learning of key lessons (good and bad) from strategies that have been tried before.

Miyamoto Musashi's concept of "knowing the way of all professions" is a central theme in his book *The Book of Five Rings*. Musashi believed that to achieve mastery in any discipline, one must understand the underlying principles and philosophies that guide various professions and arts. This approach can lead to a deeper understanding of one's own discipline and enable the application of insights from other fields to improve performance. Here's what Musashi meant by 'knowing the way of all professions':

- **Understanding universal principles.** Musashi believed that the core principles that lead to mastery are consistent across different fields. By understanding these universal principles, such as strategy, timing, and adaptability, one can apply them effectively in any profession.

- **Drawing parallels between disciplines.** Musashi encouraged finding connections and similarities between different professions. For example, the principles of timing and distance in martial arts can also be applied to other areas like negotiation in business or diplomacy.
- **Broadening perspectives.** By studying other professions and arts, individuals can gain new perspectives and insights that may not be immediately apparent within their own field. This broader view can lead to innovative solutions and a more well-rounded approach to one's own discipline.
- **Adapting techniques.** Musashi believed that learning from other professions could provide new techniques and methods that could be adapted to one's own practice. This cross-disciplinary learning can lead to improvements and advancements in any field.
- **Achieving mastery.** Ultimately, Musashi's idea of 'knowing the way of all professions' is about seeking mastery in one's own discipline by drawing knowledge from a wide range of sources. This holistic approach can lead to a more profound and comprehensive understanding of one's craft.

By studying the principles and techniques of various professions, Musashi believed that individuals could become more skilled and versatile practitioners in their own fields. This cross-disciplinary knowledge can contribute to overall personal and professional growth.

5. **Clearly Define What Counts as a Gain and What Counts as a Loss.** Musashi was clear that a cost-benefit analysis was essential when developing a strategy. The strategist must know what is at stake and what constitutes success. This may not necessarily be a clearly defined physical end-state and could well be some sort of perception, feeling or 'honour'. Similarly, the consequences of failure must be understood. The graver these consequences then the more resource and effort should be applied. Musashi was of the view that it was preferable to 'lose an arm rather than take a cut to the neck.'

When Miyamoto Musashi said "know what counts as a gain and know what counts as a loss," he was emphasising the importance of discerning the true value of outcomes in any situation, whether in combat or other aspects of life. This principle involves understanding when to pursue certain actions and when to avoid them, recognising the difference between beneficial and detrimental decisions. Here are some key aspects of what Musashi meant by this statement:

- **Strategic decision-making.** Knowing what counts as a gain or loss requires careful consideration of the long-term and short-term consequences of actions. Musashi emphasised the need to think strategically and prioritise actions that lead to overall success.
- **Evaluating risks and rewards.** Musashi encouraged weighing the potential risks and rewards of a given course of action. Being able to assess whether the potential gain is worth the risk of loss is essential for making informed decisions.
- **Learning from experience.** Understanding what counts as a gain or loss can be informed by past experiences and learning from previous successes and failures. This reflective approach helps individuals make better decisions in the future.
- **Knowing when to yield or retreat.** Sometimes, a gain may not be immediate victory, but rather preserving one's strength or resources for future opportunities. Musashi's teachings suggest knowing when to step back or avoid unnecessary conflict can be a strategic gain.
- **Recognising hidden gains or losses.** Sometimes, an action may seem beneficial at first but could lead to negative consequences later on. Conversely, an immediate loss may bring long-term benefits. Musashi taught the importance of recognising these subtleties.
- **Balancing aggression and caution.** Knowing when to press forward aggressively or hold back cautiously can determine the success or failure of a plan. Musashi believed in finding the right balance between these two approaches.

By understanding what counts as a gain or a loss in various situations, individuals can make better decisions that align with their goals and objectives. This principle is crucial for strategic thinking and achieving success in both combat and other areas of life.

6. **Develop Intuitive Judgment Ability**. Musashi was clear that the complexity and confusion of battle often prevented logical decision-making based on evidence and observation. Sometimes it was necessary to act on intuition, particularly when tempo was required. At the strategic level, decisions often have to be made in an information vacuum or semi-vacuum. When Miyamoto Musashi said to develop "intuitive judgment ability," he was advocating for cultivating a deep, instinctive understanding of situations and making swift, accurate and terse decisions based on that understanding without having to wait for a full information picture. This concept aligns closely with the idea of *mushin*, or "no-mind," which emphasises clear, unencumbered thinking that allows individuals to act spontaneously and effectively. Here are some key aspects of what Musashi meant by developing intuitive judgment ability:

- **Cultivating experience and knowledge.** Intuitive judgment often arises from a foundation of experience and knowledge. Through practice and experience in one's craft, individuals can internalise patterns and nuances, which in turn informs their instincts.
- **Trusting one's instincts.** Musashi encouraged trusting one's instincts and making decisions based on gut feelings when appropriate. This can lead to faster and more effective responses, particularly in high-pressure situations.
- **Understanding the underlying principles.** Developing intuitive judgment ability requires a deep understanding of the underlying principles of one's craft, whether it be martial arts, strategy, or another field. This understanding helps individuals recognise opportunities and risks quickly.
- **Being present in the moment.** Intuitive judgment relies on being fully present and aware of the situation. This mindfulness allows individuals to perceive subtle cues and respond appropriately.
- **Reducing hesitation and overthinking.** Through the development of intuitive judgment, individuals can reduce hesitation and overthinking. This allows for more fluid and natural decision-

making, which can be especially important in fast-paced or dynamic situations.

- **Learning from experience.** Intuitive judgment is also shaped by learning from one's experiences. Reflecting on past successes and failures helps to refine instincts and improve decision-making over time.
- **Balancing rationality and intuition.** While rational analysis is important, Musashi believed in balancing it with intuitive judgment. This combination allows individuals to make decisions that are not only logical but also informed by instinct.

Musashi's teaching to develop intuitive judgment ability encourages individuals to trust their instincts, learn from experience, and remain present in the moment. This leads to quicker, more effective decision-making and can improve performance in both combat and other aspects of life.

7. **Perceptions Matter**. When Miyamoto Musashi said "perceptions matter," he was highlighting the significance of one's awareness and understanding in determining the success of actions, whether in combat or other aspects of life. This principle emphasises the importance of perception in shaping strategy and decision-making. Here are some key aspects of what Musashi meant by this statement:

- **Situational awareness.** Perceptions involve observing and understanding the environment, the opponent, and the context of the situation. By being aware of these factors, individuals can make more informed strategic decisions.
- **Anticipating the opponent.** Perceiving the opponent's movements, intentions, and strategies allows one to anticipate their actions and respond effectively. This can give an individual a significant advantage in combat.
- **Understanding timing and distance.** Perceptions enable one to gauge the optimal timing and distance for engaging the opponent. This understanding is crucial for executing effective attacks and defences.
- **Assessing risk and opportunity.** Perceptions allow individuals to

evaluate risks and opportunities in any given situation. By recognising when to take action and when to hold back, one can make better strategic choices.

- **Recognising patterns and tendencies.** By paying attention to patterns and tendencies in the opponent's behaviour or the situation, one can adapt and adjust strategies accordingly.
- **Mindfulness and presence.** Musashi's emphasis on perceptions also involves being mindful and fully present in the moment. This state of awareness allows one to respond instinctively and fluidly to changing circumstances.
- **Integrating perception and action.** Musashi believed that perceptions and activity are interconnected. Understanding both the situation and the opponent influences how one acts and responds. Therefore, perceptions guide and inform one's actions.

Musashi's statement emphasises the importance of perception in shaping effective activity. By cultivating awareness and understanding, individuals can make better decisions and achieve greater success in combat and other areas of life.

8. **Take Note of Details.** Musashi underlined the importance of mindfulness and paying attention to details in his teachings. When Musashi said to "take note of even the trivial," he likely meant that one should pay attention to every small detail and aspect of life, training, and combat. Here are a few possible meanings and reasons why Musashi may have said this:

- **Attention to Detail.** In both martial arts and life, the smallest detail can often make a significant difference. Whether in a fight or a business negotiation, being aware of even the smallest nuances can lead to an advantage.
- **Holistic Understanding.** Paying attention to every detail allows one to see the bigger picture more clearly. When you observe and understand the smallest elements of a situation, you can better understand how they fit into the whole.
- **Continuous Learning.** Observing and learning from even the smallest things helps to cultivate a mindset of continuous

improvement and humility. There is always something new to learn or observe, even in seemingly trivial matters.

- **Adaptation and Flexibility.** Noticing the small and seemingly insignificant details allows you to adapt more effectively to changes in your environment. This can be critical in both combat and life.
- **Respect for the Process.** Paying attention to the trivial can show respect for the process, whether it is a martial art, craft, or business endeavour. Focusing on details can lead to mastery over time.

In essence, Musashi's teaching encourages mindfulness, precision, and continuous learning in all aspects of life. By paying attention to the small and seemingly insignificant, you can gain a deeper understanding of the world around you and improve your skills.

9. **Do Nothing that is Unnecessary**. Economy of effort is a quintessential principle of war, and many strategists pinpoint this facet as a foundation principle. Musashi was no different and was clear that when duelling, every movement, or lack of movement, must contribute to winning the battle. In Musashi's world there was absolutely no room for wasted effort.

When Miyamoto Musashi said "do nothing that is unnecessary," he was advocating for efficiency and effectiveness in all actions, whether in combat or other aspects of life. This principle is centred around the idea of avoiding waste, distraction, and excess in order to focus on what truly matters and achieve one's goals more directly and successfully. Here are some key aspects of what Musashi meant by this statement:

- **Eliminating wasteful actions.** Musashi encouraged focusing on actions that directly contribute to one's objectives and avoiding those that do not. This includes removing unnecessary movements or techniques in combat that could expose one to danger or waste energy.
- **Streamlining decision-making.** Making clear and concise decisions without unnecessary deliberation or hesitation can lead to more effective outcomes. Musashi's teachings state the importance of acting with purpose and clarity.
- **Focusing on the goal.** By doing nothing unnecessary, individuals

can concentrate their efforts and resources on achieving their goals. This approach helps maintain focus and avoid distractions that can hinder progress.

- **Simplifying strategies.** Complex strategies can sometimes lead to confusion and inefficiency. Musashi advocated for simplicity in planning and execution, ensuring that each action has a clear purpose and contributes to the overall strategy.
- **Improving performance.** By eliminating unnecessary actions, individuals can perform more efficiently and effectively, whether in combat or other areas of life. This can lead to quicker responses and more decisive outcomes.
- **Being mindful of resources.** Musashi's principle of doing nothing unnecessary extends to resource management as well. By conserving resources and using them wisely, individuals can sustain themselves for longer and be better prepared for future challenges.

Overall, Musashi's teaching to "do nothing that is unnecessary" encourages individuals to adopt a minimalist and focused approach in their actions. This can lead to greater efficiency, clarity, and effectiveness in achieving one's goals.

Musashi's Eleven Techniques

In addition to his nine principles, Musashi also wrote about his techniques for fighting. While more akin to martial arts moves, there are nevertheless some valuable strategic lessons to be derived from these techniques.

1. **Invoke Fear**. Musashi's first technique was psychological in nature and mandated the requirement to invoke fear in an adversary and an antagonist. He suggested several methods for achieving this from 'making something small appear big' or by a 'surprise attack on the opponent's flank.' He implied that different methods would be required for different opponents, and it was necessary to truly comprehend an adversary, so their fears were well understood. Musashi believed that exploiting an opponent's fears was essential for victory. Modern leaders must determine what their adversaries fear most and develop plans that target this fear. Contemporary Western theories and toolsets rarely mention the need to invoke fear in adversaries

and therefore this technique advocated by Musashi is well worth considering.

Miyamoto Musashi invoked fear in many of his duels and encounters due to his reputation as an undefeated swordsman and his unpredictable fighting style. One particular example of where Musashi invoked fear was in his duel against Sasaki Kojiro, a renowned swordsman known for his long sword techniques.

Musashi arrived late to the duel, which took place on Ganryu Island in 1612, and used this psychological tactic to unsettle Kojiro. When Musashi did arrive, he was calm and unhurried, contrasting with Kojiro's agitated state. Musashi's reputation as a master strategist and his calm demeanour would have further intensified Kojiro's fear and anxiety before the duel even began. Ultimately, Musashi defeated Kojiro in a single strike, further solidifying his reputation and invoking fear in other swordsmen who would consider challenging him in the future.

A historical example of a leader invoking fear in their adversary to gain strategic advantage is Genghis Khan, the founder of the Mongol Empire. Genghis Khan and his generals used psychological warfare, particularly the strategy of spreading fear and terror among their enemies, as a key tactic in their military campaigns.

During the Mongol invasion of the Khwarezmian Empire, Genghis Khan's army besieged the city of Nishapur. In order to intimidate the defenders and demoralise other cities in the region, the Mongols engaged in extreme brutality. They were known to massacre entire populations of cities that resisted, leaving behind piles of skulls as a grim warning to others. In the case of Nishapur, after a protracted siege, the Mongols eventually captured the city. In retaliation for the death of one of Genghis Khan's relatives, the Mongols executed nearly the entire population, an estimated 1.7 million people according to some accounts, though the exact number is debated. The sheer scale of this violence was intended to strike terror into the hearts of other cities and regions, effectively making them surrender without a fight to avoid a similar fate.

The fear that Genghis Khan instilled through such actions led many cities and kingdoms to surrender pre-emptively, knowing they could not withstand a Mongol siege and fearing the consequences of resistance. This fear-based strategy allowed the Mongols to expand their empire rapidly, with minimal resistance in many areas, thereby conserving their resources and focusing their efforts on the most strategic targets. Genghis Khan's use of fear was not just about immediate tactical victories but also about creating a psychological impact that would facilitate the Mongol Empire's expansion with less direct military confrontation.

A modern example of a leader invoking fear in their adversary to gain a strategic advantage can be seen in Russia's President Vladimir Putin during the early stages of the invasion of Ukraine in 2022. Putin utilised the threat of Russia's nuclear capabilities as a tool to intimidate not only Ukraine but also Western nations. This tactic was aimed at deterring NATO and other countries from intervening directly in the conflict.

Putin's veiled threats to use nuclear weapons created a climate of fear and uncertainty. The fear was not just about the immediate possibility of nuclear warfare but also about the broader consequences such as regional instability and economic turmoil. By instilling this fear, Putin limited Western support for Ukraine, thereby gaining a strategic advantage on the ground by reducing the likelihood of direct military opposition from NATO.

While this approach has had mixed results—Western nations continued to support Ukraine through sanctions and military aid—the nuclear rhetoric was a significant factor in shaping the cautious responses from various global powers. This illustrates how fear can be used as a strategic tool in modern geopolitical conflicts.

One example of a business leader invoking fear in their adversary to gain a strategic advantage is Elon Musk's approach in the electric vehicle (EV) market. Musk, CEO of Tesla, has consistently used aggressive strategies that instil fear in competitors to maintain and expand Tesla's dominance in the EV sector. In 2018, during what Musk called "production hell," Tesla was ramping up the production of the Model 3, the company's first mass-market vehicle. Many analysts and competitors doubted Tesla's ability to meet its production targets. However, Musk used the situation to create an atmosphere of fear and urgency, both internally and externally.

Musk set highly ambitious production targets that were far beyond what traditional automakers thought possible. By aiming to produce 500,000 cars annually, Musk effectively signalled to competitors that Tesla was willing to push the boundaries of what was feasible, potentially outpacing them and capturing a larger market share. This aggressive goal instilled fear in competitors that Tesla could dominate the EV market.

Musk has frequently cut prices on Tesla vehicles, sometimes unexpectedly. These price cuts often force competitors to scramble and re-evaluate their pricing strategies, creating uncertainty and fear. For instance, Tesla's price reductions in China and other markets have put pressure on traditional automakers and newer EV companies, signalling that Tesla is prepared to aggressively defend and expand its market position.

Musk is known for his provocative statements on social media, particularly Twitter/X. His tweets can send shockwaves through the stock market and influence public perception. For example, Musk's announcement that he was considering taking Tesla private at $420 per share ("funding secured") caused significant turmoil among investors and competitors. While the deal didn't materialise, the statement created fear and uncertainty, impacting Tesla's stock and those of other automakers.

Through these tactics, Musk has created an environment where competitors must constantly anticipate Tesla's next move, leading them to operate under a cloud of fear and uncertainty. This strategic use of fear has allowed Tesla to maintain a dominant position in the EV market and continue to drive the industry's direction

2. **Maintain Tempo**. Musashi instructed his followers to ensure that 'after strongly striking one of the opponents, face against the other strongest opponent immediately.' This maintenance of tempo was designed to keep an enemy off-balance and reactive and thus preventing them from seizing the initiative. In strategic terms, this could be interpreted as always presenting problems and issues to the adversary, so their planning and cerebral energy is being continually expended on dealing with the 'here and now' thus preventing them from focussing on the future.

Miyamoto Musashi was a master of timing and rhythm in his duels, often maintaining the tempo of the fight to his advantage. Again, the duel against Sasaki Kojiro on Ganryu Island highlights Musashi's techniques.

In this duel, Musashi used a boat oar as his weapon, which was shorter than Kojiro's *nodachi* (a long sword). Musashi's strategy involved keeping the distance between himself and Kojiro closer than Kojiro preferred, nullifying the advantage of Kojiro's longer weapon. By controlling the range and maintaining a tight, aggressive tempo, Musashi was able to strike quickly and effectively with his shorter weapon. Musashi's use of timing and rhythm, along with his ability to control the distance, allowed him to defeat Kojiro with a single, well-timed strike, highlighting his exceptional skill in maintaining tempo during combat.

A modern instance of a strategic leader maintaining tempo to gain a strategic advantage is Jeff Bezos, the founder of Amazon, and his approach to the rapid expansion of Amazon's services and infrastructure. Jeff Bezos has consistently driven Amazon with a high-tempo strategy, which has been a crucial factor in the company's success and dominance across multiple industries.

Amazon's pace of innovation is one of its key competitive advantages. The company rapidly launches new products, services, and features, often overwhelming competitors who cannot keep up. For example, Amazon Web Services (AWS) became the dominant player in cloud computing largely because of its fast tempo in rolling out new services and features, allowing it to stay ahead of competitors like Microsoft and Google.

The rapid expansion of Amazon Prime is another example of using fast tempo to gain an advantage. Bezos aggressively pushed the growth of Prime, launching the service in 2005 and continuously adding features like free two-day shipping, video streaming, and exclusive deals. The fast tempo of adding value to Prime made it a must-have service, leading to a massive subscriber base that locked customers into the Amazon ecosystem, making it difficult for competitors to catch up.

Amazon's investment in building a highly efficient logistics and delivery network is another instance where speed played a critical role. Bezos pushed Amazon to develop same-day and next-day delivery options faster than any competitor. The rapid build-out of fulfilment centres, coupled with innovations like Amazon Prime Air (drone delivery) and partnerships with local delivery services, allowed Amazon to outpace traditional retailers and even other e-commerce companies, gaining a significant competitive edge.

Amazon's acquisition strategy, including the purchase of Whole Foods in 2017, was executed with a fast tempo to quickly establish a physical retail presence and integrate it with its online platform. This move caught competitors off-guard, allowing Amazon to rapidly expand into the grocery market and apply its logistics and data expertise to physical retail.

Through these high-tempo strategies, Bezos kept Amazon on the offensive, constantly moving faster than competitors in innovation, service expansion, and logistics. This relentless pace has enabled Amazon to dominate in e-commerce, cloud computing, and beyond, while forcing competitors to react rather than innovate on their own terms

A classic historical example of a strategic leader using fast tempo to gain a strategic advantage is Blitzkrieg (lightning war), a military strategy employed by Nazi Germany during the early years of World War II. The most notable example of this tactic in action was the German invasion of France in 1940.

In the year 1940, Nazi Germany sought to conquer France quickly, as it had been a formidable adversary during World War I. The German military, led by Adolf Hitler and his generals, particularly Heinz Guderian, developed and executed a strategy that relied on speed, surprise, and overwhelming force to achieve their objectives before the French and their British allies could effectively respond.

Blitzkrieg involved rapid movement and coordination between different branches of the military—infantry, tanks (Panzer divisions), and air support (Luftwaffe). The goal was to penetrate deep into enemy territory with surprise, bypassing and encircling enemy forces rather than engaging them in protracted battles.

The fast tempo of the German advance was designed to shock and demoralise the enemy. By moving so swiftly, the Germans aimed to create confusion and panic among the French and British forces, who were unable to reorganise or mount an effective defence in time. The Germans concentrated their forces at specific points along the front, particularly through the Ardennes Forest, which the French believed was impassable for tanks. This allowed the Germans to break through weak points in the French defences and exploit their rapid advance to encircle and isolate large portions of the French and British armies.

The Blitzkrieg strategy was devastatingly effective. Within six weeks, German forces had bypassed the heavily fortified Maginot Line, encircled the bulk of the French Army, and captured Paris. France was forced to surrender on June 22, 1940, an astonishingly swift victory considering the prolonged stalemate of World War I.

The speed and decisiveness of the Blitzkrieg stunned the world and forced a rapid re-evaluation of military tactics and strategies. It instilled fear in Germany's enemies and demonstrated the power of fast tempo in modern warfare. Blitzkrieg's success was largely due to its ability to outpace the enemy's decision-making processes, effectively overwhelming them before they could react. This use of fast tempo gave Germany a significant strategic advantage in the early stages of World War II.

3. **Mountain-Sea**. 'Do not use the same technique over and over again in the same fight. When the opponent is expecting mountain become the sea, when expecting sea become a mountain.' Musashi and other ancient strategists were scornful of 'standard operating procedures' as these were predictable and allowed an adversary to pre-empt or react effectively. Modern strategists must strive to implement plans that are unexpected, unorthodox, or surprising to the enemy. Contemporary Western approaches have become quite predictable, particularly in military campaigns, so there is much to be said for adopting unorthodox and unexpected approaches.

Miyamoto Musashi's "Mountain-Sea" principle is a metaphorical conceptual tenet which he discussed in his book *The Book of Five Rings* to describe the adaptability and the importance of being both strong and flexible in combat and not doing what the enemy expects. An example of Musashi using this principle can be seen in his duel against Shishido Baiken, a master of the *kusarigama* (a sickle and chain weapon).

In the ensuing and all critical duel, Musashi faced an opponent wielding a complex and dangerous weapon that combined both a sickle and a weighted chain. Baiken's fighting style was unpredictable and aggressive, requiring Musashi to adjust his strategy and approach accordingly. Instead of directly attacking Baiken head-on, Musashi used his adaptability and flexibility to assess the situation and find openings in Baiken's technique. Musashi kept his distance and carefully observed Baiken's movements, analysing his attacks and searching for patterns. By using the "Mountain-Sea" principle, Musashi was able to remain solid and stable like a mountain while being fluid and adaptable like the sea. He ultimately managed to defeat Baiken by exploiting his opponent's weaknesses and timing his counterattacks precisely. This duel demonstrated Musashi's mastery of combining strength and flexibility in his approach, embodying the "Mountain-Sea" principle in his combat style.

One of the most famous historical examples of a strategic leader using unexpected tactics to gain a strategic advantage is Hannibal's victory at the Battle of Cannae in 216 BCE during the Second Punic War. Hannibal Barca, the Carthaginian general, was one of the most brilliant military strategists of the ancient world. During the Second Punic War, he led a daring campaign against Rome, marching his army, including war elephants, across the Alps into Italy. Despite facing a much larger Roman force, Hannibal repeatedly defeated Roman armies using innovative and unexpected tactics.

By 216 BCE, Rome had raised a massive army to crush Hannibal once and for all. The Roman force, numbering around 80,000 soldiers, was nearly double the size of Hannibal's 50,000 men. Confident in their numerical superiority, the Roman commanders sought a decisive engagement.

Hannibal employed an ingenious tactical formation known as the "double envelopment." He deliberately positioned his troops in a crescent-shaped formation with his weaker infantry at the centre and his stronger cavalry and veteran troops on the flanks. As the battle commenced, Hannibal's centre gradually gave ground, drawing the Roman legions deeper into his formation. The Romans, seeing what they thought was a retreat, pressed forward aggressively.

Once the Romans were fully engaged and their formations were stretched thin, Hannibal's cavalry, led by his brother Hasdrubal, attacked and routed the Roman cavalry on the wings. With the Roman flanks thus exposed, Hannibal's elite infantry on the sides wheeled inward, encircling the Romans. The Carthaginian forces closed in from all sides, trapping the Roman army in a tight pocket. Unable to manoeuvre, the Roman soldiers were systematically slaughtered.

The Battle of Cannae was one of the most devastating defeats in Roman history. Out of 80,000 Roman soldiers, it is estimated that over 50,000 were killed. Hannibal's unexpected tactics not only led to a significant military victory but also inflicted a psychological blow on Rome, shaking its confidence and causing widespread panic.

Hannibal's victory at Cannae became a classic example of the effective use of unexpected tactics to gain strategic advantage. The battle is still studied in military academies around the world as a prime example of brilliant and unconventional warfare. Hannibal's ability to surprise his enemies and exploit their weaknesses, despite being outnumbered, demonstrated the power of unexpected tactics in achieving strategic success

One notable business example of a strategic leader using unexpected tactics to gain a strategic advantage is Steve Jobs and the launch of the first iPhone in 2007. Before the iPhone's release, the mobile phone industry was dominated by companies like Nokia, Motorola, and BlackBerry. These companies focused primarily on hardware features like battery life, durability, and physical keyboards. The market was highly competitive, but innovation was largely incremental, with little disruption to the *status quo*.

The most unexpected aspect of the iPhone was that it combined several devices—a mobile phone, an iPod (for music), and an internet communication device—into one. While smartphones existed before, they were primarily aimed at business users (like BlackBerry) and were not seen as consumer friendly. The iPhone's integration of these features in a sleek, user-friendly design was revolutionary and unexpected in a market dominated by single-function devices.

The iPhone's touch interface was a radical departure from the physical keyboards and styluses used by competitors. Jobs eliminated the need for a physical keyboard entirely, replacing it with a multi-touch screen that allowed users to interact directly with the device using their fingers. This was unexpected at the time, as many believed a physical keyboard was essential for typing on a mobile device. The touchscreen interface fundamentally changed user expectations and set a new standard for smartphones.

Another unexpected move was the introduction of the App Store in 2008, which created a platform for third-party developers to create and sell apps directly to iPhone users. This turned the iPhone into not just a device but a platform for innovation, dramatically expanding its capabilities and creating a new revenue stream for Apple. Competitors were caught off guard by how quickly the App Store grew, and it took them years to develop comparable ecosystems.

While competitors were focused on selling as many units as possible at various price points, Jobs positioned the iPhone as a premium product, with a higher price tag. This was unexpected in a market that was being increasingly commoditised. The premium strategy helped Apple capture significant profits, even with a smaller market share, and positioned the iPhone as a status symbol.

The iPhone revolutionised the mobile phone industry, rendering many competitors' products obsolete almost overnight. Companies like Nokia and BlackBerry, which had dominated the market, struggled to adapt to the new paradigm that Apple had created. The unexpected tactics used in the iPhone's launch transformed Apple from a niche computer maker into one of the most valuable companies in the world. The iPhone became the cornerstone of Apple's business, leading to massive growth in revenue and profits. Steve Jobs' unexpected tactics with the iPhone launch not only gave Apple a significant strategic advantage but also reshaped the entire technology industry, influencing everything from hardware design to software ecosystems

4. **Crush the enemy**. 'When an enemy is defeated, he does not yield at the heart. Make sure the enemy is beaten at heart and defeated beyond doubt. Crush once, crush fast. Never let the enemy recover.' Musashi was simply stating that the enemy had to feel defeated and accept that they were beaten. Pushing an enemy back was not enough; they had to completely lose the

will to fight. The Taliban in Afghanistan is a really good example of where they were regularly beaten in battles and pushed back but still retained a strong will to fight and were able to recuperate and recover in Pakistani safe havens. Perhaps the best example though is the Vietnam War where the US Forces rarely conceded a battle but lost the war anyway.

Miyamoto Musashi's "crush the enemy" principle is a concept that involves decisively and completely defeating an opponent without hesitation but crucially inflicting such a psychological blow that they accept they are beaten. An example of Musashi using this principle can be seen in his duel against Ito Ittosai, one of the most skilled swordsmen of his time.

During the duel, Musashi employed his "crush the enemy" principle by engaging Ito Ittosai in a manner that aimed to dominate and overpower him quickly and decisively. Musashi attacked with ferocity and precision, using his signature unpredictability to keep Ittosai off balance. His strategy was to apply relentless pressure, leaving Ittosai with little time to react or adapt to his attacks.

Musashi's goal was to eliminate any possibility of a drawn-out or prolonged fight, as he believed in asserting control from the outset to maintain the upper hand. By executing his attacks with determination and commitment, Musashi physically overwhelmed Ittosai with such ferocity that his mind no longer wanted to fight. This duel highlights Musashi's ability to crush his enemy by being assertive, confident, and unyielding in his approach, ensuring a definitive and unambiguous victory over his opponent.

A modern instance of a strategic leader crushing an adversary and completely destroying their will to fight is the U.S.-led coalition's campaign during the First Gulf War in 1991, particularly under the leadership of U.S. General H. Norman Schwarzkopf. In August 1990, Iraq, under the leadership of Saddam Hussein, invaded and annexed Kuwait. This aggressive move was condemned globally, leading to the formation of a large coalition of 35 nations, led by the United States, to force Iraq to withdraw from Kuwait.

The coalition initiated the war with an overwhelming air campaign on January 17, 1991. Over 42 days, coalition forces launched more than 100,000 sorties, dropping a massive amount of ordnance on Iraqi military targets, command and control centres, communication networks, and infrastructure. This relentless bombing campaign was designed to cripple Iraq's ability to wage war and to destroy the morale of Iraqi forces by making it clear that resistance was futile. The precision and scale of the air strikes were unprecedented and left Iraqi forces and leadership demoralised and disoriented.

In the aftermath of the air campaign, the coalition launched a ground offensive on February 24, 1991. General Schwarzkopf executed a "left-hook" strategy, where coalition forces conducted a rapid and unexpected manoeuvre through the desert to outflank and encircle the Iraqi forces. The ground war lasted only 100 hours, with coalition forces overwhelming the Iraqi military. The speed and decisiveness of the coalition's advance further crushed the Iraqi army's will to fight. Many Iraqi soldiers surrendered without a fight, and entire units were destroyed or captured with minimal resistance.

Throughout the campaign, the coalition employed psychological operations to weaken the resolve of Iraqi troops. This included dropping leaflets urging Iraqi soldiers to surrender, broadcasting messages that explained the hopelessness of their situation, and showcasing the overwhelming military power of the coalition forces. These efforts, combined with the devastation wrought by the air campaign, effectively destroyed the morale of Iraqi forces. By the time the ground invasion began, many Iraqi soldiers were ready to surrender, and some even abandoned their positions before encountering coalition forces.

The military campaign was so overwhelming that it effectively destroyed Iraq's ability to continue the fight. The rapid collapse of the Iraqi military, combined with the psychological impact of the coalition's overwhelming force, left Saddam Hussein with no choice but to accept a ceasefire. The Iraqi army was not only physically defeated but also psychologically broken. The coalition's strategy ensured that the Iraqi forces had no realistic hope of victory or even meaningful resistance. This complete destruction of will to fight led to a quick end to the conflict.

The Gulf War significantly weakened Saddam Hussein's regime, although he remained in power. However, the defeat left a lasting impression on the Iraqi military and the region, demonstrating the overwhelming superiority of U.S. and coalition forces and the futility of resisting such a coalition. General Schwarzkopf's leadership and strategy during the First Gulf War provide a clear example of how a well-planned and executed military campaign can crush an adversary's will to fight, leading to a decisive and swift victory

A business example of a strategic leader crushing an adversary and completely destroying their will to fight, can be seen in the commercial tactics employed by Jeff Bezos and Amazon against the bricks-and-mortar retail giant Toys "R" Us. In the early 2000s, Toys "R" Us was the dominant toy retailer, a household name with a vast network of physical stores. However, as e-commerce began to rise, the retail landscape started to change, and Amazon, under Jeff Bezos' leadership, was quickly becoming a major player in online retail.

In 2000, Toys "R" Us entered into a 10-year partnership with Amazon, allowing Amazon to be the exclusive online distributor of Toys "R" Us products. The deal was meant to leverage Amazon's growing online presence while allowing Toys "R" Us to focus on its physical stores.

Over the years Amazon began to expand its toy offerings beyond the Toys "R" Us exclusives. Amazon gradually diversified its product range and partnered with other toy manufacturers, which diluted the exclusivity of Toys "R" Us's products on Amazon's platform. This move was unexpected and put Toys "R" Us at a disadvantage as it was increasingly losing its competitive edge in online retail.

In 2004, Toys "R" Us sued Amazon for breach of contract, claiming that Amazon had violated the exclusivity agreement by allowing other toy retailers to sell on its platform. This legal battle led to the dissolution of their partnership in 2006. However, by this time, Amazon had already built a robust infrastructure for selling toys online, and Toys "R" Us was left struggling to compete on its own.

Amazon continued to innovate in e-commerce, using advanced technology, data analytics, and a highly efficient logistics network to offer lower prices, faster delivery, and a better customer experience. Toys "R"

Us, on the other hand, was slow to adapt to the digital age, relying heavily on its physical stores and failing to build a strong online presence.

Amazon's dominance became particularly evident during the holiday seasons. With aggressive pricing, extensive product selections, and convenient online shopping, Amazon increasingly became the go-to destination for holiday shoppers. This put immense pressure on Toys "R" Us, whose traditional holiday sales were crucial for its profitability.

By 2017, Toys "R" Us had filed for bankruptcy, burdened by massive debt and unable to compete with Amazon's efficiency and market reach. In 2018, Toys "R" Us announced it would close all of its U.S. stores, marking the end of the once-iconic retailer. Amazon emerged as the dominant force in toy retail, capturing a significant share of the market that Toys "R" Us once led. The complete closure of Toys "R" Us demonstrated Amazon's ability to not only outcompete but also utterly dismantle a former industry leader.

Jeff Bezos and Amazon's strategy effectively crushed Toys "R" Us, destroying its will to fight by leveraging superior technology, market presence, and logistics to dominate the retail space. The fall of Toys "R" Us serves as a stark example of how a strategic leader can completely overpower an adversary in the modern business world

5. **Attack first**. 'If the conflict is unavoidable attacking first is twice as advantageous as waiting.' Musashi, once again, was advocating for being proactive rather than reactive. Miyamoto Musashi's "attack first" principle involves taking the initiative in combat and being the first to attack to gain an advantage over the opponent. An example of Musashi using this principle can be seen in his duel against Yoshioka Seijuro, the head of the Yoshioka school of swordsmanship.

In the ensuing duel, Musashi faced an established and respected swordsman from a prominent school. Musashi knew he had to act quickly and decisively to overcome Seijuro. Instead of waiting for Seijuro to make the first move, Musashi immediately attacked with a strong, aggressive approach, catching Seijuro off guard. Musashi's initial attack disrupted Seijuro's plans and forced him onto the defensive, giving Musashi control of the tempo of the fight. By attacking first, Musashi was able to maintain the momentum and keep Seijuro on his back foot, ultimately leading to a swift victory. This duel demonstrates how Musashi's "attack first" principle allowed him to dictate the pace of the fight and gain a strategic advantage over his opponent from the very beginning.

A prominent case study of a strategic leader striking first to gain a strategic advantage is General Douglas MacArthur's amphibious landing at Incheon during the Korean War in September 1950.

In the early stages of the Korean War, North Korean forces had successfully invaded South Korea and captured much of the country, pushing South Korean and United Nations (UN) forces into a small perimeter around the port city of Pusan in the southeast. The situation was dire for the UN forces, and a counteroffensive was desperately needed.

General Douglas MacArthur, the Supreme Commander for the Allied Powers (SCAP) in the Far East, conceived an ambitious plan to conduct a surprise amphibious landing at Incheon, a port city on the west coast of Korea, far from the front lines. This was a highly risky manoeuvre due to Incheon's challenging tides and heavily fortified positions.

The operation, codenamed Operation Chromite, was launched on September 15, 1950. The landing force, consisting of U.S. Marines and Army units, executed the operation with precision and stealth, catching the North Korean forces off guard. The landing was successful despite the logistical challenges and heavy resistance from the enemy.

The Incheon landing achieved several critical objectives. The landing allowed UN forces to cut off and disrupt North Korean supply lines and communication routes. This isolated and weakened the North Korean forces in the southern part of Korea. The landing also relieved the pressure on the Pusan Perimeter, allowing UN forces to break out and launch counteroffensives. The surprise attack at Incheon dramatically shifted the strategic momentum in favour of the UN forces. Within weeks, UN forces advanced rapidly and recaptured Seoul, the capital of South Korea, forcing North Korean troops into a chaotic retreat.

The audacity of the Incheon landing had a profound psychological impact on the enemy. It demonstrated the ability of the UN forces to strike decisively and unpredictably, undermining the confidence of the North Korean leadership and disrupting their campaign plans. The success of the Incheon landing was a turning point in the Korean War. It allowed the UN forces to transition from a defensive posture to an offensive one, leading to the recapture of South Korea's capital and a significant strategic shift in the war.

By attacking first and achieving surprise, MacArthur's strategy effectively reversed the North Korean momentum and forced them into a reactive stance. This had lasting implications for the course of the war and the overall balance of power in the region. General MacArthur's decision to launch the surprise attack at Incheon exemplifies how attacking first, especially in an unexpected and strategically advantageous location, can secure a decisive advantage and significantly alter the course of a conflict

A prominent business example of a strategic leader who used a pre-emptive attack to gain a strategic advantage is Amazon's approach to entering the grocery sector, particularly through its acquisition of Whole Foods in 2017. Before the acquisition, Amazon was a dominant force in e-commerce and cloud computing through its Amazon Web Services (AWS) platform. However, it had little presence in the bricks-and-mortar retail space, especially in the grocery sector, which was still largely controlled by established chains like Walmart and Kroger.

On June 16, 2017, Amazon declared that it would acquire Whole Foods for $13.7 billion. This move was unexpected and shook the grocery industry. It was a pre-emptive strike aimed at gaining a foothold in the grocery market before competitors could strengthen their own digital and e-commerce strategies in this sector. The acquisition was seen as a bold move to disrupt the grocery market. By integrating Whole Foods' physical stores with Amazon's technology and logistics capabilities, Amazon aimed to blend online and offline shopping experiences, offering new services like delivery of fresh groceries through Amazon Prime.

Amazon's strategy included using its technology to enhance the grocery shopping experience. For example, integrating Amazon's data analytics and technology into Whole Foods allowed for better inventory management and personalised customer experiences. The introduction of cashier-less payment systems and smart pricing was a part of this tech integration.

The acquisition allowed Amazon to gather valuable consumer data from Whole Foods' customers, which could be used to refine its retail strategies and improve targeted marketing efforts. This data provided a competitive edge over other grocery retailers who lacked such advanced data capabilities. Following the key and significant acquisition, Amazon adjusted Whole Foods' pricing strategy to align more with its own competitive pricing model. This move not only disrupted the traditional grocery pricing structure but also made Whole Foods more competitive with other mainstream grocers.

Amazon leveraged Whole Foods' locations to enhance its delivery network. This included the integration of grocery delivery services with Amazon Prime, thereby creating a more seamless shopping experience and increasing customer loyalty. The acquisition of Whole Foods created immediate disruption in the grocery sector. Competitors were forced to respond quickly to the new competitive landscape, which included adapting to Amazon's innovative delivery and pricing models.

Amazon solidified its presence in the grocery market and continued to innovate in the retail space. The integration of Whole Foods helped Amazon push its Amazon Fresh and grocery delivery services, further consolidating its dominance in both the digital and physical retail markets. The move set off a wave of consolidation and strategic adjustments among other major retailers, who sought to counter Amazon's growing influence. This included investments in technology, e-commerce, and logistics to better compete with Amazon's newly strengthened position.

Amazon's strategic decision to acquire Whole Foods can be seen as a pre-emptive attack on the grocery industry. By moving first, Amazon disrupted the status quo, leveraged its technological advantages, and positioned itself as a formidable competitor in the grocery sector

6. **Stand Strong**. 'Hopping and bouncing most of the time is unnecessary as sword fights take place in all sorts of terrains.' Miyamoto Musashi's "stand strong" principle involves maintaining composure and resilience in

the face of an opponent's attacks. It stresses the importance of not yielding ground and staying firm and steady during combat.

An example of Musashi using this principle can be seen in his duel against Denshichiro Yoshioka, a skilled swordsman and member of the Yoshioka school. This duel took place after Musashi had already defeated Denshichiro's brother, Seijuro Yoshioka, which added to the intensity of the situation. During the duel, Denshichiro came at Musashi with determination and aggression, seeking to avenge his brother's defeat. Musashi, however, remained calm and composed throughout the encounter. He held his ground and did not allow Denshichiro's attacks to unsettle him. By standing strong and holding his position, Musashi was able to assess Denshichiro's movements and respond with precise and effective counterattacks.

Musashi's ability to stay rooted and unwavering in the face of his opponent's aggression allowed him to successfully control the duel and ultimately defeat Denshichiro. This duel exemplifies Musashi's mastery of the "stand strong" principle, which enabled him to withstand the pressure and turn the fight to his advantage.

A notable example of a strategic leader utilising strong defence to gain a strategic advantage is the defensive strategy employed by General Georgy Zhukov during the Battle of Stalingrad in World War II. The Battle of Stalingrad was a turning point in World War II and one of the largest and deadliest battles in history. It was fought between Nazi Germany and the Soviet Union from August 23, 1942, to February 2, 1943. Adolf Hitler's goal was to capture Stalingrad (now Volgograd) to secure the eastern front and gain control of the oil-rich Caucasus region.

Zhukov, the Soviet commander, implemented a strong defensive strategy within the city. Stalingrad was heavily fortified, with Soviet troops making extensive use of the urban terrain for defensive purposes. Buildings, factories, and even ruins were used to create strongpoints and defensive positions. Despite facing overwhelming German forces and a severe shortage of supplies, Soviet forces under Zhukov held their positions tenaciously. The Soviet defence was marked by fierce, close-quarters combat, which neutralised many of the Germans' advantages in mobility and firepower.

Zhukov employed a defence-in-depth strategy, using layers of defensive positions to slow and attrite the German advance. This approach exhausted German resources and personnel while inflicting heavy casualties. Zhukov also took advantage of the harsh Russian winter. The severe cold and snow conditions further strained the already overstretched German forces and contributed to their logistical difficulties.

On November 19, 1942, Zhukov launched Operation Uranus, a massive Soviet counteroffensive that encircled the German 6th Army in Stalingrad. This operation was meticulously planned to exploit the weaknesses in the German flanks and encircle the enemy. The Soviet counteroffensive trapped approximately 300,000 German troops in a pincer movement, cutting them off from supplies and reinforcements. The Germans were forced to fight a desperate defensive battle inside the encirclement, which significantly weakened their fighting capacity.

The strong defence and subsequent counteroffensive had a profound effect on Soviet morale. The successful defence of Stalingrad was a significant morale booster for the Soviet Union and symbolised resilience and Soviet strength. The prolonged and intense defence led to a high attrition rate among German forces. The encirclement and eventual surrender of the 6th Army marked one of the most significant defeats for Nazi Germany, with massive losses in both personnel and equipment along with the attendant humiliation.

The Soviet victory at Stalingrad marked a turning point in World War II on the Eastern Front. It ended the German offensive into the Soviet Union and began a series of Soviet offensives that would eventually lead to the defeat of Nazi Germany. Zhukov's use of a strong defensive strategy, coupled with the successful counteroffensive, provided the Soviet Union with a strategic advantage. The battle demonstrated the effectiveness of strong, well-organised defensive positions and the ability to turn defence into a successful counterattack. General Zhukov's leadership during the Battle of Stalingrad exemplifies how a strategic leader can use a strong defensive posture not only to hold off a superior enemy but also to create conditions for a decisive counteroffensive, ultimately gaining a strategic advantage

A notable business example where a strategic leader used strong defence to gain a strategic advantage is Microsoft's strategy during the antitrust lawsuit with the U.S. Department of Justice (DOJ) in the late 1990s and early 2000s. In the late 1990s, Microsoft faced a significant antitrust lawsuit from the U.S. Department of Justice and several state attorneys general. The core issue was whether Microsoft had used its dominant position in the PC operating system market to stifle competition, particularly through its bundling of Internet Explorer with Windows.

Microsoft, under the leadership of CEO Steve Ballmer and Chief Counsel Brad Smith, mounted a vigorous legal defence. The company employed a team of top lawyers and experts to challenge the allegations and argue that its practices were legal and beneficial to consumers. Microsoft engaged in a comprehensive public relations campaign to sway public opinion and political support. The company argued that its integration of software was driven by innovation and efficiency, not anti-competitive behaviour. They also lobbied extensively to influence policymakers and regulators.

Despite the legal challenges, Microsoft continued to focus on innovation and product development. The company invested heavily in new technologies and expanded its product offerings, which helped to reinforce its position in the market and demonstrate that it was committed to advancing technology rather than monopolising it. Microsoft defended its market position by strengthening its presence in other strategic areas, such as enterprise solutions and server software. By diversifying its product portfolio and reinforcing its market leadership in these areas, Microsoft was able to mitigate the potential impact of the antitrust case on its overall business.

In 2001, Microsoft reached a settlement with the DOJ and the state plaintiffs. The settlement imposed various restrictions and requirements on Microsoft's business practices, including making it easier for PC manufacturers to offer competing software. Microsoft accepted the terms but managed to avoid a breakup of the company, which was one of the original remedies sought by the DOJ. Microsoft adapted its business practices to comply with the settlement terms while maintaining its competitive edge. This included allowing greater flexibility for software manufacturers and continuing to focus on product innovation and customer satisfaction.

By employing a strong defensive strategy, Microsoft was able to maintain its leadership position in the software industry. The company's ability to adapt and continue innovating ensured that it remained competitive and avoided significant disruptions to its business operations. The settlement allowed Microsoft to continue its core operations and growth trajectory without the severe penalties or structural changes that could have arisen from a more aggressive antitrust ruling.

The defensive strategy and subsequent settlement allowed Microsoft to focus on expanding its business into new areas such as cloud computing and enterprise services, contributing to its long-term success and market dominance. Microsoft's approach during the antitrust lawsuit is a prime example of how a company can use strong defence—through legal strategies, public relations efforts, and strategic business moves—to mitigate the impact of legal challenges and maintain a competitive advantage

7. **Distant-near**. 'Imagine things far as if they are near and imagine the distant view of things that are near (from above).' Miyamoto Musashi's "distant-near" principle, as described in *The Book of Five Rings*, refers to controlling the distance between oneself and the opponent during combat. It involves alternating between staying far enough to avoid danger and closing the distance quickly when the opportunity for attack arises.

An example of Musashi using this principle can be seen in his duel against a skilled swordsman named Ganryu. In this duel, Musashi demonstrated his ability to control the range of the fight effectively. Musashi started the duel by keeping his distance from Ganryu, staying out of reach of his opponent's attacks. This cautious approach allowed Musashi to observe Ganryu's movements and technique without putting himself in immediate danger. By staying distant initially, Musashi could gauge his opponent's strengths and weaknesses.

Once Musashi identified an opening, he quickly closed the distance and launched a surprise attack, catching Ganryu off guard. This sudden shift from distant to near allowed Musashi to exploit his opponent's vulnerabilities and take control of the fight. Musashi's mastery of the "distant-near" principle in this duel enabled him to manage the range of the encounter effectively and defeat Ganryu with strategic precision. This approach showcases how Musashi used distance control to his advantage in combat.

A modern example of a strategic leader using distance, manoeuvre, and close combat to gain a strategic advantage is General David Petraeus' strategy during the Iraq War, particularly the surge strategy implemented in 2007. By 2006, Iraq was experiencing intense sectarian violence and insurgency, leading to a deteriorating security situation. The U.S. military, under President George W. Bush, decided to implement a new strategy to stabilise the country and gain control over the rapidly deteriorating security situation.

General David Petraeus, who was appointed as the Commander of U.S. Central Command in early 2007, advocated for a troop surge. This involved deploying an additional 30,000 U.S. troops to Iraq, increasing the overall presence to about 160,000 troops. This increase in troop numbers allowed for greater security coverage and more flexibility in operations. The surge involved not just adding troops but also repositioning them to create a larger, more effective security footprint. U.S. forces were spread out to cover previously underserved areas, particularly in Baghdad and the surrounding provinces where violence was most intense.

Petraeus employed a counterinsurgency strategy known as "Clear-Hold-Build." This approach required clearing areas of insurgents (clear), maintaining security and stability (hold), and then rebuilding infrastructure and fostering local governance (build). This strategy required manoeuvring forces through complex urban and rural environments to root out insurgent cells and stabilise regions. U.S. forces were integrated more deeply into local communities. Soldiers began conducting more frequent foot patrols and engaging with local populations to build trust and gather intelligence. This manoeuvring through local areas helped in identifying and targeting insurgent activity.

In addition to broader counterinsurgency operations, U.S. forces engaged in direct raids and operations against high-value targets, including key insurgent leaders and bomb-making facilities. This close combat approach was essential in disrupting insurgent networks and reducing their operational capabilities. In cities like Baghdad, close combat included intense urban engagements to clear insurgent strongholds and secure neighbourhoods. This close-quarters combat was critical in reducing the immediate threat posed by insurgents and stabilising key areas.

The surge strategy significantly reduced violence in Iraq. By late 2007 and into 2008, the number of attacks and casualties decreased, and the overall security situation improved. The increase in troop numbers and the application of counterinsurgency tactics were instrumental in achieving this stabilisation. The successful implementation of the surge strategy provided a strategic advantage by regaining control over contested areas, reducing the operational space available to insurgents, and rebuilding local governance and security forces. This created a more stable environment, which allowed for political and economic development to proceed.

The success of the surge strategy had significant implications for U.S. policy and military strategy. It demonstrated the of a well-executed counterinsurgency strategy and influenced future military and political decisions in the region. General Petraeus' use of distance (through strategic repositioning and increasing troop numbers), manoeuvre (with the clear-hold-build strategy and engagement with local populations), and close combat (through targeted raids and urban warfare) exemplifies a modern application of these principles to gain a strategic advantage in a complex and volatile environment

A compelling business example of a strategic leader using distance, manoeuvre, and close combat to gain a strategic advantage is Netflix's strategy in the video rental and streaming industry, particularly under CEO Reed Hastings. In the early 2000s, Netflix was a small DVD rental company competing against established video rental giants like Blockbuster. The traditional video rental market was dominated by physical stores, and Blockbuster was the leading player with a large network of retail outlets.

Netflix initially set itself apart from Blockbuster by offering DVD rentals by mail. This allowed customers to rent DVDs without having to visit a physical store, which was a significant advantage in terms of convenience and reduced late fees. This distance from the traditional model of in-store rentals was Netflix's first strategic move. Netflix also introduced a subscription model with no late fees, a significant departure from Blockbuster's fee-based rental system. This model provided an added layer of convenience and predictable cost for consumers, creating initial traction and a loyal customer base.

As technology evolved, Netflix manoeuvred by transitioning from DVD rentals to streaming video in 2007. This move leveraged emerging internet technology and permitted Netflix to offer instant access to a vast library of content, bypassing the need for physical media and physical infrastructure. Recognising the growing importance of exclusive content, Netflix began investing heavily in original programming, starting with "House of Cards" in 2013. This strategic manoeuvre further differentiated Netflix from competitors and provided unique value to its subscribers, making it difficult for traditional competitors to match.

Netflix involved itself in close combat by aggressively pricing its streaming service and investing in marketing to rapidly expand its subscriber base. This put significant pressure on traditional rental companies and even other streaming services. Netflix's strategic moves directly impacted Blockbuster, which struggled to adapt to the changing market. Blockbuster's attempt to launch its own DVD rental by mail service and later a streaming service was too little, too late. Netflix's well-executed strategy in both the digital space and content creation made it the dominant player, leading to Blockbuster's decline and eventual bankruptcy.

Netflix jockeyed as a dominant player in the entertainment industry, transforming from a DVD rental service into a leading global streaming platform with a vast library of content, including highly acclaimed original series and films. Netflix's strategic approach effectively disrupted the traditional video rental market and set new standards for how media content is consumed. It forced competitors to innovate rapidly or face obsolescence.

By continuously evolving its strategy to stay ahead of industry trends, Netflix has maintained a competitive edge and expanded its influence globally. Its success in manoeuvring and adapting to new technologies has cemented its position as a major player in the entertainment industry. Netflix's strategy illustrates how a company can use distance from traditional business models, manoeuvre through technological and market changes, and engage in close combat with competitors to gain and maintain a strategic advantage

8. **Use Three Methods to See**. Miyamoto Musashi's "three methods of seeing" principle is a concept he described in *The Book of Five Rings*. It involves three approaches to perceiving a situation: seeing the overall strategy (broad view), seeing the opponent's intentions (narrow view), and seeing the immediate opportunities in the fight (close view). These methods allow a swordsman to adapt and respond effectively during combat.

An example of Musashi utilising his "three methods of seeing" principle can be seen in his duel against an opponent using a different weapon style, such as when he faced a practitioner of the spear. In such a duel, Musashi would apply the three methods as follows:

- **Broad view:** Musashi first assesses the overall situation, including the opponent's weapon style, stance, and movement. He recognises the advantages and disadvantages of facing a spear and considers how the duel may play out.
- **Narrow view:** Musashi then focuses on the opponent's intentions, looking for signs of their strategy and tactics. He observes the opponent's posture, grip, and footwork to understand how they plan to attack and defend.
- **Close view:** Finally, Musashi homes in on the immediate opportunities in the fight. He stays vigilant and watches for openings in the opponent's defence, changes in their stance, or moments of vulnerability that he can exploit.

By employing all three methods of seeing, Musashi could adapt to the situation, anticipate his opponent's moves, and seize opportunities as they arose. This comprehensive approach to perceiving the duel allowed Musashi to maintain control and achieve victory against a variety of opponents.

An illustrative example of a strategic leader utilising broad, narrow, and close views of a situation to gain a strategic advantage is Satya Nadella's leadership of Microsoft. When Satya Nadella became CEO of Microsoft in 2014, the company was facing several challenges, including declining relevance in the mobile space, competition in cloud computing, and internal organisational issues. Nadella needed to transform Microsoft to regain its competitive edge and drive future growth.

Nadella recognised the broader trend of cloud computing becoming central to business operations and technological innovation. He understood that the future of technology was moving away from traditional software and hardware towards cloud services. This broad view led him to prioritise cloud computing as a core strategic focus for Microsoft. Nadella also identified the need for a cultural transformation within the Microsoft conglomerate. He prioritised creating a growth mindset across the organisation, which involved broadening employees' perspectives and encouraging a more collaborative and innovative culture.

Nadella narrowed Microsoft's focus on developing and expanding its Azure cloud platform. He invested heavily in Azure to compete with Amazon Web Services (AWS), leveraging Microsoft's existing enterprise customer base and technical expertise. This targeted approach allowed Microsoft to make significant gains in the cloud market, positioning Azure as a strong competitor to AWS. Nadella made targeted acquisitions to enhance Microsoft's cloud and productivity offerings. For example, the acquisition of LinkedIn in 2016 was a strategic move to integrate professional networking with Microsoft's enterprise solutions, and the acquisition of GitHub in 2018 helped strengthen Microsoft's position in the developer community.

Nadella paid close attention to the execution and integration of Microsoft's productivity tools like Office 365. He ensured that these tools were seamlessly integrated with cloud services, improving customer experience and driving adoption. This close view on operational details allowed Microsoft to deliver immediate value and reinforce its competitive position.

Nadella tackled immediate operational and organisational challenges, such as streamlining the company's structure and addressing internal conflicts. By focusing on these close-up issues, he was able to improve efficiency, foster a more collaborative environment, and enhance overall company performance.

Under Nadella's leadership, Microsoft successfully transitioned to a cloud-first strategy, with Azure becoming one of the leading cloud platforms in the market. This shift significantly boosted Microsoft's revenue and market position. Nadella's emphasis on a growth mindset and cultural transformation revitalised Microsoft's internal dynamics, leading to increased innovation and employee engagement.

The strategic focus on cloud computing and productivity tools, combined with effective operational execution, positioned Microsoft for long-term growth and relevance in a rapidly evolving technology landscape. Satya Nadella's use of broad, narrow, and close views demonstrates how a strategic leader can integrate various levels of analysis to drive comprehensive transformation and gain a significant strategic advantage

A prime example of a military strategic leader using broad, narrow, and close views to gain a strategic advantage is General Dwight D. Eisenhower during the D-Day invasion of Normandy on June 6, 1944, in World War II. The D-Day invasion, known as Operation Overlord, was a pivotal moment in World War II. The goal was to establish a Western front against Nazi Germany by landing Allied forces on the beaches of Normandy, France. The operation required meticulous planning and execution to succeed against a formidable and well-entrenched enemy.

Eisenhower, as Supreme Commander of the Allied Expeditionary Force, adopted a broad view of the situation by considering the overall strategic picture. This involved coordinating with multiple Allied nations, integrating diverse military branches, and planning a massive amphibious assault across a broad front. Eisenhower orchestrated a broad strategy involving extensive deception operations to mislead the Germans about the invasion's true location. Operation Fortitude, part of this deception, created a fake army group to divert German attention away from Normandy. This broad strategic perspective ensured that the main invasion force faced less resistance than it otherwise might have.

On D-Day itself, Eisenhower needed a more focused, narrow view to manage the tactical aspects of the landings. This involved precise coordination of landing forces on five separate beaches (Utah, Omaha, Gold, Juno, and Sword) and managing the immediate challenges and opportunities each beach presented. Eisenhower's narrow view during the landings allowed him to address specific tactical issues as they arose, such as dealing with unexpected strong German resistance at Omaha Beach and coordinating the deployment of airborne troops behind enemy lines. This focused approach was crucial for the success of the landings and the establishment of a secure beachhead.

Eisenhower maintained close oversight of the operation by receiving updates from field commanders and responding to immediate operational challenges. His ability to stay closely connected with on-ground realities allowed him to make timely decisions, such as adjusting the deployment of reinforcements and addressing logistical issues. Eisenhower's close interaction with his commanders and troops helped boost morale and ensure that the complex operation proceeded smoothly. His leadership in addressing the immediate needs of the forces on the ground was crucial for overcoming difficulties and achieving success.

The broad, narrow, and close perspectives employed by Eisenhower led to the successful establishment of a foothold in Normandy, which was crucial for the subsequent liberation of Western Europe. The successful execution of D-Day significantly weakened German forces and opened a new front in the war, contributing to the eventual defeat of Nazi Germany. The invasion marked a turning point in World War II and demonstrated the effectiveness of a multifaceted strategic approach.

Eisenhower's ability to integrate broad strategic planning with detailed tactical and operational management exemplified how a leader can use different levels of perspective to achieve a strategic advantage in complex and high-stakes situations. Eisenhower's approach during the D-Day invasion shows how a strategic leader can use broad, narrow, and close views to effectively manage and execute a complex operation, gaining a significant strategic advantage in warfare

9. **Cut the enemy**. 'The final goal is cutting the enemy, usually starting from the neck. No matter how the fight is going, never forget your final

goal.' Selection and maintenance of the aim is the overriding principle of war in Western doctrine and it is clear that Musashi agrees with this foundational principle as well.

Miyamoto Musashi's "cut the enemy" principle involves the idea of striking decisively and accurately in combat to defeat an opponent. It emphasises delivering a direct and effective attack to neutralise the enemy swiftly. An example of Musashi using his "cut the enemy" principle can be seen in his duel against an experienced swordsman named Arima Kihei. This duel was one of the first significant challenges Musashi faced, and it took place when Musashi was still a young swordsman.

Musashi's strategy in this duel was straightforward and aggressive. He aimed to cut Arima Kihei quickly and decisively. When the duel began, Musashi immediately closed the distance and delivered a powerful, direct strike to Arima's head, killing him instantly. This swift and decisive action demonstrated Musashi's commitment to the "cut the enemy" principle. By focusing on delivering a strong, accurate strike at the right moment, Musashi was able to secure a quick victory over his opponent and establish his reputation as a formidable swordsman.

A classic example of a military strategic leader focusing on a single critical priority to achieve strategic success is General Ulysses S. Grant's campaign to capture Vicksburg during the American Civil War (1861-1865). Vicksburg, Mississippi, was a crucial stronghold on the Mississippi River, which was essential for controlling the central part of the United States during the Civil War. The city's capture would split the Confederacy in two and give the Union control over the Mississippi River, significantly impacting the Confederacy's ability to transport troops and supplies.

General Grant identified the capture of Vicksburg as the single most critical objective in the Western Theatre of the Civil War. Unlike other operations that might have diluted focus, Grant concentrated all efforts and resources on this goal. He understood that Vicksburg was a linchpin for Confederate control over the Mississippi River and that its capture would have a decisive impact on the war.

Grant's strategy involved surrounding Vicksburg and cutting it off from reinforcements and supplies. This approach included a combination of military manoeuvres and siege tactics. He meticulously planned and executed a series of operations to place Vicksburg under siege, isolating it from the outside world. Grant maintained relentless pressure on the Confederate forces, ensuring that Vicksburg's defenders were unable to break the siege or receive external support. His ability to keep the city surrounded and under constant attack was crucial in wearing down the defenders and breaking their will to continue resisting.

Grant employed innovative tactics to overcome natural obstacles and logistical challenges. For instance, he used a series of manoeuvres to bypass Confederate defences and achieve a position of advantage. His ability to adapt to changing circumstances and leverage Union resources effectively was key to the campaign's success. Grant's leadership and coordination with his subordinates ensured that all aspects of the siege operation were executed efficiently. His focus on Vicksburg allowed him to effectively manage and direct his forces towards achieving the singular objective.

The successful capture of Vicksburg on July 4, 1863, delivered a significant strategic victory for the Union. The fall of the city split the Confederacy in two and gave the Union full control over the Mississippi River. The victory at Vicksburg, combined with the Union's success at Gettysburg a day earlier, marked a turning point in the Civil War. It bolstered Union morale and significantly weakened the Confederate war effort.

The success of the Vicksburg campaign solidified Grant's reputation as a decisive and effective military leader, eventually leading to his appointment as Commander of all Union armies and contributing to the eventual Union victory in the Civil War. Grant's singular focus on the capture of Vicksburg demonstrates how a strategic leader's dedication to a single critical priority can deliver substantial strategic success, shaping the course of a major conflict.

A notable commercial example of a strategic leader focusing on a single critical priority to deliver strategic success is Howard Schultz's approach at Starbucks during his time as CEO in the early 2000s. By the early 2000s, Starbucks had experienced rapid expansion, but the company faced challenges related to maintaining the quality of its coffee and the customer experience. Some critics and customers felt that the rapid growth had diluted the brand's core identity and customer experience.

Schultz, who had stepped down as CEO in 2000 but returned in 2008, made it his single critical priority to reinvigorate Starbucks' core coffee experience. He recognised that the company's success was built on the quality of its coffee and the unique in-store experience. Schultz highlighted the need to improve the in-store environment and customer service. This involved investing in better training for baristas, upgrading store interiors, and ensuring that every store maintained the high standards of product quality and customer service that had originally defined Starbucks. Schultz also focused on innovation in the coffee products offered. This included refining the espresso preparation process and introducing new beverages that would enhance the overall quality and appeal of Starbucks' offerings.

Schultz's strategy included renovating existing stores to align with the brand's high standards and enhancing barista training programs. This commitment to quality helped restore the company's reputation and improve customer satisfaction. Under Schultz's leadership, Starbucks saw a significant turnaround. The renewed focus on the coffee experience helped re-establish the brand's premium image and loyalty among customers. The emphasis on quality and customer service resonated well, leading to increased sales and profitability.

The single-minded focus on quality not only addressed immediate concerns but also set a foundation for long-term success. Starbucks continued to grow and expand globally, maintaining its position as a leading coffee retailer with a strong brand identity. Schultz's focus on a single critical priority—enhancing the quality of the coffee experience—helped restore Starbucks' brand identity and customer loyalty. This strategic shift was crucial in addressing the issues arising from rapid expansion.

The emphasis on quality and customer experience contributed to Starbucks' financial recovery and growth. The company reported improved financial performance and continued expansion, both in existing markets and internationally. By realigning the company's strategy around its core product, Starbucks reinforced its leadership position in the coffee industry. The focus on maintaining high standards helped differentiate Starbucks from competitors and solidified its reputation as a premium coffee brand. Howard Schultz's focus on the critical priority of quality coffee experience illustrates how a leader's commitment to a single, crucial element of the business can deliver significant strategic success and drive long-term growth

10. **Manipulate timing**. This dictum states 'Always control your timing and the enemy's timing.' Musashi would often arrive late on purpose for a duel in order to demoralise his enemy. By timing, he also meant one must look at the enemy and predict the enemy's next move based on the enemy's past movements.

Miyamoto Musashi's "manipulate timing" principle involves controlling the pace and rhythm of combat to gain an advantage over the opponent. This includes using various techniques to disrupt the enemy's timing and maintain control over the flow of the fight.

An example of Musashi using his "manipulate timing" principle can be seen in his duel against Yoshioka Matashichiro, a member of the Yoshioka school of swordsmanship.

In this duel, Musashi faced a skilled and determined opponent who sought to avenge the defeat of his school. Musashi understood the importance of controlling the tempo of the fight and disrupting Matashichiro's plans. To achieve this, Musashi used feints and unpredictable movements to manipulate Matashichiro's timing.

Musashi assiduously engaged in sudden advances or retreats, changing the distance and angle of attack abruptly. This caused Matashichiro to react defensively and lose his rhythm. By constantly shifting the pace and rhythm of the fight, Musashi kept his opponent off balance and unable to establish a consistent strategy. As a result, Musashi was able to seize the initiative and create openings in Matashichiro's defence. Ultimately, Musashi's ability to manipulate timing played a key role in his victory over Matashichiro, showcasing his mastery of controlling the pace and flow of combat.

A significant World War II example of a strategic leader manipulating timing to deliver strategic success is General George S. Patton's execution of the Third Army's counteroffensive during the Battle of the Bulge in December 1944. The Battle of the Bulge, fought from December 16, 1944, to January 25, 1945, was a major German offensive through the Ardennes Forest in Belgium. The Germans aimed to split the Allied lines and capture the vital Belgian port of Antwerp. The surprise attack created a "bulge" in the Allied front line, and the situation became critical for the Allies.

When the German offensive began, Patton's Third Army was in the Lorraine region of France, and the Allies were initially caught off guard. Patton, known for his bold and aggressive tactics, recognised the urgency of the situation and understood that timely intervention was crucial. Patton quickly reoriented his forces to respond to the German threat. Despite challenging winter weather and logistical difficulties, he managed to pivot his army from its position in Lorraine to the Ardennes. Patton's Third Army executed a remarkable rapid advance to relieve the besieged town of Bastogne, which was a key point in the German offensive.

One of Patton's key tactical advantages was his ability to manipulate timing with respect to weather. The Allies had been suffering from poor visibility due to fog and heavy snow, which had hindered air support and movement. Patton managed to time his counterattack to coincide with a break in the weather, allowing Allied aircraft to provide air support and reconnaissance. Patton's Third Army launched its counteroffensive on December 26, 1944, effectively timing the attack to capitalise on the Germans' extended supply lines and fatigue. His forces cut through German lines, disrupting their advance and pushing them back.

Patton's timing was crucial in the relief of Bastogne, where the 101st Airborne Division was encircled by German forces. The rapid advance of Patton's troops lifted the siege and provided a significant morale boost to the Allies. The counteroffensive, executed with precise timing and coordination, effectively halted the German advance and began to push them back. This marked a turning point in the battle, leading to the eventual Allied victory in the Battle of the Bulge.

Patton's manipulation of timing and rapid response was pivotal in defeating the German offensive. The success of the counteroffensive significantly weakened German forces and contributed to the overall Allied victory in the Western Front. By effectively timing the counterattack and leveraging the break in weather conditions, Patton helped preserve Allied territorial gains and reinforced the Allies' position in Europe.

Patton's impactful and canny use of timing during the Battle of the Bulge reinforced his reputation as a dynamic and capable commander. His actions demonstrated the importance of timing and rapid manoeuvring in achieving strategic military success. General Patton's adept manipulation of timing during the Battle of the Bulge exemplifies how a strategic leader can leverage precise timing to turn the tide of a critical battle and secure significant strategic advantages

A notable business instance of a strategic leader manipulating timing to achieve success is Luca di Montezemolo's strategy at Ferrari during the early 2000s. In the early 2000s, Ferrari was in a crucial period of transition. The company had been struggling to dominate the Formula 1 racing scene despite its strong brand and historical success. The late 1990s had seen a decline in Ferrari's performance, and the company needed a strategic overhaul to return to winning ways.

Luca di Montezemolo, Chairman of Ferrari since 1991, understood that timing was critical for Ferrari's return to dominance in Formula 1. He strategically timed the overhaul of the team by bringing in new leadership and technical staff at a pivotal moment. In 2000, he appointed Jean Todt as Team Principal and Ross Brawn as Technical Director, while also retaining Rory Byrne as Chief Designer. This timing allowed Ferrari to rebuild its team with fresh perspectives and a unified strategy.

Ferrari strategically timed the introduction of new car technology to align with the F1 calendar. The launch of the Ferrari F2000 and subsequent models was meticulously planned to maximise performance in the upcoming racing seasons. Di Montezemolo and his team timed their development cycles to ensure that Ferrari's cars were at their peak during critical points in the racing season. This included optimising car performance for key races and ensuring that advancements were implemented at the most strategic times.

As Ferrari began to see success on the track, Di Montezemolo timed the promotion of Ferrari's Formula 1 achievements to bolster the brand's image and appeal. The success in Formula 1 was used as a marketing tool to enhance Ferrari's reputation in the consumer car market. Ferrari's strategic manipulation of timing led to a period of dominance in Formula 1. Ferrari won the Constructors' Championship in 2000, 2001, 2002, and 2003, with Michael Schumacher securing the Drivers' Championship in 2000, 2001, 2002, and 2003.

The timing of Ferrari's success on the racetrack helped reinforce its brand image as a leader in performance and innovation. This had a positive spillover effect on its consumer car sales and overall brand prestige. The strategic timing and execution during this period established a strong foundation for Ferrari's continued success in Formula 1 and contributed to the company's long-term brand strength and market position. Luca di Montezemolo's ability to manipulate timing, from personnel changes to car development and brand positioning, demonstrates how effective timing can be a critical factor in achieving strategic success in a competitive industry.

11. **Pommel to the head**. Musashi made swords with extra sharp edges on the pommels so that he could hit the enemy's head from the back side after striking with the blade. He also promoted the idea that one should hit the enemy's head, hands, and legs by using the arms and head if the blade strike missed the target. Musashi made it clear with his explanation of this technique that other non-traditional or 'lower yield' weapons can have an important part to play in any strategy and that the primary weapon should not be considered the only means of inflicting damage on an enemy.

Miyamoto Musashi's "pommel to the head" principle is a specific tactic that involves using the pommel of the sword as a striking weapon against the opponent, rather than just relying on the blade. This technique can catch an opponent off guard and provide a strategic advantage. An example of Musashi using his "pommel to the head" principle can be seen in one of his many duels against skilled swordsmen. In these duels, Musashi often used unconventional and unexpected techniques to surprise his opponents and gain the upper hand.

During a duel against a particularly skilled swordsman, Musashi faced an opponent who was well-versed in traditional swordplay and expected a conventional fight. Instead of adhering to the expected sword techniques,

Musashi employed his "pommel to the head" principle to break the opponent's guard.

As the duel progressed, Musashi found an opening and quickly closed the distance between himself and his opponent. Instead of striking with the blade, Musashi used the pommel of his sword to strike the opponent's head. This unexpected move stunned the opponent and allowed Musashi to quickly follow up with a decisive blow, securing the victory.

Musashi's use of the "pommel to the head" principle demonstrated his ability to adapt and innovate in combat, using every part of his weapon to his advantage and catching his opponents off guard with unconventional tactics.

A notable World War I example of a strategic leader using a secondary attack to achieve strategic success is General Ferdinand Foch's implementation of the Hundred Days Offensive in 1918. By 1918, World War I was approaching its final phase, and the stakes were high. The Central Powers, particularly Germany, were launching a series of offensives on the Western Front, attempting to break the Allied lines before American forces could fully arrive and reinforce the Allies. The Allies were in a precarious position but had not yet mounted a decisive counter-offensive.

General Ferdinand Foch, the Supreme Allied Commander, orchestrated a comprehensive strategy that involved a series of coordinated offensives by Allied forces. Foch's strategy aimed to capitalise on the growing strength of the Allied forces, including fresh American troops, and to exploit the overstretched German lines. While the main Allied offensives were planned around key locations like the Argonne Forest and the Hindenburg Line, Foch also utilised secondary attacks to distract and weaken the German forces. The Meuse-Argonne Offensive, which was initiated in late September 1918, was one of these secondary but crucial attacks. This offensive was intended to divert German resources and attention from the main Allied push. The Meuse-Argonne Offensive involved a large-scale attack by American and French forces against German positions in the Argonne Forest and the Meuse River region. Though not the primary focus of the overall Allied strategy, this offensive was strategically important for stretching German defences and causing significant attrition.

Foch's use of secondary attacks was part of a coordinated plan to apply pressure on multiple fronts. The Hundred Days Offensive was characterised by a series of attacks, including the Meuse-Argonne Offensive, which worked together to exhaust and disorganise German forces. These secondary attacks complemented the main offensives, ensuring that German forces could not concentrate their defences effectively.

The secondary attack in the Meuse-Argonne, combined with other Allied offensives, was successful in breaking through German lines and pushing the Central Powers back. The relentless pressure from multiple fronts overwhelmed German defences. The Hundred Days Offensive, which included both primary and secondary attacks, led to the collapse of the German military and the eventual armistice on November 11, 1918. The success of these offensives, including secondary attacks like the Meuse-Argonne, was crucial in hastening the end of the war.

The use of secondary attacks effectively depleted German resources and contributed to the overall success of the Allied strategy. The coordinated offensives forced the Germans into a defensive posture, undermining their ability to sustain the war effort. General Ferdinand Foch's employment of secondary attacks, such as the Meuse-Argonne Offensive, demonstrates how strategic leaders can use these secondary operations to complement primary offensives and achieve overall strategic success in warfare.

A prominent business example of a strategic leader using secondary activity to achieve success is Jack Ma's strategy at Alibaba Group during its expansion into the online payment market with Alipay. In the early 2000s, Alibaba was primarily known as an online marketplace connecting buyers and sellers. However, to build trust and facilitate transactions on its platform, Alibaba needed a secure and reliable payment system. At the time, the online payment market in China was underdeveloped, with few established players.

Alibaba's prime focus was on growing its e-commerce platform, Alibaba.com, and Taobao, its consumer-to-consumer marketplace. The company aimed to capture market share in the rapidly growing Chinese e-commerce market. Recognising the limitations of existing payment solutions and the need for a secure payment system to support its e-commerce growth,

Jack Ma initiated the development of Alipay in 2004. This was a secondary approach to the problem of online payment security, separate from Alibaba's core e-commerce business.

Alipay was designed to address issues of trust and security in online transactions. It introduced features such as escrow services, where funds were held by Alipay until both parties confirmed that a transaction was completed satisfactorily. This innovative approach helped build confidence among users.

Alipay was integrated into Alibaba's e-commerce platforms, providing a seamless and secure payment experience for users. This integration facilitated growth in Alibaba's core e-commerce business by making transactions more efficient and trustworthy. Over time, Alipay expanded beyond Alibaba's platforms, offering services to other merchants and consumers. This secondary attack on the broader financial services market helped establish Alipay as a leading player in digital payments in China.

Alipay became one of China's largest and most successful online payment systems, with a significant share of the market. Its success strengthened Alibaba's position in the e-commerce sector by resolving a critical barrier to online transactions. The introduction of Alipay contributed to the growth of Alibaba's entire ecosystem, including its e-commerce platforms, financial services, and other ventures. It provided Alibaba with a competitive edge and allowed it to offer a comprehensive suite of services.

Alipay's success extended beyond China, with the company making significant inroads into international markets and expanding its services to include financial products like loans and wealth management. Jack Ma's strategic use of a secondary activity through the development of Alipay highlights how addressing a complementary market need—in this case, online payments—can deliver significant strategic success and enhance the overall strength of a core business.

MUSASHI'S STRATEGIC CONCEPTS

Musashi added some strategic concepts to his principles and techniques. These writings are much more philosophical in nature and group together some of the principles and techniques.

Understanding the Fundamentals. Musashi stresses the significance of understanding the fundamentals of strategy. Whether in martial arts or life, a strong foundation is crucial. Knowing the basics provides the groundwork for effective and nuanced strategic thinking. The modern world makes this easy as information is but a click away on the internet. There is no shortcut to this instruction by Musashi and it requires daily reading and the studying of a wide array of material to build a vibrant and diverse knowledge base.

Holistic Approach. Musashi encourages the application of strategic thinking in all aspects of life. The practitioner is urged to see strategy as a holistic approach that encompasses daily decision-making and interactions. This is a hugely important concept as it is simply not possible to switch a strategic mindset on and off. The implications of this for the modern strategist are profound as our daily lives outside of work tend to be quite simple with easy transport, shopping, entertainment, and support. This means complex problems that require strategy to solve are quite rare unless the strategist actively seeks them out. It is essential that anyone trying to improve their strategic mindset does this. For example, there are online innovation challenges (such as those hosted by HeroX and Innocentive), escape room challenges, or even running a small hobby business.

Adaptability and Fluidity. Musashi highlights the importance of adaptability and fluidity in strategy. The strategist should be able to adjust to changing circumstances and flow around obstacles, much like water in a river flowing around or over rocks. In the modern context this means not being wedded to rigid or linear processes or Standard Operating Procedures (SOPs) and having the self-awareness and humility to acknowledge when the desired results or outcomes are not being achieved. Unfortunately, modern organisations, and particularly the military, love linear toolsets and step-by-step guides. Musashi is clear that these are detrimental to the formulation and implementation of strategy.

Intuitive Action. Musashi advocates for a state of intuitive action where the mind is clear, and actions are spontaneous. This aligns with the concept of *Mushin*, a state of no-mind or no-form, where the strategist is free from preconceived notions and can respond naturally to the situation at hand. We should be quite clear that in the modern context this does not negate the need to think through a problem and plan carefully. What Musashi is articulating is the need to avoid blindly applying templates or previous experience to a complex problem. Instead, in the analysis and planning phases the mind should be allowed to spontaneously wander and dream as it is here that innovative solutions and new, unexpected ways of tackling problems can be found. In the modern world, this can be achieved though meditation, saunas, massage, gym workouts, watching television or any other activity that allows the mind to free itself from rigid thought.

Practical Application. Strategy is meant to be practical and applicable. Musashi underlines the importance of hands-on experience and actual practice. The strategist must not only understand the principles but embody them through continuous training and application. This is a problem for military leaders as they rarely get to develop and implement strategy for real, so training takes on an urgent dimension. But Musashi is clear, that training must be as close to the real thing as possible, and the preference is always for actual problems rather than artificial constructs. There are many ways to achieve this, and Artificial Intelligence (AI) is now providing rich virtual environments for training.

Balance and Harmony. Achieving balance and harmony in one's actions is a key aspect of Musashi's Way of Strategy. This involves balancing opposing forces, understanding the interplay of different elements, and finding harmony in one's approach to conflicts and challenges. In the modern context this is about understanding that while the end state of a strategy may be vague or difficult to define, it must achieve a new balanced reality and *status quo*. Harmony may not be possible, but a period of calm must be the minimum outcome. Any strategy must leave things better, or it will have failed.

No-Form (*Mushin*). Musashi introduces the concept of "No-Form," a state of mind free from preconceived notions and attachments. In strategic terms, this involves being open to various possibilities and not being bound by rigid plans. A strategist in the state of No-Form can adapt instantly to changing circumstances.

Timing and Opportunity. Timing is crucial in the Way of Strategy. Musashi stresses the importance of seizing the opportune moment. This involves patience, keen observation, and the ability to act decisively when the time is right. In simple terms, Musashi is stating the requirement to be proactive and force adversaries to react to your activity. He advises practitioners to be aware of the ebb and flow of a situation, striking when the timing is optimal. Understanding the rhythm of a conflict allows for precise and effective actions.

No Waste Strategy. Musashi advises against wasteful actions and unnecessary movements. The strategist should be economical and efficient in their approach. Every action should have a purpose and contribute to the overall strategy. As all strategists will know, there is never enough resource to do everything well. Musashi knew this and was clear that every single action, no matter how minor, must make a meaningful contribution to the desired end state or vision.

Continuous Improvement. The Way of Strategy involves a path of continuous improvement. Musashi encourages the strategist to refine their skills, learn from experiences, and adapt their approach based on lessons gained. Mastery is a journey of constant refinement, adaptation, and evolution. Musashi is clear that training and learning must never stop.

The Five Rings

Musashi divides his teachings into five books, or rings, each representing a different element of strategy and underpinned by the principles, techniques and concepts described above. The five rings are Earth, Water, Fire, Wind, and the Void. Each ring corresponds to a specific aspect of strategy, providing a holistic framework to develop a strategic mindset that can be used to tackle complex problems.

Earth (*Chi*). Musashi associates Earth with the foundation of strategy. This involves understanding the terrain, the environment, the politics, potential adversaries, allies, neutrals, and the wider situation. It is about knowing your own strengths and weaknesses and adapting your approach accordingly. Musashi encourages a thorough understanding of the Earth, which serves as the groundwork for effective strategy. To achieve *Chi*, the strategist must be constantly observing, measuring, and analysing the Earth to maintain a dynamic understanding of the world. This is the absolute fundamental base of a strategic mindset. Those that study or practice strategy on a regular basis will notice the similarity to PESTLE, STEEPLEMS and SWOT type analysis toolsets from modern business management processes.

Water (*Sui*). Water symbolises adaptability and fluidity. Musashi urges practitioners to be flexible in their strategies, capable of flowing around or over obstacles rather than confronting them directly. Water teaches the importance of being receptive to change and adjusting tactics based on the evolving circumstances. To achieve *Sui*, strategists must avoid the temptation to always use brute force such as military action or economic coercion.

Fire (*Ka*). Fire represents the intensity and decisiveness required in strategic actions. Musashi emphasises the need to seize opportunities and act with commitment. The strategic concept of Fire involves exploiting weaknesses in the opponent's position and maintaining relentless pressure when the time is right. Fire (*Ka*) is more than blunt offensive action or an aggressive spirit. It is more akin to applying a surgeon's scalpel at the right place at the right time under the right conditions. Get it wrong and the consequences are disastrous. Get it right and the effects are miraculous.

Wind (*Fu*). Wind signifies the ability to read and respond to the intentions of the opponent. Musashi encourages a deep understanding of human nature and the capacity to anticipate and counteract the strategies of others. The strategic concept of Wind involves psychological warfare and deception. To achieve Wind (*Fu*), the strategist must build a comprehensive understanding of human personality types and how they act under different pressures and in different situations. This can take a long time to achieve and must be multi-cultural. The only way to become expert at this is to mix, socialise and interact with many people in many different environments. Training in body language, cultural awareness and psychology can all help in this regard. Without expertise in Wind (*Fu*), the strategist will be weak and incomplete.

The Void (*Ku*). The Void is the ultimate formless state, where the strategist transcends techniques and becomes one with the situation. Musashi describes this as a state of emptiness where the mind is clear, allowing for intuitive and spontaneous action. The concept of the Void articulates the importance of mastering oneself to achieve strategic excellence. Musashi encourages the practitioner to find this void, where there is no fixed form or limitation. It is a state of emptiness that allows for limitless possibilities. This is like the concept of *Mushin* where the strategist avoids fixed templates and rigid toolsets. In the today's world, it means seeking innovative new ideas and ways of doing business and not being constrained by convention, narrow mindedness, or a lack of imagination.

CREATING A STRATEGIC MINDSET – MUSASHI'S GUIDE FOR THE MODERN STRATEGIST

Putting Musashi's five rings into practice is a daunting prospect even for the most experienced strategist. Musashi himself made it clear that constant practice, training and experience was necessary even for experts. The 5-step process below is designed to help create a strategic mindset through experience and learning.

Musashi would be turning in his grave if he saw the linear guide below given that a core element of his teaching was about adaptation, fluidity, and 'no-form'. Unfortunately, books are read in a linear fashion so that is how this guide is presented. Please note, that constant looping back and adaptation are always required!

Step 1: Continually Improve Your Knowledge and Understanding of the Earth (Chi)

This is the foundation of all good strategies and the source of strength for all great strategists. Musashi was clear that one must learn and 'know things'. This means reading widely, and not just texts with which the strategist is comfortable or knowledgeable and make a concerted effort to experience new things and new situations. In short - read, travel, experience and explore as much as one can. The more exotic and outlandish the better. Understanding the world around you is a dynamic and continuous process that involves curiosity, awareness, and an open mind. Here are some practical suggestions to help you gain a deeper understanding of the Earth (*Chi*):

Cultivate Curiosity. Approach the world with a curious mindset. Ask questions, seek to understand different perspectives, and explore topics that pique your interest. Try new hobbies and sports and accept unusual invitations from friends and colleagues. Visit museums and art galleries. Curiosity is the driving force behind learning and understanding.

Read Widely. Read books, articles, and news from a diverse range of sources. Exposure to different ideas, cultures, and viewpoints broadens your understanding of the world. Don't be arrogant or culturally prejudiced. Remember, the adversary thinks they are right, and you are wrong. Understand their point of view, even if you don't agree with it. Consider reading both fiction and non-fiction to gain varied insights.

Stay Informed. Keep yourself informed about current events, global issues, and developments in various fields. Stay updated on news from reliable sources to understand the context and implications of events happening around the world. But also read highly biased reports to better understand how other people think and perceive the world.

Engage in Critical Thinking. Develop your critical thinking skills by questioning information, evaluating evidence, and considering alternative viewpoints. Critical thinking allows you to analyse and interpret information more effectively.

Travel and Explore. If possible, travel to different places and immerse yourself in new cultures. Experiencing diverse environments first hand can provide valuable insights into the complexities of the world and help you appreciate cultural differences. Try learning a new language.

Connect with People. Build connections with people from different backgrounds, cultures, and perspectives. Engage in meaningful conversations, listen actively, and learn from others' experiences. Building diverse relationships enhances your understanding of the human experience.

Learn from History. Study history to understand the context and historical events that have shaped the present. History provides valuable lessons and insights into the patterns of human behaviour and societal development.

Educate Yourself. Pursue education and persistent learning. Whether through formal education, online courses, or self-directed learning, acquiring knowledge in various fields contributes to a well-rounded understanding of the world.

Be Open-Minded. Approach new ideas with an open mind. Be willing to reconsider your beliefs and perspectives based on new information. Open-mindedness allows for intellectual growth and adaptability.

Engage in Discussions and Debates. Participate in discussions and debates on a variety of topics. Engaging with others in a respectful and constructive manner encourages the exchange of ideas and promotes deeper understanding.

Seek Different Perspectives. Actively seek out viewpoints that differ from your own. Exposure to diverse perspectives helps you challenge assumptions, broaden your understanding, and appreciate the complexity of issues.

Reflect on Your Own Beliefs. Periodically reflect on your own beliefs, values, and biases. Understand how your background and experiences influence your worldview. Self-awareness is crucial for developing a more nuanced understanding of the world.

Stay Humble. Acknowledge that the world is vast and complex, and no one has all the answers. Approach your quest for understanding with humility, recognising that there is always more to learn and discover.

Remember that understanding the world and gaining '*Chi*' is an ongoing and evolving process. Embrace the journey of exploration and discovery and stay committed to learning from the diverse and dynamic tapestry of the world around you.

*Step 2: Embrace the Void (*Ku*) at Least Once per Day to Improve Ingenuity and Innovation*

Musashi was insistent on the necessity of releasing the mind to wander and ponder without restraint. His strong advice was to use techniques that allowed the mind to move away from concentrating on the here and now. Modern science has shown that disengaging the mind from the present through techniques such as mediation or alternative pursuits is the key to accessing the creative sub conscious. The key to this endeavour is to find something that works for you as everyone is different. For some it will be the calm of say a sauna and massage. For others it will be the brutal intensity of a gym workout. You will know it when you see it! It's that eureka or 'light bulb' moment when the mind makes a sudden unprompted leap to a creative concept or idea. T E Lawrence referred to it as 'the flash of a kingfisher across a pond.' Improving your innovation and creativity involves cultivating a mindset that embraces curiosity, experimentation, and a willingness to explore new ideas. Here are some practical strategies to enhance your innovation and creativity:

Diversify Your Experiences. Exposure to diverse experiences can stimulate creativity. Engage in activities outside your comfort zone, travel, meet new people, and try new hobbies. Different perspectives and experiences can inspire innovative thinking.

Encourage a Growth Mindset. Embrace a growth mindset, believing that your abilities and intelligence can be developed through dedication and hard work. This mindset fosters resilience, a willingness to learn from failures, and a commitment to continuous improvement.

Challenge Assumptions. Question assumptions and conventional wisdom. Often, innovation arises when one can challenge existing norms and explore alternative ways of thinking. Be open to questioning the status quo.

Embrace Failure as a Learning Opportunity. View failure not as a setback, but as a valuable learning opportunity. Analyse failures to understand what went wrong, extract lessons, and use that knowledge to improve future endeavours.

Develop a Creative Environment. Surround yourself with a creative and stimulating environment. This could include inspiring artwork, diverse reading materials, and spaces that encourage free thinking. A conducive environment can foster innovative ideas.

Practice Mindfulness and Reflection. Cultivate mindfulness practices to stay present and focused. Reflecting on your thoughts and experiences can help you gain insights and make connections that contribute to creative thinking.

Collaborate and Brainstorm. Collaborate with diverse individuals who bring different perspectives and skills to the table. Engage in brainstorming sessions where ideas flow freely without judgment. Collective creativity often leads to innovative solutions.

Set Aside Dedicated Time for Creativity. Allocate specific time in your schedule for creative thinking and problem-solving. This intentional focus allows your mind to delve into creative processes without distractions.

Use Creative Techniques. Explore creative techniques such as mind mapping, lateral thinking, or brainstorming exercises. These methods can help break mental barriers and stimulate novel ideas.

Seek Inspiration from Different Disciplines. Look beyond your own field for inspiration. Draw insights and ideas from diverse disciplines, as cross-pollination of ideas from different domains often leads to innovative solutions.

Read and Consume Creatively. Read books, articles, and content that challenge your thinking and stimulate creativity. Explore different genres and expose yourself to a variety of perspectives and ideas.

Develop a Creative Ritual. Establish a ritual or routine that signals your mind to enter a creative mode. It could be a specific time of day, a particular environment, or even a creative warm-up activity that prepares your mind for innovation.

Continuous Learning. Stay curious and commit to lifelong learning. Acquiring knowledge in diverse fields can provide you with a broad foundation for creative thinking and problem-solving.

Experiment and Iterate. Embrace a mindset of experimentation. Don't be afraid to try new things, iterate on existing ideas, and refine your approach based on feedback and results.

*Step 3: Improve Your Understanding of People to Achieve Expertise in Wind (*Fu*)*

Understanding people and their behaviours is a multifaceted and ongoing process that involves a combination of empathy, observation, communication, and self-awareness. Here are some practical methods to enhance your understanding of people:

Practice Active Listening. Actively listen to what others are saying without interrupting. Pay attention to both verbal and non-verbal cues. Reflecting back what you've heard can demonstrate your understanding and encourage further communication.

Observe Non-Verbal Cues. Non-verbal communication, including body language, facial expressions, and gestures, provides valuable insights into emotions and intentions. Pay attention to these cues to better understand the underlying feelings or attitudes.

Ask Open-Ended Questions. Encourage meaningful conversations by asking open-ended questions. These questions invite people to share more about themselves, their experiences, and their perspectives, providing you with a deeper understanding.

Cultivate Empathy. Empathy involves putting yourself in someone else's shoes and understanding their feelings and perspectives. Practice empathy by considering the emotions and experiences of others, which can foster stronger connections and understanding.

Be Mindful of Cultural Differences. Recognise and respect cultural variations in communication styles and behaviours. People from different cultures may express themselves in diverse ways, and understanding these differences can enhance your overall comprehension.

Read Books on Psychology and Human Behaviour. Reading books on psychology, human behaviour, and communication can provide valuable insights into the complexities of human nature. Choose books written by reputable authors or experts in the field.

Take Courses or Attend Workshops. Consider taking courses or attending workshops on psychology, communication, or interpersonal skills. These educational experiences can deepen your understanding of human behaviour and provide practical tools for improvement.

Build Self-Awareness. Comprehending others begins with understanding yourself. Reflect on your own emotions, motivations, and behaviours.

Increased self-awareness allows you to relate better to others and recognise common patterns in human behaviour.

Seek Diverse Experiences. Engage with people from different backgrounds, cultures, and perspectives. Exposure to diverse experiences broadens your understanding of various behaviours and helps you appreciate the richness of human diversity.

Practice Patience. Building a deep understanding of people takes time. Be patient and allow relationships to develop naturally. Avoid making quick judgments and give others the space to express themselves authentically.

Consider Individual Differences. Recognise that each person is unique, and behaviours may be influenced by a variety of factors such as personality, upbringing, and personal experiences. Avoid making assumptions and approach each individual with an open and broad mindset.

Reflect on Your Interactions. After interactions, take a moment to reflect on the dynamics, communication patterns, and emotions involved. This reflection can enhance your awareness and contribute to continuous improvement in understanding people.

*Step 4: Develop Techniques for Dealing with Immovable Obstacles so Your Strategy can Flow Like Water (*Sui*)*

Musashi advocated for strategies that flowed around or over immovable obstacles like water flowing around or over rocks in a stream. Dealing with immovable obstacles at work can be challenging, but with a consistent approach, you can navigate these situations more effectively. Here are some techniques to help you handle immovable obstacles:

Assess the Situation. Take a step back and assess the nature of the immovable obstacle. Understand the reasons behind its resistance or inflexibility. Consider the organisational dynamics, policies, or individuals involved.

Seek Understanding. Engage in open and honest communication to understand the perspectives of those contributing to the obstacle. Listen actively, ask questions, and seek to comprehend their concerns or reasons for resistance.

Build Relationships. Cultivate positive relationships with key stakeholders, decision-makers, or individuals associated with the immovable obstacle. Strong relationships can facilitate a more collaborative approach and open avenues for finding common ground.

Find Common Ground. Identify areas of common ground or shared goals with the parties involved. Highlighting shared interests can create a foundation for collaboration and compromise.

Present Alternatives. Propose alternative solutions or approaches that address the concerns of those contributing to the obstacle. Providing viable alternatives demonstrates your commitment to finding a resolution and allows for more flexibility in problem-solving.

Highlight Consequences. Clearly articulate the potential consequences of maintaining the immovable obstacle. This could include impacts on productivity, morale, or the overall success of a project. Presenting the consequences can encourage reconsideration.

Engage Leadership Support. If the immovable obstacle is deeply ingrained, seek support from leadership. Present your case and provide evidence to demonstrate the need for change. Leadership involvement can lend weight to your efforts and initiate a broader discussion.

Leverage Data and Evidence. Use data and evidence to support your position. Data-driven arguments can be persuasive and provide an objective basis for decision-making. Presenting compelling evidence strengthens your case.

Build a Coalition. Identify and enlist the support of colleagues or like-minded individuals who share your concerns. A coalition can amplify your voice, demonstrate broader support, and increase the likelihood of influencing change.

Negotiate and Compromise. One ought to be willing to negotiate and find compromises. Understand that a complete removal of the obstacle may not be feasible, but finding middle ground can lead to a more workable solution.

Develop Patience and Persistence. Dealing with immovable obstacles often requires patience and persistence. Stay committed to your goal and be prepared for a gradual process of influencing change.

Adapt to the Environment. Evaluate whether adapting to the existing environment, within certain limits, is a viable option. Sometimes, adjusting your approach or expectations can make it easier to work within the constraints.

Seek External Support. If internal efforts are not yielding results, consider seeking external support. This could involve consulting with mentors, seeking advice from industry experts, or exploring external resources that may provide insights or assistance.

Know When to Let Go. Recognise when a situation may be truly immovable, and it may be in your best interest to let go. Assess the impact on your well-being and professional growth and consider alternative paths if necessary.

*Step 5: Learn When to Strike with Fire (*Ka*) to Gain and Maintain the Initiative*

Taking aggressive and proactive action to solve a problem involves a combination of strategic planning, assertiveness, and a results-oriented mindset. Here are some effective methods to approach problems with a proactive and aggressive stance and apply Fire (*Ka*) at the right time:

Define Clear Objectives. Clearly define the objectives you aim to achieve through your aggressive and proactive actions. Having a clear vision of what success looks like provides a guiding framework for your efforts.

Gather Information. Equip yourself with comprehensive information about the problem. Conduct thorough research, gather relevant data, and understand the root causes and contributing factors. Informed decisions are key to effective problem-solving.

Set Priorities. Prioritise the most critical aspects of the problem that require immediate attention. Focus your aggressive actions on addressing high-priority issues to have a more significant impact on the overall solution.

Develop a Plan. Develop a plan that outlines the steps you need to take to address the problem aggressively. Define specific actions, timelines, and resource requirements. A well-structured plan serves as a roadmap for your proactive efforts.

Take Swift and Decisive Action. Be decisive and take swift action to implement your plan. Procrastination can hinder progress, so demonstrate a sense of urgency in tackling the problem head-on.

Anticipate and Mitigate Risks. Identify potential risks and challenges that may arise during the problem-solving process. Develop contingency plans to mitigate risks, ensuring that your proactive actions remain effective in the face of unexpected obstacles.

Engage Stakeholders. Involve relevant stakeholders early in the process. Communicate your plans, gather input, and build a coalition of support. Engaging stakeholders ensures alignment with organisational goals and increases the likelihood of successful implementation.

Be Assertive in Communication. Communicate assertively about the problem and your proposed solutions. Clearly articulate your position, express the urgency of the matter, and convey the potential benefits of your proactive actions. Confidence in communication inspires confidence in your approach.

Leverage Resources Effectively. Make efficient use of available resources, whether they be financial, human, or technological. Allocate resources strategically to maximise their impact on the problem-solving process.

Monitor Progress Actively. Regularly monitor the progress of your actions. Track key performance indicators, assess the effectiveness of implemented solutions, and be ready to adjust your approach based on real-time feedback.

Adaptability and Flexibility. Be adaptable and flexible in your approach. Recognise when adjustments are needed and be willing to modify your strategy based on changing circumstances or new information.

Demonstrate Tenacity. Display tenacity and persistence in pursuing your goals. Overcoming challenges often requires determination and a willingness to persevere in the face of setbacks.

Celebrate Small Wins. Acknowledge and celebrate incremental successes along the way. Recognising achievements, no matter how small, boosts morale and reinforces a positive and results-driven culture.

Seek Feedback and Continuous Improvement. Solicit feedback from stakeholders and team members. Use feedback to identify areas for improvement and refine your approach. Continuous learning and improvement are integral to maintaining a proactive and aggressive problem-solving stance.

Reflect and Learn. After the resolution of the problem, take time to reflect on the entire process. Analyse what worked well, identify areas for improvement, and capture lessons learned for future challenges.

Remember that taking aggressive and proactive action is not synonymous with being impulsive. It involves a calculated and strategic approach to problem-solving that advocates decisiveness, assertiveness, and a commitment to achieving tangible results.

Tackle a Complex Problem Once per Week to Build Experience

Simple and contrived training exercises are of little use. Musashi advocated for real world experience as the only assured way of developing expertise. Tackling a complex problem requires a systematic approach in order to maximise the learning experience. Here is a step-by-step guide to help you navigate complex problems and learn from the experience:

Understand the Problem and Understand Yourself. Begin by thoroughly understanding the problem. Define the problem statement, identify its scope, and gather relevant information. Break down the problem into its components and understand the relationships between different elements. Understand your own strengths, weaknesses, knowledge gaps and limitations regarding the problem.

Research and Gather Information. Conduct research to gather more information about the problem. Consult various sources, gather data, and seek insights from experts or relevant literature. A comprehensive understanding of the problem is crucial for developing effective solutions.

Define Goals and Objectives. Clearly define your goals and objectives. What are you trying to achieve by solving this problem? Establishing clear goals provides a direction for your efforts and helps measure success.

Be Clear on the Consequences of Failure. Understanding the consequences of failure is an important aspect of decision-making and risk management. It allows the assessment of potential risks and enable preparation for different outcomes.

Identify Stakeholders. Identify and involve relevant stakeholders who are affected by or can contribute to the resolution of the problem. Consider perspectives from different stakeholders to ensure a comprehensive understanding of the issue.

Brainstorm and Generate Ideas. Engage in brainstorming sessions to generate a wide range of ideas and potential solutions. Encourage creativity, and don't dismiss any idea initially. This phase is about exploring possibilities without judgment.

Prioritise and Analyse Solutions. Evaluate and prioritise the generated ideas based on feasibility, impact, and alignment with your goals. Analyse the strengths and weaknesses of each solution. Consider short-term and long-term implications.

Break Down the Problem into Manageable Parts. If the problem is a complex one, it can be broken it down into smaller and more manageable segments. Addressing each component individually can make the overall problem-solving process more manageable.

Develop a Strategy. Develop a strategic plan for solving the problem. Outline the steps you need to take, allocate resources, and set timelines. Consider the sequencing of activities and dependencies between different steps.

Experiment and Iterate. Don't be afraid to experiment with different solutions. Iterate on your initial ideas based on feedback and results. This iterative approach allows you to refine your strategy and adapt to changing circumstances.

Collaborate and Communicate. Collaborate with others who can contribute valuable insights and expertise. Effective communication is essential for ensuring that everyone involved understands the problem, the chosen strategy, and their roles in the solution.

Anticipate Challenges. Anticipate potential challenges or obstacles that may arise during the implementation of your solution. Develop contingency plans and strategies for addressing unforeseen issues.

Implement and Monitor. Begin implementing your solution while closely monitoring progress. Establish key performance indicators (KPIs) to measure success. Regularly assess whether the implemented solution is achieving the desired outcomes.

Seek Feedback. Seek feedback from stakeholders and other relevant parties throughout the process. Feedback provides valuable insights, helps identify areas for improvement, and ensures that your approach remains responsive to changing dynamics.

Celebrate Success and Learn from Failure. Acknowledge and celebrate successes along the way. Additionally, learn from failures and setbacks. Use these experiences to refine one's problem-solving skills and inform future approaches to complex problems.

Reflect and Iterate. After solving the problem, take time to reflect on the entire process. Identify lessons learned, areas for improvement, and insights gained. This reflection prepares you for future problem-solving endeavours.

Remember that tackling complex problems is an ongoing process that requires adaptability and a willingness to learn. By approaching the problem systematically and incorporating feedback, you increase the likelihood of finding effective and sustainable solutions.

MUSASHI – A SUMMARY

Strategists in the modern world must work hard to create a strategic mindset in themselves and their supporting team. Musashi's "*The Book of Five Rings*" provides advice and insights on how to achieve this. But it is not an easy undertaking and requires dedication, perseverance, and a lifelong commitment to excellence. Musashi's key tenets are below.

- Musashi advocated for a strategic mindset rather than a defined methodology for tackling complex problems.
- He was of the view that every complex problem was completely unique and therefore could not be solved with templates, rules,

toolsets, or procedures.

- Musashi stated that rigid approaches stifle innovation, creativity, and initiative but also give adversaries ample opportunity to guess what is coming next and take appropriate pre-emptive action or enable effective countermeasures.
- Earth (*Chi*). Musashi associates Earth with the foundation of strategy. This involves understanding the terrain, the environment, the politics, potential adversaries, allies, neutrals, and the wider situation. It is about knowing your own strengths and weaknesses and adapting your approach accordingly.
- Water (*Sui*). Water symbolises adaptability and fluidity. Musashi urges practitioners to be flexible in their strategies, capable of flowing around or over obstacles rather than confronting them directly. Water teaches the importance of being receptive to change and adjusting tactics based on the evolving circumstances.
- Fire (*Ka*). Fire represents the intensity and decisiveness required in strategic actions. Musashi underlines the need to seize opportunities and act with commitment. The strategic concept of Fire involves exploiting weaknesses in the opponent's position and maintaining relentless pressure when the time is right.
- Wind (*Fu*). Wind signifies the ability to read and respond to the intentions of the opponent. Musashi encourages a deep understanding of human nature and the capacity to anticipate and counteract the strategies of others. The strategic concept of Wind involves psychological warfare and deception. To achieve Wind (*Fu*), the strategist must build a comprehensive understanding of human personality types and how they act under different pressures and in different situations.
- Void (*Ku*). Musashi described this as a state of emptiness where the mind is clear, allowing for intuitive and spontaneous action. The concept of the Void emphasises the importance of mastering oneself to achieve strategic excellence. Musashi encourages the practitioner to find this void, where there is no fixed form or limitation. It is a state of emptiness that allows for limitless

possibilities. In the today's world, it means seeking innovative new ideas and ways of doing business and not being constrained by convention, narrow mindedness, or a lack of imagination and innovation.

MUSASHI'S GUIDE TO CREATING A STRATEGIC MINDSET

*Step 1 Continually Improve Your Knowledge and Understanding of the Earth (*Chi*)*

- Cultivate Curiosity.
- Read Widely.
- Stay Informed.
- Engage in Critical Thinking.
- Travel and Explore.
- Connect with People.
- Learn from History.
- Educate Yourself.
- Be Open-Minded.
- Engage in Discussions and Debates
- Seek Different Perspectives.
- Reflect on Your Own Beliefs.
- Stay Humble.

*Step 2 Embrace the Void (*Ku*) at Least Once per Day to Improve Ingenuity and Innovation*

- Diversify Your Experiences.
- Encourage a Growth Mindset.
- Challenge Assumptions.
- Embrace Failure as a Learning Opportunity.
- Develop a Creative Environment.
- Practice Mindfulness and Reflection.
- Collaborate and Brainstorm.
- Set Aside Dedicated Time for Creativity.

- Use Creative Techniques.
- Seek Inspiration from Different Disciplines.
- Read and Consume Creatively.
- Develop a Creative Ritual.
- Continuous Learning.
- Experiment and Iterate.

*Step 3 Improve Your Understanding of People to Achieve Expertise in Wind (***Fu***)*

- Practice Active Listening.
- Observe Non-Verbal Cues.
- Ask Open-Ended Questions.
- Cultivate Empathy.
- Be Mindful of Cultural Differences.
- Read Books on Psychology and Human Behaviour.
- Take Courses or Attend Workshops.
- Build Self-Awareness.
- Seek Diverse Experiences.
- Practice Patience.
- Consider Individual Differences.
- Reflect on Your Interactions.

*Step 4 Develop Techniques for Dealing with Immovable Obstacles so Your Strategy can Flow Like Water (***Sui***)*

- Assess the Situation.
- Seek Understanding.
- Build Relationships.
- Find Common Ground.
- Present Alternatives.
- Highlight Consequences.
- Engage Leadership Support.
- Leverage Data and Evidence.

- Build a Coalition.
- Negotiate and Compromise.
- Develop Patience and Persistence.
- Adapt to the Environment.
- Seek External Support.
- Know When to Let Go.

*Step 5 Learn When to Strike with Fire (*Ka*) to Gain and Maintain the Initiative*

- Define Clear Objectives.
- Gather Information.
- Set Priorities.
- Develop a Plan.
- Take Swift and Decisive Action.
- Anticipate and Mitigate Risks.
- Engage Stakeholders.
- Be Assertive in Communication.
- Leverage Resources Effectively.
- Monitor Progress Actively.
- Adaptability and Flexibility.
- Demonstrate Tenacity.
- Celebrate Small Wins.
- Seek Feedback and Continuous Improvement.
- Reflect and Learn.

Chapter Two

The Mahabharata

"Success that is obtained by negotiations and other means is the best. Success which is secured by creating disunion amongst the enemy is temporary. Success secured by battle is the worst."

—Vyasa, Bhishma Parva

In This Chapter

- About *The Mahabharata*.
- The Strategic Concepts within *The Mahabharata*.
- Creating a Strategic Mindset - *The Mahabharata's* Advice for the Modern Strategist.
- The *Mahabharata* – A Summary

About *The Mahabharata*

The *Mahabharata* is one of the greatest epics in world literature and a central text in the Indian literary and cultural tradition. It is a multifaceted work encompassing themes such as duty, righteousness, love, betrayal, and the struggle between good and evil. Composed over several centuries, it is largely attributed to the sage Vyasa and comprises over 100,000 verses, making it one of the longest poems in the world. The *Mahabharata* tells the story of a great war between two branches of a royal family, the Kauravas and the Pandavas, for control of the kingdom of Hastinapura.

The exact historical context of the *Mahabharata* is difficult to determine, as its composition likely spanned several centuries, beginning around the 8th century BCE and continuing until around the 4th century CE. It is a compilation of numerous stories and traditions that reflect the culture, values, and beliefs of ancient India. The epic is set in a mythological past and features an array of human and divine characters.

The *Mahabharata* delves into various philosophical and ethical themes. These include:

- ***Dharma* (Righteousness)**. The concept of *dharma*, or righteousness, is central to the epic. Characters often struggle with their duty to family, society, and their own moral compass. The text explores the complexities of *dharma* through the experiences of its protagonists.
- ***Karma* and Fate**. The epic examines the relationship between *karma* (actions) and fate, showing how the choices characters make have consequences in their lives.
- **The *Bhagavad Gita***. One of the most revered sections of the *Mahabharata* is the *Bhagavad Gita*, a philosophical and spiritual dialogue between the warrior Arjuna and the god Krishna. It addresses questions of duty, ethics, and the nature of the self, providing guidance on how to navigate life's challenges.
- **Family and Relationships**. The epic revolves around the intricate relationships among family members, including themes of loyalty, betrayal, and reconciliation. The conflict between the Pandavas and Kauravas is essentially a family feud taken to its extreme.

The story centres on the rivalry between the five Pandava brothers (Yudhishthira, Bhima, Arjuna, Nakula, and Sahadeva) and the hundred Kaurava brothers (led by Duryodhana) over the throne of Hastinapura. The epic culminates in the great war of Kurukshetra, where the Pandavas and Kauravas engage in a fierce battle with the fate of the kingdom at stake. This battle serves as the backdrop for the ethical dilemmas faced by the characters.

The god Krishna plays a pivotal role as Arjuna's charioteer and spiritual guide. He provides Arjuna with the teachings of the *Bhagavad Gita*, which offer an exploration of duty, righteousness, and the nature of life.

The *Mahabharata* had a profound impact on Indian culture and continues to be a source of inspiration for literature, art, theatre, and film. Its themes and characters have been reinterpreted in various forms across generations. The epic's exploration of complex moral and ethical dilemmas remains relevant in contemporary discussions of personal and societal values.

The *Mahabharata* is a multifaceted epic that weaves together mythology, philosophy, and history to create a rich tapestry of human experience. Its enduring legacy is a testament to its profound insights into the nature of life and the challenges faced by individuals in their pursuit of righteousness and wisdom. From these challenges a number of strategic concepts can be determined.

The Strategic Concepts within *The Mahabharata*

***Dharma* (Righteousness).** Central to the *Mahabharata* is the concept of *dharma*, or righteousness. The characters in the epic grapple with moral dilemmas and ethical choices, highlighting the importance of aligning one's actions with the principles of *dharma*. Strategic decisions, according to the *Mahabharata*, should be grounded in moral and ethical considerations. Strategists must therefore have a set of values and standards on which to base their actions. These cannot be ambiguous or flexible but must be the bedrock of everything the strategist undertakes. The basis of these values and standards can be built upon a range of guiding principles from religion to cultural beliefs, but they are enduring and immovable.

In reality, this is far harder to achieve than the *Mahabharata* makes out. The human tendency to use the Ends to justify the Means appears to be endemic across all cultures and takes concerted effort, not to mention checks and balances, to ensure this attitude does not prevail. However, there is surprising commonality around the world as to what constitutes ethical conduct. In order to create a strategic mindset, strategists should establish four to ten values and standards that they will live their life by. These must be personalised to the individual but could include values such as integrity, loyalty to the constitution, treating everyone equally, or putting others first.

Strategic Planning and Vision. The *Mahabharata* underlines the significance of strategic planning and foresight. The key protagonists Bhishma, Drona, and Krishna are portrayed as master strategists who carefully plan their moves on the battlefield. The importance of setting long-term goals and having a clear vision for the future is a recurring theme not only in the *Mahabharata* but many other strategic texts as well. To create a strategic mindset, one must constantly be looking to the future and establishing a vision of what this new reality will look like. A word of caution here as the temptation is to go into great detail but this would be a mistake. The treatise clearly posits that the vision of the future is more about feelings and perceptions than a purely physical outcome.

Alliance Building. The formation of alliances plays a crucial role in the epic, *Mahabharata*. Various factions seek support and form strategic partnerships to strengthen their positions. The concept of alliance building is presented as an essential aspect of strategic thinking, emphasising the power of collaboration to achieve common goals.

Understanding the Enemy. The *Mahabharata* highlights the need to thoroughly understand one's opponents. This involves studying their strengths, weaknesses, motivations, and strategies. Characters like Vidura and Krishna provide insights into the psychological and strategic aspects of dealing with adversaries.

Adaptability and Flexibility. The characters in the *Mahabharata* often face unpredictable challenges. The ability to adapt to changing circumstances and improvise in the face of adversity is highlighted as a crucial strategic skill. Characters like Arjuna showcase the importance of flexibility in tactics, operations and strategies.

Deception and Diplomacy. Diplomacy and strategic deception are woven into the fabric of the *Mahabharata*. Characters employ various forms of deceit to achieve their goals, highlighting the pragmatic aspects of strategy. Krishna's role as a diplomat and strategist exemplifies the use of clever tactics to achieve a higher purpose.

Leadership and Decision-Making. The epic explores different leadership styles and the impact of leadership on strategic outcomes. Characters like Yudhishthira and Duryodhana demonstrate contrasting leadership qualities, shedding light on the consequences of decisions made under pressure.

Role of Wisdom and Counsel. Seeking wise counsel is a recurring theme in the *Mahabharata*. Characters often turn to mentors, advisors, and sages for guidance. The importance of wise decision-making, informed by experienced counsel, is portrayed as a key factor in successful strategic endeavours.

The Influence of Fate and Destiny. While strategic planning is crucial, the *Mahabharata* also acknowledges the role of fate and destiny in shaping events. Characters grapple with the idea that certain outcomes are beyond their control, highlighting the complexity of the interplay between free will and destiny in strategic pursuits. This concept is quite unique and actually hugely important as strategies operate in complex, chaotic and confusing environments where the unexpected is likely to happen with regularity. In order to create a strategic mindset, strategists must be comfortable with surprises, unexpected setbacks, fleeting opportunities and decision-making in a semi-vacuum.

War Ethics and Conduct. The *Mahabharata* delves into the ethical considerations of war. The discourse between Arjuna and Krishna in the *Bhagavad Gita*, a central part of the *Mahabharata*, addresses the moral aspects of conflict and the responsibility that comes with wielding power. The principles of just war and ethical conduct on the battlefield are explored in depth.

In summary, the *Mahabharata* offers a rich tapestry of strategic concepts that encompass ethical considerations, alliance building, adaptability, and the influence of fate. The epic provides timeless lessons on leadership, decision-making, and the complexities of navigating the moral and strategic dimensions of life.

Creating a Strategic Mindset – Advice from the *Mahabharata* for the Modern Strategist

Akin to Musashi's Five Rings, the temptation to use the *Mahabharata* as a linear guide or rigid process must be avoided. The steps below are designed to assist strategists in creating a strategic mindset and should not be followed in a linear or slavish manner.

Step 1: Determine Your Personal Values

Personal values and standards are the guiding principles that shape our behaviour, decisions, and interactions with others. They provide a framework for understanding ourselves and our goals, helping us live a fulfilling and meaningful life. This step will explore the importance of determining personal values and standards, the process of identifying them, and how they impact various aspects of our lives.

The Importance of Personal Values

- **Guidance for Decision-Making.** Personal values serve as a moral compass, helping us make choices that align with our beliefs and aspirations. When faced with complex decisions, having clear values allows us to navigate challenges more effectively.
- **Sense of Purpose.** Knowing our values helps us define our purpose and goals in life. When we understand what matters most to us, we can set meaningful objectives and work towards them.
- **Self-Awareness.** Identifying our values fosters self-awareness and introspection. It enables us to understand our strengths and weaknesses and to recognise how our actions align with our beliefs.
- **Authenticity.** Living according to our values allows us to be true to ourselves. When we align our behaviour with our beliefs, we cultivate authenticity and integrity.

- **Resilience.** Personal values provide a foundation for resilience in the face of adversity. When we encounter challenges, our values can offer strength and motivation to persevere.

The Process of Identifying Personal Values

- **Self-Reflection.** Start by reflecting on your life experiences, both positive and negative. Consider moments when you felt most fulfilled and when you felt most challenged. Identify the underlying values that influenced these experiences.
- **Identify Core Values.** Make a list of values that resonate with you. These could include honesty, compassion, respect, perseverance, and others. Narrow down the list to a few core values that are most important to you.
- **Assess Priorities.** Determine how your values influence your priorities in different areas of your life, such as career, relationships, and personal growth. Consider how you want to allocate your time and energy to align with your values.
- **Seek Feedback.** Ask trusted friends, family members, or mentors for feedback on your values. They may offer insights into your strengths and how you embody your values.
- **Re-evaluate Over Time.** Personal values may evolve as you grow and experience new situations. Periodically reassess your values to ensure they remain relevant and reflective of your current beliefs.

Impact of Personal Values

- **Relationships.** Personal values guide how we interact with others. When our values align with those of our loved ones, friends and colleagues, it fosters mutual respect and understanding. Misalignments may lead to conflicts that require communication and compromise.
- **Career Choices.** Values play a significant role in career decisions. People who choose careers aligned with their values tend to experience higher job satisfaction and a sense of fulfilment.
- **Personal Growth.** Personal values drive our desire for growth and

improvement. When we prioritise values such as continuous learning or self-discipline, we can achieve personal and professional development.

- **Social Responsibility.** Our values also guide our engagement with society and our contributions to the community. They influence our stance on social issues and our willingness to take action.

Determining personal values and standards is a vital aspect of self-discovery and personal growth and therefore essential for a strategic mindset. By reflecting on our beliefs and aligning our actions with our values, we can lead more authentic and fulfilling lives. Our values shape our relationships, career choices, and contributions to society, making it essential to understand and embrace them. As we evolve, our values may change, so regular self-assessment is crucial to ensure that we continue to live in accordance with our true selves.

In the Indian epic *Mahabharata*, one notable example of a protagonist determining their personal values is seen in the character of Arjuna during the events of the *Bhagavad Gita*. This sacred text is a conversation between Arjuna, one of the Pandava princes, and Lord Krishna, who serves as his charioteer and guide.

As the epic's climactic battle, the Kurukshetra War, approaches, Arjuna faces a profound moral and ethical dilemma. He finds himself standing on the battlefield, ready to fight against his own relatives, teachers, and friends on the opposing side. Torn between his duty as a warrior (*Kshatriya*) and his love and respect for his family and mentors, Arjuna experiences deep inner conflict.

Arjuna questions the righteousness of the war and the consequences of killing his kin, expressing his doubts and concerns to Krishna. This moment is a critical point where Arjuna evaluates his personal values and struggles to reconcile his duty with his moral beliefs.

In response, Krishna imparts wisdom to Arjuna through the teachings of the *Bhagavad Gita*. Krishna encourages Arjuna to fulfil his duty as a warrior and fight for righteousness and truth underlining the importance of acting selflessly and without attachment to the results of his actions. Krishna also teaches Arjuna about different paths of spiritual growth, including the path of knowledge, action, and devotion.

Arjuna ultimately resolves his inner conflict by aligning his personal values with his duty as a warrior and his untrammelled faith in Krishna's guidance. This allows him to proceed with the battle with clarity and determination, demonstrating his acceptance of his responsibilities and his commitment to righteousness.

This example from the *Mahabharata* showcases how a protagonist, Arjuna, navigates a complex moral dilemma and determines his personal values by seeking guidance, reflecting on his beliefs, and ultimately choosing a path that aligns with his duty and sense of justice.

A modern example where the *Mahabharata's* guidance on determining personal values delivered strategic success can be seen in Nelson Mandela's leadership during the transition from apartheid to democracy in South Africa. South Africa was under apartheid, a system of institutionalised racial segregation and discrimination, from 1948 until the early 1990s. Nelson Mandela, a key leader of the African National Congress (ANC), was imprisoned for 27 years for his opposition to apartheid. Upon his release in 1990, Mandela faced the enormous challenge of leading South Africa through a peaceful transition to democracy.

The *Mahabharata* emphasises the importance of *dharma* (righteousness or duty) and the need for leaders to align their actions with their moral and ethical values, even in the face of adversity. Mandela's approach to leadership during this critical period can be seen as being influenced by these principles.

Despite suffering immensely under apartheid, Mandela chose the path of reconciliation and nonviolence, reflecting the *Mahabharata's* emphasis on the importance of *dharma* over vengeance. He recognised that a peaceful transition was essential for the future of South Africa, where all citizens could coexist, regardless of race.

Mandela's personal values, which were centred around forgiveness, compassion, and the unification of a divided nation, mirrored the lessons from the *Mahabharata*. He rejected the notion of revenge against the white minority, understanding that the cycle of hatred and retribution would only lead to further suffering. Instead, he advocated for a "rainbow nation" where all races could live together in harmony.

Mandela's leadership was driven by a deep sense of moral duty to his people and his country. He believed that the end of apartheid should not result in the reversal of roles but rather in the establishment of a fair and just society for everyone. This approach was aligned with the *Mahabharata's* teachings on the responsibilities of a leader to uphold *dharma* and work for the greater good.

Mandela's adherence to these values was crucial in achieving a peaceful transition in South Africa. His ability to prioritise reconciliation over retribution helped prevent a potential civil war and allowed for the establishment of a democratic government. In 1994, Mandela became South Africa's first black president in the country's first multiracial elections. His leadership ensured that South Africa moved towards a more inclusive society rather than descending into chaos and conflict. The Truth and Reconciliation Commission, which he supported, played a key role in healing the nation by allowing victims of apartheid to share their stories and perpetrators to seek amnesty.

Nelson Mandela's approach to leadership during South Africa's transition from apartheid to democracy is a modern example of how the *Mahabharata's* guidance on determining and adhering to personal values can lead to strategic success. By aligning his leadership with principles of *dharma*, forgiveness, and reconciliation, Mandela was able to guide South Africa through one of the most challenging periods in its history, ultimately achieving a peaceful and just outcome.

Step 2: Practice Describing End States in Terms of Feelings and Perceptions

Strategic end states are goals or visions that an organisation, team, or individual aims to achieve over the long term. While they can often be defined in quantitative terms such as revenue targets, market share, or operational metrics, describing them in terms of feelings and perceptions can offer a more holistic and meaningful perspective. This approach emphasises the human aspect of success and the impact on individuals' experiences, ultimately leading to more effective strategies and higher engagement. In this step, we will explore the importance of describing strategic end states in terms of feelings and perceptions, how to do so effectively, and the benefits this approach offers.

The Importance of Describing Strategic End States in Terms of Feelings and Perceptions

- **Human-Centric Perspective.** Describing strategic end states in terms of feelings and perceptions puts people at the centre of the vision. It prioritises the emotional and psychological impact of achieving these goals, recognising that success is not solely about tangible outcomes but also about human experiences.
- **Enhanced Motivation and Engagement.** When people understand how strategic end states will make them feel, they are more likely to be motivated and engaged. This emotional connection can drive individuals to work towards the vision with passion and commitment.
- **Clearer Communication.** Translating strategic end states into feelings and perceptions makes them more relatable and easier to understand. It allows leaders to communicate their vision in a way that resonates with their audience and aligns everyone towards a common goal.
- **Better Alignment.** By focusing on how achieving strategic end states will make people feel, organisations can ensure that their goals align with the values, beliefs, and aspirations of their team members and stakeholders.

How to Describe Strategic End States in Terms of Feelings and Perceptions

- **Identify Desired Emotions.** Consider the emotions and feelings that you want people to experience when the strategic end state is achieved. This could inculcate a sense of accomplishment, pride, trust, or belonging.

- **Visualise the Impact.** Imagine the impact that achieving the end state will have on individuals, teams, and stakeholders. How will their perceptions change? What experiences will they have?
- **Use Descriptive Language.** Choose language that evokes emotions and paints a vivid picture of the desired future. For example, instead of saying, "Increase customer satisfaction by 20%," you could describe it as, "Create experiences that leave customers feeling valued and understood."
- **Connect to Values and Purpose.** Link the strategic end state to the organisation's values and purpose. Explain how achieving the end state aligns with these core principles and contributes to the greater good.
- **Engage Stakeholders.** Involve stakeholders in the process of defining strategic end states. Ask for their input on how they envision the future and how it will make them feel. This collaborative approach can enhance buy-in and support.

Benefits of Describing Strategic End States in Terms of Feelings and Perceptions

- **Stronger Commitment.** When people understand how achieving strategic end states will positively impact their feelings and perceptions, they are more likely to commit to the vision and work towards it.
- **Improved Adaptability.** Describing and explaining, end states in emotional terms allows for more flexible and adaptive strategies. It focuses on the experience rather than rigid metrics, enabling adjustments along the way to better achieve the desired feelings.
- **Enhanced Leadership.** Leaders who can articulate strategic end states in terms of feelings and perceptions are more likely to inspire and motivate their teams. This approach fosters trust and strengthens relationships.
- **Greater Customer Loyalty.** When strategic end states include creating positive feelings for customers, it can lead to higher satisfaction and loyalty. Customers who have a positive emotional

experience are more likely to remain loyal and advocate for the brand.

Describing strategic end states in terms of feelings and perceptions offers a unique and powerful approach to vision setting. By focusing on the human experience and emotional impact, organisations and individuals can create more compelling and meaningful goals. This approach fosters stronger commitment, adaptability, and customer loyalty, ultimately leading to greater success and fulfilment.

In the Indian epic *Mahabharata*, one notable example of a strategic end state being described as a feeling or emotion can be found in the character of Yudhishthira, the eldest of the Pandava brothers. Yudhishthira's strategic goal throughout the epic is to establish and maintain *dharma* (righteousness and justice) in the world, which is intertwined with his personal values and the well-being of his family and kingdom.

Yudhishthira's quest for *dharma* can be seen as both a strategic end state and an emotional aspiration. His desire for peace, justice, and righteousness shapes his actions and decisions throughout the epic. This feeling of responsibility toward *dharma* is a driving force behind his participation in the Kurukshetra War, where he fights not only to reclaim his rightful inheritance, but also to establish moral order.

After the war, Yudhishthira's strategic goal shifts towards restoring peace and stability in the kingdom. His emotional state reflects a sense of sorrow and remorse for the destruction and loss of life caused by the war. Despite achieving victory, he experiences mixed emotions about the heavy cost of the conflict.

Ultimately, Yudhishthira's strategic end state can be described as a deep longing for peace, justice, and righteousness. His journey involves navigating the complexities of achieving this state while upholding his values and responsibilities as a leader. The emotional fulfilment of this end state is characterised by his sense of duty, moral obligation, and compassion for his people.

Yudhishthira's experience highlights how a strategic end state in the *Mahabharata* can be closely tied to feelings and emotions, such as the desire for justice and the emotional burden of war and loss. His story underscores the intricate relationship between strategic goals and the emotional journey of the characters in the epic.

An example in the business world where the *Mahabharata's* guidance on describing end states in terms of feelings and perceptions has delivered strategic success can be seen in Apple's approach to product design and marketing, particularly with the iPhone.

In the treatise *Mahabharata*, the concept of describing end states in terms of feelings and perceptions emphasises the importance of understanding and influencing the emotions and experiences of people. Rather than focusing solely on the technical or material aspects of a goal, this approach prioritises how individuals will feel and perceive the outcome.

When Steve Jobs introduced the first iPhone in 2007, Apple didn't just market it as a device with impressive technical specifications. Instead, the focus was on how the iPhone would make users feel and how it would transform their lives. The marketing and design strategy revolved around the following key elements.

Apple emphasised the joy, simplicity, and empowerment that users would experience with the iPhone. The product was positioned as not just a phone but a revolutionary device that would change the way people connect with the world, capture memories, and express themselves.

Apple's design philosophy centred on creating a seamless and intuitive user experience. The company understood that the perception of the product's ease of use and elegance would be more impactful than any technical specification. This focus on how users would feel when interacting with the product led to innovations like the touch interface, the App Store, and the sleek, minimalist design.

Apple cultivated a brand image that resonated with feelings of innovation, creativity, and exclusivity. The iPhone was marketed as a status symbol, appealing to consumers' desires to be part of a forward-thinking, elite group. This perception was crucial in establishing brand loyalty and driving the iPhone's global success.

Apple's marketing often projected a vision of the future where their products played a central role. The iPhone was depicted as a tool that would enable a more connected, efficient, and enjoyable life. This forward-looking perspective created anticipation and excitement among consumers, aligning their feelings with the end state Apple envisioned.

Apple's strategy of focusing on feelings and perceptions paid off immensely. The iPhone became not just a successful product but a cultural phenomenon. Consumers didn't just buy the iPhone because of its features; they bought into the experience and the emotions associated with owning an Apple product. This emotional connection helped Apple achieve and maintain a dominant position in the smartphone market.

Apple's approach with the iPhone is a prime example of how the *Mahabharata's* guidance on describing end states in terms of feelings and perceptions can lead to strategic success in business. By understanding and influencing how customers would feel and perceive the product, Apple created a powerful brand and a loyal customer base, achieving long-term success in a highly competitive market.

Step 3: Determine the Types of People and Organisations You Will Work With

Working with good people and organisations is crucial for personal and professional growth, productivity, and job satisfaction. Identifying these qualities can lead to more positive relationships, collaboration, and career opportunities. Here are some key factors to consider when determining whether a person or organisation is good to work with.

Values Alignment. Shared values form the foundation of successful partnerships. Look for individuals and organisations whose values align with your own, whether that's a commitment to integrity, social responsibility, innovation, or work-life balance. When your values align, you're more likely to work well together and achieve shared goals.

Reputation and Track Record. Research the reputation and history of the individual or organisation. Positive reviews, testimonials, and references can provide insight into their reliability, ethics, and past performance. A good reputation is often a strong indicator of an organisation or individual you can trust.

Communication. Effective communication is essential in any collaboration. Look for partners who are clear, open, and transparent in their communication. They should be willing to listen, provide feedback, and engage in meaningful dialogue.

Expertise and Experience. Consider the expertise and experience of the individual or organisation. Those with a proven track record in their field are more likely to bring valuable insights and skills to the table. Make sure their expertise complements your own and aligns with the goals of the collaboration.

Integrity and Trustworthiness. Integrity is a key trait in determining good people and organisations to work with. Trustworthy individuals and organisations are honest, keep their promises, and operate ethically. Look for signs of integrity in their business practices and interpersonal interactions.

Collaborative Approach. Good partners work well with others and value collaboration. They are open to new ideas, willing to share credit, and capable of working towards a common goal. Look for evidence of a collaborative mindset in their previous projects and interactions.

Cultural Fit. Consider whether there is a cultural fit between you and the organisation or individual. This includes not only professional culture, such as work habits and management styles, but also social and cultural norms. A good cultural fit can enhance productivity and satisfaction.

Growth and Development. Look for individuals and organisations that prioritise growth and development, both for themselves and their partners. Those who invest in learning, improvement, and professional development are more likely to contribute positively to your work and help you grow as well.

Responsiveness and Adaptability. Responsiveness and adaptability are important traits in good partners. They should be willing to adjust to changing circumstances and respond quickly and positively to challenges or opportunities.

Conflict Resolution Skills. Good people and organisations handle conflicts constructively and professionally. Look for partners who can resolve differences amicably and maintain healthy working relationships.

Financial Stability. For organisational partnerships, financial stability is an important consideration. An organisation that is financially stable is more likely to fulfil its commitments and maintain a healthy working relationship.

Shared Vision and Goals. When choosing to work with someone, ensure that you share a common vision and goals. This shared focus helps maintain alignment and commitment to achieving mutual success.

Finding good people and organisations to work with involves assessing their values, reputation, communication skills, integrity, and collaborative approach. By considering these factors, you can build positive, productive, and successful professional relationships.

In the Indian epic *Mahabharata*, one example of a protagonist determining which type of people they will work with, and those they will not, can be seen in the character of Yudhishthira, the eldest of the Pandava brothers. Yudhishthira is rightly idolised for his adherence to *dharma* (righteousness and justice), and his decisions regarding whom he will align with reflect his commitment to these values.

An example of this occurs in Yudhishthira's interactions with Karna, a skilled warrior who is known to have animosity toward the Pandavas due to his loyalty to their rival, Duryodhana. Despite Karna's prowess in battle, Yudhishthira chooses not to work with him due to Karna's association with Duryodhana and his actions against the Pandavas.

Yudhishthira's decision to distance himself from Karna can be seen as a reflection of his adherence to moral principles. Karna, while being a noble character in many ways, has pledged his loyalty to Duryodhana and is seen as an enemy to the Pandavas. Additionally, Karna had made vows to kill Arjuna, Yudhishthira's brother, which further cements Yudhishthira's decision to keep Karna at a distance.

Yudhishthira's approach to selecting allies is guided by his commitment to *dharma*. He seeks to surround himself with individuals who share his values and goals, such as his brothers and trusted advisors like Krishna and Vidura. These choices help Yudhishthira stay true to his principles and achieve his strategic objectives in the epic.

This example demonstrates how Yudhishthira uses his values as a guide for determining which types of people he will work with and those he will not. His choices are rooted in his commitment to righteousness and justice, which ultimately shape his alliances and relationships throughout the epic.

A pertinent example from more recent history where principles akin to the *Mahabharata's* guidance on choosing the right allies and team members led to strategic success, can be found in the Indian independence movement, specifically the leadership of Mahatma Gandhi during the Salt March (Dandi March) in 1930.

In the *Mahabharata*, wise counsel is often given on choosing allies and companions who are trustworthy, morally upright, and share common goals. These values resonate with Gandhi's careful selection of individuals and groups to work with during the non-violent struggle for Indian independence.

In 1930, Mahatma Gandhi launched the Salt March as a direct-action campaign against the British salt tax, a symbol of the broader struggle against British rule. The march was a pivotal event in the Indian independence movement, characterised by strategic brilliance and deep moral conviction.

Gandhi selected individuals for the Salt March who were committed to the principles of non-violence and civil disobedience. He ensured that those who joined him were not only physically capable but also mentally prepared to face the potential consequences, including imprisonment or violence, without retaliating. This mirrored the *Mahabharata's* emphasis on the moral character of allies.

Gandhi's march included people from diverse backgrounds—men and women, young and old, Hindus and Muslims, rich and poor. This inclusivity was strategic, as it symbolised the unity of India and the collective desire for independence, reflecting the *Mahabharata's* advice on forging alliances with those who share a common purpose.

Gandhi's role in the march was not just that of a leader but also of a mentor. He guided his followers with patience and wisdom, much like the guidance given to the Pandavas in the *Mahabharata* by Lord Krishna. His ability to inspire and maintain discipline among the marchers was crucial to the movement's success.

Gandhi carefully chose the initial group of 78 people who would accompany him on the march. These were individuals who were not only loyal and dedicated but also capable of influencing others. This decision ensured that the march had the desired impact and garnered widespread attention. The Salt March was a resounding success in terms of its strategic objectives. It galvanised the Indian population against British rule and brought international attention to the Indian independence movement. The British authorities were forced to confront the moral and political implications of their colonial policies, leading to increased pressure for reform.

Mahatma Gandhi's success in the Salt March is an example of the *Mahabharata's* guidance on choosing the right people to work with. By selecting individuals who embodied the values of non-violence, shared a common vision for India's future, and could act as role models for the nation, Gandhi was able to create a powerful and effective movement that played a crucial role in India's eventual independence.

Step 4: Learn How to Read People and Situations

The ability to read people and situations is an invaluable skill that can enhance interpersonal relationships, decision-making, and problem-solving. By understanding others' emotions, intentions, and motivations, we can navigate social interactions more effectively and adapt our behaviour to achieve our goals. This step will explore the importance of reading people and situations, strategies for developing this skill, and how it can benefit various aspects of our lives.

The Importance of Reading People and Situations

- **Improved Communication.** Understanding people's emotions and intentions allows for more effective and empathetic communication.

It helps us tailor our words and actions to suit the needs and preferences of others.

- **Better Conflict Resolution.** By accurately assessing situations and understanding the perspectives of all parties involved, we can resolve conflicts more effectively and find mutually beneficial solutions.
- **Enhanced Decision-Making.** Reading people and situations provides insights into potential outcomes and risks. This awareness can lead to more informed decisions and better judgment.
- **Stronger Relationships.** Building meaningful connections requires empathy and understanding. Reading people and situations helps us connect with others on a deeper level and cultivate trust.

Strategies for Reading People and Situations

- **Observe Nonverbal Cues.** Pay attention to body language, facial expressions, and gestures. These nonverbal cues can reveal a person's emotions, level of engagement, and intentions.
- **Listen Actively.** Practice active listening by focusing on the speaker, asking clarifying questions, and summarising what you've heard. This helps you understand others' perspectives and intentions.
- **Watch for Patterns.** Notice patterns in people's behaviour over time. Consistent actions or reactions can provide insights into their values, beliefs, and motivations.
- **Consider Context.** Take into account the context of the situation. People's behaviour can vary depending on the circumstances, so understanding the broader context is essential.
- **Pay Attention to Tone.** The tone of voice can convey a lot about a person's emotional state and intentions. Listen for changes in pitch, pace, and volume to gain insights.
- **Empathise.** Put yourself in others' shoes to understand their emotions and perspectives. Empathy helps you connect with others and navigate situations more effectively.
- **Ask Open-Ended Questions.** Open-ended questions encourage

others to share their thoughts and feelings more freely. This can provide valuable insights into their perspectives.

- **Stay Curious.** Approach interactions with a sense of curiosity and openness. Avoid making assumptions and be willing to ask questions and seek clarification.

Benefits of Reading People and Situations

- **Enhanced Emotional Intelligence.** Reading people and situations contributes to emotional intelligence, which involves understanding and managing emotions—both our own and those of others.
- **Improved Leadership.** Leaders who can read people and situations can better guide their teams, address concerns, and foster a positive work environment.
- **Increased Persuasion and Influence.** Understanding others' emotions and motivations can help you tailor your arguments and appeals to persuade and influence more effectively.
- **Greater Personal Growth.** Reading people and situations encourages self-awareness and reflection. It helps us understand our own behaviour and how it impacts others.
- **Stronger Social Connections.** Being able to read people and situations helps us build and maintain strong relationships based on trust, understanding, and respect.

Reading people and situations is a multifaceted skill that enhances communication, decision-making, and relationships. By observing nonverbal cues, listening actively, and empathising with others, we can gain valuable insights into their emotions and intentions. This skill is beneficial in various aspects of life, from personal relationships to professional settings. Cultivating the ability to read people and situations can lead to greater emotional intelligence, leadership, and personal growth.

In the Indian epic *Mahabharata*, one character who is known for reading people and situations effectively, is Lord Krishna. As an avatar of the god Vishnu and a central figure in the epic, Krishna possesses exceptional insight and wisdom that allows him to navigate complex situations and understand people's motivations and intentions.

One notable example of Krishna's ability to read people and situations effectively occurs during the *Udyoga Parva*, the book of efforts and negotiations. In this section, Krishna serves as a mediator and envoy for the Pandavas, attempting to negotiate a peaceful resolution with the Kauravas before the outbreak of the Kurukshetra War.

Krishna visits the court of the Kauravas and engages in discussions with Dhritarashtra, Duryodhana, and other key figures. He proposes a peaceful settlement that would allow the Pandavas to reclaim a portion of their kingdom, thus avoiding a devastating war. During these negotiations, Krishna demonstrates his ability to read the intentions and attitudes of the Kaurava leaders:

- **Understanding Duryodhana's stubbornness:** Krishna recognises Duryodhana's arrogance and unwillingness to compromise, despite the potential consequences of war. He sees Duryodhana's determination to maintain power and control, which ultimately leads to the failure of peace negotiations.
- **Perceiving the fears and hopes of Dhritarashtra:** Krishna understands the conflicting emotions of Dhritarashtra, the blind king of the Kauravas. Dhritarashtra desires peace and the safety of his sons, but he is also swayed by their ambitions and desires.
- **Assessing the positions of other key figures:** Krishna gauges the perspectives of other influential figures in the Kaurava court, such as Bhishma and Drona, understanding their loyalties and concerns.

Krishna's ability to read the situation effectively informs his actions and decisions throughout the epic. Despite his efforts to broker peace, he realises that war is inevitable due to Duryodhana's intransigence. Krishna then shifts his focus to supporting the Pandavas in the upcoming conflict, offering them guidance and strategic advice.

This example demonstrates how Krishna's keen perception and understanding of people and situations play a crucial role in his role as a mediator and advisor in the *Mahabharata*. His insight helps him navigate the complexities of the epic and guide the Pandavas toward victory.

A modern example where the *Mahabharata's* guidance on learning to read people and situations has delivered strategic success is in the field of international diplomacy, particularly the Cuban Missile Crisis of 1962. This event is often cited as one of the most critical moments of the Cold War and exemplifies the importance of understanding the motivations, intentions, and psychology of others to achieve a strategic outcome.

The Cuban Missile Crisis occurred in October 1962, when the United States discovered that the Soviet Union was secretly installing nuclear missiles in Cuba, just 90 miles from the U.S. coast. This development brought the world to the brink of nuclear war, as the U.S. perceived the missiles as an immediate and unacceptable threat. President John F. Kennedy and his administration were faced with a grave situation that required not only a firm response but also a deep understanding of the Soviet Union's intentions and the potential consequences of any U.S. action.

Kennedy and his advisors worked to understand Soviet Premier Nikita Khrushchev's motivations. They recognised that Khrushchev was attempting to counterbalance U.S. nuclear capabilities in Europe and bolster Soviet prestige. By reading the situation, Kennedy understood that Khrushchev likely did not want a nuclear war but was instead trying to gain a strategic advantage.

Kennedy had to balance the need to remove the missiles from Cuba with the need to avoid triggering a nuclear conflict. His decision to impose a naval blockade (termed a "quarantine") on Cuba, rather than launching an immediate military strike, reflected a deep understanding of the situation. The blockade allowed time for negotiations and signalled U.S. resolve without immediately escalating to war.

Kennedy's administration engaged in careful back-channel communications with the Soviet Union, using both official and unofficial channels to convey messages. This allowed them to gauge Khrushchev's willingness to negotiate and to propose a face-saving solution for the Soviet Union—removing U.S. missiles from Turkey in exchange for the withdrawal of Soviet missiles from Cuba.

Kennedy understood the need to manage domestic and international perceptions. He was careful to present the blockade as a defensive measure, which helped to garner support from U.S. allies and the United Nations.

By understanding the perspectives of both allies and adversaries, he was able to maintain a united front.

After several tense days, Khrushchev agreed to remove the Soviet missiles from Cuba in exchange for a U.S. commitment not to invade Cuba and the secret removal of U.S. missiles from Turkey. The crisis was resolved without a nuclear confrontation, and the world stepped back from the brink of war.

The Cuban Missile Crisis is a clear example of the *Mahabharata's* wisdom on the importance of understanding people and situations to navigate complex and potentially catastrophic scenarios. Kennedy's ability to read Khrushchev's intentions, anticipate global reactions, and carefully calibrate his response was key to achieving a strategic victory without resorting to war. This episode highlights how deep situational awareness and insight into the motivations of others can lead to successful conflict resolution.

Step 5: Demonstrate Cerebral Flexibility

Cerebral flexibility, also known as cognitive flexibility, is the ability to adapt one's thinking to new and changing situations, solve problems in innovative ways, and shift perspectives when necessary. This attendant skill is essential for navigating the complexities of modern life and can lead to improved decision-making, creativity, and emotional resilience. Developing cerebral flexibility involves challenging one's mind through varied experiences and practices. This step will explore the importance of cerebral flexibility, strategies for developing it, and how it can benefit individuals in various aspects of their lives.

The Importance of Cerebral Flexibility

- **Enhanced Problem-Solving.** Cerebral flexibility allows individuals to approach problems from different angles, leading to more creative and effective solutions.
- **Adaptability.** Life is unpredictable, and being able to adjust one's thinking to new circumstances helps individuals navigate changes and challenges more effectively.

- **Improved Decision-Making.** By considering multiple perspectives and alternatives, individuals with cerebral flexibility make more informed and balanced decisions.
- **Emotional Resilience.** Cognitive flexibility enables individuals to cope with stress and setbacks more effectively, maintaining emotional balance in the face of adversity.

Methods for Developing Cerebral Flexibility

- **Expose Yourself to New Experiences.** Engage in a variety of activities, such as traveling, trying new hobbies, or learning about different cultures. Exposure to diverse experiences broadens your perspective.
- **Challenge Your Beliefs.** Question your assumptions and beliefs regularly. Consider alternative viewpoints and seek out information that challenges your existing views.
- **Practice Mindfulness.** Mindfulness meditation helps you become aware of your thoughts and emotions without judgment. This awareness allows you to see situations from a fresh perspective.
- **Engage in Critical Thinking.** Sharpen your critical thinking skills by analysing information, identifying biases, and evaluating arguments. Practice solving puzzles and brain teasers to keep your mind sharp.
- **Read Widely.** Read books and articles from various genres and topics to expand your knowledge and challenge your thinking.
- **Learn a New Language.** Learning a new language can improve cognitive flexibility by exposing you to different ways of thinking and communicating.
- **Collaborate with Others.** Working with people from diverse backgrounds and perspectives can broaden your understanding and introduce you to new ways of thinking.
- **Embrace Uncertainty.** Accepting uncertainty and ambiguity can help you become more comfortable with change and open to new possibilities.

- **Practice Perspective-Taking.** Put yourself in others' shoes to understand their point of view. This exercise enhances empathy and helps you see situations from different angles.

Benefits of Cerebral Flexibility

- **Increased Creativity.** Cerebral flexibility encourages innovative thinking and the generation of new ideas.
- **Improved Learning and Memory.** Flexibility in thinking can enhance learning and memory retention, as the brain is better able to make connections between different pieces of information.
- **Enhanced Communication.** Being able to adapt your thinking to different situations and perspectives can improve your ability to communicate effectively with others.
- **Greater Success in Personal and Professional Life.** Cognitive flexibility can lead to greater adaptability and success in both personal and professional life by enabling you to respond effectively to new challenges.

Developing cerebral flexibility is an important aspect of personal and intellectual growth. By challenging your beliefs, seeking diverse experiences, and practicing critical thinking, you can enhance your cognitive adaptability and creativity. This skill can lead to improved problem-solving, decision-making, and emotional resilience. Cultivating cerebral flexibility not only enriches one's life but also helps one navigate the complexities of the modern world with grace and confidence.

In the Indian epic *Mahabharata*, one character who demonstrates cerebral flexibility is Arjuna, one of the Pandava brothers. Arjuna's adaptability in both thought and action is evident in several situations throughout the epic, particularly in his willingness to consider and embrace new perspectives and strategies.

One notable example of Arjuna's cerebral flexibility occurs during the conversation with Lord Krishna in the *Bhagavad Gita*, which takes place on the battlefield of Kurukshetra. As the war is about to begin, Arjuna is overcome with doubt and moral conflict about fighting against his own relatives, teachers, and friends. He questions the righteousness of the war and whether he should proceed.

Krishna's teachings in the *Bhagavad Gita* challenge Arjuna's initial perspective and help him reframe his understanding of duty, righteousness, and the nature of life and death. Through this conversation, Arjuna demonstrates cerebral flexibility by:

- **Adopting a new understanding of duty (*dharma*):** Arjuna learns that his duty as a warrior is to fight for righteousness and protect dharma. He realises that his actions should be selfless and detached from the outcomes.
- **Embracing different paths of spiritual growth:** Krishna introduces Arjuna to various paths of spiritual growth, including the paths of knowledge, action, and devotion. Arjuna's openness to these teachings allows him to broaden his perspective on life and spirituality.
- **Changing his approach to the battle:** By the end of the conversation, Arjuna's mindset shifts from one of hesitation and fear to one of determination and clarity. He understands that he must fulfil his duty without attachment to the results.

Arjuna's ability to adapt his thinking and embrace Krishna's teachings showcases his cerebral flexibility. This flexibility allows him to resolve his internal conflict and approach the battle with a renewed sense of purpose and conviction. Arjuna's journey in the *Bhagavad Gita* highlights the importance of being open to new ideas and perspectives, especially when faced with challenging situations. His willingness to change his mind set and approach, demonstrates the value of cerebral flexibility in achieving personal growth and success.

A modern example that reflects the *Mahabharata's* guidance on cerebral flexibility, particularly the ability to adapt strategies and approaches based on the situation, is the evolution of Apple's business strategy under Steve Jobs, after his return to the company in 1997. When Steve Jobs returned to the Apple conglomerate in 1997, the company was struggling. Apple was on the brink of bankruptcy, with a fragmented product line, declining market share, and fierce competition from Microsoft and other PC manufacturers.

The situation required not just a strong leader but someone capable of cerebral flexibility—adapting and changing strategies dynamically to fit the challenges at hand.

Apple had an overly complex product line with numerous models that confused consumers and diluted the brand. One of Jobs' first moves was to streamline Apple's product line. He reduced the number of products by 70%, focusing on four core areas: consumer desktops (iMac), consumer laptops (iBook), professional desktops (Power Mac), and professional laptops (PowerBook). This clarity allowed Apple to focus its resources and marketing efforts effectively.

At the time, the focus in the tech industry was heavily on hardware specifications, but Apple was losing out to competitors who could offer better specs at lower prices. Jobs shifted the company's focus toward design, user experience, and brand appeal. This was a significant strategic shift, emphasising aesthetics, simplicity, and integration between hardware and software. The introduction of the iMac in 1998, with its innovative design and ease of use, exemplified this new approach and revitalised Apple's brand.

Apple was traditionally a computer company, but the personal computer market was becoming increasingly competitive with slim margins. Jobs demonstrated cerebral flexibility by moving Apple beyond computers into new markets. This included the launch of the iPod in 2001, which revolutionised the music industry, and later the iPhone in 2007, which the mobile phone industry. These products were not just new revenue streams; they reshaped entire industries and cemented Apple's position as an innovation leader.

In the late 1990s, technology companies largely operated in product silos without integrated ecosystems. Jobs envisioned and developed an ecosystem that interconnected all of Apple's products and services. iTunes, the App Store, iCloud, and the integration between iPhones, iPads, Macs, and other Apple devices created a seamless user experience. This strategic shift locked users into the Apple ecosystem, leading to long-term customer loyalty and recurring revenue.

Steve Jobs' ability and skilful dexterity to adapt and change strategies dynamically—guided by a flexible, cerebral approach—allowed him to navigate Apple through its most challenging period. By simplifying the product line, focusing on design and user experience, expanding into new markets, and creating an integrated ecosystem, Jobs didn't just save Apple; he turned it into one of the most valuable companies in the world. This success mirrors the *Mahabharata's* lessons on the importance of cerebral flexibility—adapting one's strategies to the evolving realities of the battlefield, or in this case, the marketplace.

Step 6: Practice Deception and Diplomacy

Deception and diplomacy have been intertwined throughout history, as nations and leaders navigate the complex world of international relations. Diplomacy is the art of negotiating and managing relationships between countries to achieve mutual benefits and maintain peace. Deception, on the other hand, involves the use of tactics such as misinformation, ambiguity, or manipulation to achieve specific strategic goals. While deception can play a role in diplomacy, it raises ethical and practical concerns. This step will explore the role of deception in diplomacy, its ethical implications, and the balance between achieving strategic goals and upholding ethical standards.

The Role of Deception in Diplomacy

- **Achieving Strategic Goals.** In certain situations, deception can be used as a tool to achieve strategic goals in international relations. For example, disinformation campaigns or misleading signals, can be employed to gain an advantage during negotiations or to influence the actions of other parties.
- **Maintaining Secrecy.** Diplomacy often involves sensitive information that must be kept confidential. Deceptive tactics can be used to protect classified information or strategic interests.
- **Gaining Leverage.** Diplomatic negotiations may involve complex power dynamics. Deception can be employed to gain leverage over the opposing party or to create uncertainty in their decision-making.

- **Avoiding Conflict.** In some cases, deception can help avoid direct confrontation or conflict by allowing parties to maintain face-saving narratives or to manage difficult situations discreetly.

Ethical Implications of Deception in Diplomacy

- **Trust and Credibility.** Deceptive tactics can erode trust and credibility in diplomatic relationships. Once trust is compromised, it becomes challenging to maintain effective communication and collaboration.
- **Long-Term Consequences.** While deception may yield short-term gains, it can lead to long-term consequences such as damaged relationships, reputational harm, and retaliation from other parties.
- **Ethical Standards.** Diplomats and leaders are expected to uphold ethical standards in their conduct. Deception challenges these standards and can lead to questions about the integrity of their actions.
- **Transparency and Accountability.** Modern diplomatic practices recommend transparency and accountability. Deception undermines these values and can lead to a lack of confidence in diplomatic institutions.

Balancing Strategic Goals with Ethical Standards

- **Use Deception Sparingly.** If deception is necessary for strategic reasons, it should be employed judiciously, cannily and with a clear understanding of the potential risks and consequences.
- **Maintain Ethical Boundaries.** Diplomats should adhere and cling assiduously to ethical boundaries and avoid tactics that could harm innocent parties or violate international laws and norms.
- **Consider Alternative Strategies.** Whenever possible, explore alternative strategies that do not involve deception. Honest negotiation and open dialogue can often yield more sustainable and mutually beneficial outcomes.
- **Uphold Transparency.** Even when employing deceptive tactics, strive to maintain transparency with allies and partners. This helps

preserve trust and cooperation in the long run.

- **Reflect on Long-Term Impact.** Assess the long-term impact of deception on relationships and international stability. Consider whether short-term gains are worth potential long-term costs.

Deception and diplomacy are complex and often intertwined, with deception sometimes serving as a tool to achieve strategic goals. However, the ethical implications of deception cannot be ignored, as it can erode trust, damage relationships, and compromise transparency and accountability. Diplomats and leaders must strike a careful balance between achieving strategic objectives and upholding ethical standards. By using deception sparingly and considering alternative strategies, they can navigate the challenges of international relations while maintaining integrity and fostering long-term cooperation.

In the Indian epic *Mahabharata*, one character who skilfully integrates deception and diplomacy is, Lord Krishna. As an advisor and guide to the Pandavas, Krishna often uses a combination of strategic deception and diplomatic negotiation to achieve their goals and ensure victory in the Kurukshetra War. A notable example of Krishna's integration of deception and diplomacy occurs in his involvement in the killing of Drona, one of the Kaurava generals and a formidable warrior. Drona was an exceptional archer and a key military leader for the Kauravas, making him a significant obstacle for the Pandavas.

Drona's death was orchestrated through a combination of deception and diplomacy:

- **Deception:** Krishna advised the Pandavas to spread the false news that Drona's son, Ashwatthama, had died in battle. This news would greatly distress Drona, causing him to lose focus and lower his guard. The false information was delivered by Yudhishthira, known for his honesty, which made it more convincing.
- **Diplomacy:** When Drona asked Yudhishthira directly whether his son Ashwatthama had died, Yudhishthira hesitated but confirmed the statement indirectly, saying "Ashwatthama, the elephant, has died." This statement was technically true, but the emphasis was placed on the elephant's name, misleading Drona.

Distraught by the news of his son's supposed death, Drona laid down his weapons in grief and was subsequently killed by Dhrishtadyumna, one of the Pandava allies. This combination of deception and diplomacy highlights Krishna's strategic thinking and his ability to use unconventional methods to achieve victory. By advising the Pandavas to use deception in this way, Krishna was able to eliminate a key Kaurava general and turn the tide of the battle in favour of the Pandavas.

Krishna's use of deception and diplomacy in the *Mahabharata* demonstrates his pragmatic approach to achieving his objectives while navigating the complexities of war and maintaining alliances. His actions also underscore the importance of strategic thinking and adaptability in overcoming challenges.

A modern example of where principles from the *Mahabharata*—particularly those related to deception and diplomacy—have delivered strategic success can be seen in the U.S. military's use of psychological operations (psyops) and strategic deception during the Iraq War. The Iraq War, which began in 2003, involved a complex strategic environment with numerous military, political, and cultural factors. As part of its strategy, the U.S. military employed various forms of deception and psychological operations to achieve its objectives.

Prior to the invasion of Iraq, the U.S. military conducted a range of deceptive operations to mislead the Iraqi military and leadership about the actual invasion plans. For instance, there were extensive efforts to create the impression that the main assault would come from the north through Turkey, while the actual invasion was planned to come from the south through Kuwait. This deception aimed to confuse and misdirect Iraqi forces, leading them to concentrate their defences in the wrong areas. The U.S. also used psychological operations to demoralise Iraqi troops and encourage surrender. This included dropping leaflets, broadcasting messages, and using other means to persuade Iraqi soldiers to abandon their positions or surrender without engaging in actuals of combat.

After the initial invasion, the U.S. engaged in significant diplomatic efforts to gain the support of neighbouring countries and regional allies. This included building coalitions and securing bases and logistical support from countries in the region. The diplomatic efforts helped to legitimise the operation and provided strategic advantages.

The strategic use of deception and psychological operations during the Iraq War contributed to several key outcomes. The successful misdirection of Iraqi forces helped to ensure a rapid and relatively smooth advance of coalition troops, leading to the quick fall of Baghdad and the toppling of Saddam Hussein's regime. The psychological operations contributed to a significant decrease in organised resistance from Iraqi military units, as many soldiers and commanders chose to surrender rather than face the overwhelming force and psychological pressure. Diplomatic efforts helped to build a coalition of allied nations, which provided additional support and legitimacy to the operation.

The Iraq War demonstrates how principles similar to those found in the *Mahabharata*—such as using deception to mislead opponents and employing psychological tactics to influence behaviour—can be applied in modern strategic contexts. The successful execution of these strategies helped the U.S. achieve its initial military objectives and set the stage for further diplomatic and strategic efforts in the region.

Step 7: Display Strong Leadership and Decision-Making Skills

Leadership and decision-making are closely interconnected, as effective leaders are responsible for making impactful decisions that guide their organisations or teams toward success. Strong decision-making skills are essential for leaders to navigate challenges, set strategic goals, and inspire their teams. This step will explore the importance of decision-making in leadership, the traits of effective decision-makers, and the impact of leadership decisions on organisations and individuals.

The Importance of Decision Making in Leadership

- **Setting Direction.** Leaders are responsible for setting the strategic direction of an organisation or team. This involves making decisions about goals, priorities, and resource allocation.
- **Problem Solving.** Leaders often face complex problems that require thoughtful and timely decisions. Their ability to address challenges

effectively influences the overall success of their teams or organisations.

- **Inspiring and Motivating Teams.** Leaders' decisions can impact team morale and motivation. By making clear and consistent decisions, leaders provide their teams with a sense of direction and purpose.
- **Risk Management.** Leaders must assess and manage risks associated with their decisions. This involves weighing potential outcomes and making informed choices that align with their goals.
- **Stakeholder Relationships.** Leaders must consider the interests and perspectives of various stakeholders when making decisions. Balancing these interests requires thoughtful analysis and negotiation.

Traits of Effective Decision Makers

- **Critical Thinking.** Effective leaders use critical thinking to analyse situations objectively, consider multiple perspectives, and evaluate potential solutions.
- **Emotional Intelligence.** Leaders with high emotional intelligence understand their own emotions and can empathise with others. This helps them make decisions that consider the impact on their teams and stakeholders.
- **Decisiveness.** While it is important to gather information and consider options, effective leaders are able to make timely decisions and act with confidence.
- **Adaptability.** The ability to adapt to changing circumstances and revise decisions as needed is a hallmark of strong leadership.
- **Communication Skills.** Effective leaders communicate their decisions clearly and transparently to their teams and stakeholders. This builds trust and fosters collaboration.
- **Ethical Judgment.** Leaders must consider ethical implications when making decisions. Acting with integrity and adhering to ethical standards is essential for long-term success.

Impact of Leadership Decisions

- **Organisational Success.** The decisions made by leaders directly impact the success of their organisations. Strategic decisions can drive growth, innovation, and efficiency.
- **Team Performance.** Leaders' decisions affect team dynamics and performance. Thoughtful decisions can enhance collaboration, productivity, and job satisfaction.
- **Reputation and Trust.** Leaders' decisions shape the reputation of their organisations and their own credibility. Consistent, transparent, and ethical decisions build trust among employees, customers, and other stakeholders.
- **Long-Term Sustainability.** Leaders must consider the long-term impact of their decisions on their organisations and the broader community. Sustainable decisions contribute to the overall health and longevity of the organisation.

Leadership and decision-making are closely intertwined, as effective leaders guide their organisations and teams through thoughtful and strategic decisions. Strong decision-making skills enable leaders to navigate challenges, set clear goals, and inspire their teams. By combining critical thinking, emotional intelligence, adaptability, and ethical judgment, leaders can make impactful decisions that drive organisational success and build trust with stakeholders. The connection between leadership and decision-making underscores the importance of continuous learning and growth for leaders to enhance their decision-making abilities and achieve sustainable success.

In the Indian epic treatise *Mahabharata*, one character who shows strong leadership and decision-making skills is, Bhishma. As a central figure in the Kuru dynasty and a key leader in the Kurukshetra War, Bhishma's strategic acumen and decision-making abilities are evident throughout the epic.

A notable example of Bhishma's leadership and decision-making skills can be seen in his role as the commander-in-chief of the Kaurava army during the Kurukshetra War. Despite his loyalty to the Kauravas, Bhishma is known for his adherence to *dharma* (righteousness) and his impartiality in difficult situations. He commands respect from both his allies and opponents due to his integrity and honour.

Bhishma's strong leadership and decision-making skills are evident in his ability to lead the Kaurava forces effectively against the Pandavas. Some key aspects of his leadership include:

1. **Strategic Planning:** Bhishma develops battle strategies and formations to counter the Pandavas' advances. He uses his extensive knowledge of warfare and experience to devise effective tactics and position his forces advantageously.
2. **Inspiring Loyalty:** Bhishma's reputation for wisdom, honour, and righteousness inspires loyalty and respect from the soldiers and commanders under his command. His presence boosts the morale of the Kaurava forces.
3. **Managing Conflicts:** Bhishma's role as a leader often involves managing internal conflicts and disputes within the Kaurava ranks. His diplomatic skills and authority help maintain cohesion within the army.
4. **Leading by Example:** Bhishma leads from the front, displaying exceptional courage and skill in battle. His personal example motivates his troops and earns him admiration from both sides.
5. **Adaptability:** Bhishma adjusts his strategies based on the evolving situation on the battlefield. His ability to adapt and respond to changing circumstances demonstrates his agility as a leader.

Bhishma's leadership and decision-making skills are further highlighted by his principled stance on key issues, such as his insistence on following *dharma* even when it conflicts with the desires of the Kauravas. Despite his deep affection for the Pandavas, Bhishma's sense of duty compels him to lead the Kaurava forces with integrity. Overall, Bhishma's role as a leader in the *Mahabharata* showcases his strong decision-making skills, strategic thinking, and commitment to righteousness. His leadership is a significant factor in the Kaurava's efforts during the Kurukshetra War.

A modern example where the *Mahabharata's* guidance on leadership and strong decision-making skills is keenly reflected, is the 2008 financial crisis and the subsequent global economic recovery. Specifically, the role of Ben Bernanke, then Chairman of the U.S. Federal Reserve, showcases how principles akin to those found in the *Mahabharata* can lead to strategic success. The 2008 financial crisis was a severe worldwide economic crisis that led to massive financial instability, the collapse of major financial institutions, and a global recession. The challenge for leaders was to navigate through a crisis of unprecedented scale and restore economic stability.

Bernanke, an expert in economics and financial history, deeply understood the complexities of financial markets and the potential impacts of various interventions. His knowledge was critical in diagnosing the crisis accurately and identifying effective responses. Just as leaders in the *Mahabharata* made bold decisions to overcome challenges, Bernanke took decisive actions to stabilise the economy. This included implementing unconventional monetary policies such as quantitative easing (QE), which involved large-scale purchases of government and mortgage-backed securities to inject liquidity into the financial system.

Bernanke's decisions were guided by the principles of preventing a deeper economic collapse and protecting the broader economy, even though they were controversial. His leadership reflected a commitment to the greater good, much like the strategic and moral considerations in the *Mahabharata*. The *Mahabharata* also teaches the importance of adaptability in leadership. Bernanke and the Federal Reserve had to be flexible and adapt their strategies as the crisis evolved. This included adjusting interest rates, implementing emergency lending facilities, and coordinating with other central banks.

Bernanke's leadership and decision-making played a crucial role in navigating the U.S. economy through the financial crisis and setting the stage for recovery. By implementing policies that were effective in stabilising financial markets and supporting economic growth, he helped prevent a more severe economic downturn.

The recovery from the 2008 crisis, although slow, demonstrated the effectiveness of strong, decisive leadership and well-considered strategic interventions. The principles of understanding the environment, making bold and ethical decisions, and adapting to changing circumstances, as reflected in the *Mahabharata*, were starkly evident in Bernanke's approach to managing the crisis.

Step 8: Seek Out Wisdom and Counsel

Wisdom is a complex and multifaceted quality that involves a deep understanding of life, human nature, and the world around us. It is the ability to apply knowledge and experience to make thoughtful decisions, solve problems, and provide meaningful advice to others. Becoming a wise counsel requires cultivating wisdom through continuous learning, reflection, and empathy. This step will explore the importance of wisdom, how to develop it, and how to become a wise counsel to others.

The Importance of Wisdom

- **Informed Decision-Making.** Wisdom allows individuals to make well-considered decisions based on a thorough understanding of a situation and its potential consequences.
- **Conflict Resolution.** Wise individuals can navigate conflicts with tact and diplomacy, finding equitable solutions that consider the needs and perspectives of all parties involved.
- **Emotional Regulation.** Wisdom involves managing one's emotions and responding to situations thoughtfully rather than reacting impulsively.
- **Guidance and Support.** Wise people can offer valuable guidance and support to others, helping them navigate life's challenges and make sound decisions.

Developing Wisdom

- **Seek Diverse Experiences.** Exposure to a variety of experiences broadens your perspective and deepens your understanding of different cultures, ideas, and ways of life.
- **Reflect on Life Lessons.** Take time to reflect on your experiences, both positive and negative. Consider what you have learned and how you can apply these lessons to future situations.
- **Cultivate Self-Awareness.** Develop an awareness of your thoughts,

emotions, and behaviours. Understanding your own motivations and biases allows you to approach situations more objectively and with precision.

- **Practice Empathy.** Put yourself in others' shoes to understand their emotions, perspectives, and experiences. Empathy helps you connect with others and make compassionate decisions.
- **Embrace Lifelong Learning.** Continuously seek knowledge and insights from various sources, including books, lectures, podcasts, and conversations with others. Stay curious and open to new ideas.
- **Practice Patience and Thoughtfulness.** Take your time to consider different viewpoints and possible outcomes before making decisions or offering advice. Avoid rushing to judgments.
- **Develop Critical Thinking Skills.** Learn to evaluate information critically, question assumptions, and analyse situations from multiple angles.
- **Observe and Learn from Others.** Study the actions and decisions of wise individuals you admire. Observe how they handle challenges and interact with others.

Becoming a Wise Counsel

- **Listen Actively.** Pay close attention to what others are saying without interrupting or judging. Active listening allows you to understand the situation fully and offer thoughtful advice.
- **Ask Open-Ended Questions.** Encourage others to express themselves and share their thoughts and feelings. Asking open-ended questions can lead to deeper insights and understanding.
- **Offer Thoughtful Advice.** When providing guidance, consider the person's context, goals, and values. Tailor your advice to their specific situation and needs.
- **Be Honest and Constructive.** Provide honest feedback while being respectful and constructive. Focus on helping the person grow and learn from their experiences.
- **Respect Autonomy.** Recognise that others have the right to make

their own decisions. Offer support and guidance without imposing your own beliefs or values.

- **Encourage Reflection.** Help others reflect on their experiences and consider the lessons they can learn. Encourage them to think critically about their choices and potential outcomes.
- **Be Humble.** Acknowledge the limits of your knowledge and experience. Be willing to learn from others and admit when you do not have all the answers.

Developing wisdom and becoming a wise counsel requires continuous learning, reflection, and empathy. By seeking diverse experiences, practicing active listening, and offering thoughtful guidance, you can cultivate wisdom and provide valuable support to others. Wise individuals not only enhance their own lives but also positively impact the lives of those around them, fostering understanding, compassion, and thoughtful decision-making.

In the Indian epic *Mahabharata*, one character who actively seeks out wisdom and counsel is Duryodhana, the eldest son of the Kaurava king Dhritarashtra. Despite his often negative portrayal in the epic, Duryodhana understands the importance of seeking advice from wise and experienced individuals to achieve his goals.

One notable example of Duryodhana seeking wisdom and counsel occurs when he consults his uncle, Shakuni. Shakuni is a cunning and strategic advisor who plays a significant role in shaping Duryodhana's actions and decisions. Duryodhana relies heavily on Shakuni's advice, especially when it comes to his rivalry with the Pandavas.

For instance, Shakuni devises the plan to invite the Pandavas to a game of dice. The game is rigged in favour of Duryodhana and the Kauravas, allowing them to win the Pandavas' kingdom and wealth. Duryodhana follows Shakuni's counsel in this matter, despite its ethical ambiguity and the long-term consequences it has for the Kaurava-Pandava relationship.

Additionally, Duryodhana also seeks the counsel of other key figures, such as Bhishma and Drona, both of whom are respected elders and warriors. Although he often disregards their advice when it contradicts his ambitions, he recognises their expertise and values their input on military and strategic matters.

While Duryodhana's choices are often driven by his desire for power and revenge against the Pandavas, his willingness to seek out wisdom and counsel demonstrates his recognition of the importance of experienced guidance. His reliance on advisors like Shakuni, Bhishma, and Drona highlights the complex dynamics between ambition, counsel, and moral judgment in the *Mahabharata*.

A modern example where the *Mahabharata's* guidance on seeking out wisdom and counsel has delivered strategic success is the formation and execution of the 2016 Brexit referendum campaign. Specifically, the successful campaign strategies employed by the Leave.EU group, led by Dominic Cummings, illustrate the impact of seeking diverse wisdom and counsel.

The Brexit referendum, held on June 23, 2016, was a pivotal event in British history, determining whether the United Kingdom would remain in or leave the European Union. The Leave campaign, which advocated for exiting the EU, faced a formidable challenge against the "Remain campaign", which favoured staying in the EU. Dominic Cummings, the campaign director for Vote Leave, sought out and leveraged various sources of wisdom and counsel to craft a successful strategy.

Cummings and his team consulted with experts in data analysis, behavioural psychology, and political strategy. They sought insights from individuals with a deep understanding of voter behaviour and messaging. This included hiring the data analytics firm Cambridge Analytica, which provided detailed voter segmentation and targeted messaging strategies.

The campaign used sophisticated data analytics to understand voter concerns and preferences. They conducted extensive research to identify key issues and emotional triggers that resonated with different voter segments. This approach allowed them to tailor their messages more effectively than the Remain campaign.

The Leave campaign was open to advice from a variety of sources, including political strategists, economic experts, and grassroots activists. This openness to different perspectives helped them craft a message that appealed to a broad audience, addressing economic, sovereignty, and cultural concerns.

The campaign continually sought feedback and adjusted its strategy based on new information and changing circumstances. This iterative process of seeking counsel and adapting tactics was crucial in refining their approach and responding to emerging challenges.

The Leave campaign's strategy involved a mix of emotional appeals, targeted advertisements, and grassroots mobilisation. The campaign focused on the theme of reclaiming national sovereignty, which resonated with many voters. They framed EU membership as a loss of control over British laws and borders. Leveraging data-driven insights, the campaign created compelling and memorable slogans such as "Take Back Control" and used high-impact media strategies to reach target demographics. The campaign mobilised a wide network of volunteers and local activists to spread their message and engage with voters directly.

The success of the Brexit Leave campaign demonstrates the value of seeking wisdom and counsel as outlined in the *Mahabharata*. By consulting experts, utilising data-driven insights, and adapting their strategy based on diverse inputs, the Leave campaign was able to achieve a strategic victory against the odds. This modern example illustrates the enduring relevance of seeking comprehensive advice and insight to guide strategic decision-making.

Step 9: Prepare for the Unexpected

The ability to prepare for unexpected fallout, is a valuable skill that can help individuals navigate life's uncertainties and challenges with resilience and adaptability. While we cannot predict every unforeseen event, we can take proactive steps to equip ourselves with the tools and mindset needed to respond effectively. This step will explore the importance of preparing for the unexpected, practical strategies for doing so, and how it can benefit various aspects of our lives.

The Importance of Preparing for the Unexpected

- **Resilience and Adaptability.** Being prepared for unexpected situations helps us build resilience and adaptability. It allows us to navigate challenges more effectively and recover more quickly from setbacks.

- **Reduced Stress and Anxiety.** When we have contingency plans and resources in place, we are better equipped to handle surprises, which can reduce stress and anxiety in uncertain situations.
- **Improved Decision-Making.** Preparation provides us with the information and confidence needed to make informed decisions when unexpected events occur.
- **Increased Safety and Security.** By anticipating potential risks and having plans in place, we can better protect ourselves and our loved ones in emergencies.

Methodologies for Preparing for the Unexpected

- **Assess Risks.** Begin by identifying potential risks and vulnerabilities in various areas of your life, such as health, finances, career, and personal relationships. Consider how these risks might impact you.
- **Create Contingency Plans.** Develop contingency plans for different scenarios. For example, have emergency kits and evacuation plans in place for natural disasters, or set up an emergency fund for financial uncertainties.
- **Build a Support Network.** Establish a network of friends, family, or colleagues who can provide support in times of need. Having trusted people to rely on can make a significant difference during unexpected events.
- **Stay Informed.** Keep yourself informed about current events and potential risks in your area. This knowledge can help you anticipate and prepare for potential challenges.
- **Develop a Flexible Mindset.** Cultivate a mindset that embraces change and uncertainty. Practice being open to new ideas and alternative solutions when faced with unexpected situations.
- **Hone Problem-Solving Skills.** Enhance your problem-solving skills through practice and continuous learning. Being able to think critically and creatively can help you navigate unexpected challenges.
- **Maintain Physical and Mental Well-Being.** Taking care of your physical and mental health helps you stay strong and focused during

stressful times. Exercise, healthy eating, and mindfulness practices can all contribute to overall well-being.

- **Practice Financial Preparedness.** Build an emergency fund to cover unexpected expenses and ensure you have adequate insurance coverage for health, home, and other significant areas.

Benefits of Preparing for the Unexpected

- **Enhanced Confidence.** Being prepared gives you confidence in your ability to handle unexpected situations. This self-assurance can help you remain calm and focused during challenging times.
- **Quicker Recovery.** Preparation allows you to respond more swiftly to unexpected events, minimising potential damage and aiding in a quicker recovery.
- **Better Decision-Making.** When you have a plan in place, you can make decisions more effectively and efficiently, even under pressure.
- **Greater Peace of Mind.** Knowing you have prepared for potential challenges can bring peace of mind and a sense of security, allowing you to live more fully in the present.

Preparing for the unexpected is an essential aspect of navigating life's uncertainties and challenges. By assessing risks, creating contingency plans, building a support network, and maintaining physical and mental well-being, we can equip ourselves with the tools and mindset needed to respond effectively to unforeseen events. This preparation not only enhances our resilience and adaptability but also brings peace of mind and confidence in our ability to handle whatever comes our way.

In the Indian epic *Mahabharata*, one character who prepares for the unexpected is Lord Krishna, who serves as the advisor and charioteer to Arjuna and plays a key role in guiding the Pandavas throughout the epic.

One notable instance of Krishna's preparation for the unexpected, can be seen in his role in the Kurukshetra War. As the war progresses, Krishna devises and employs several strategies to ensure the Pandavas' victory, often anticipating the actions of the Kauravas and making plans to counter them effectively.

One such instance occurs during the battle against the Kaurava general Jayadratha. Jayadratha is a formidable opponent who manages to hold back the Pandava forces, particularly Arjuna, who has vowed to kill him by sunset in order to avenge the death of his son, Abhimanyu.

To counter this challenging move, Krishna prepares for the unexpected by manipulating the natural elements. As sunset approaches, Arjuna is unable to locate Jayadratha, and the chances of fulfilling his vow begin to diminish. To buy more time, Krishna creates an illusion of an eclipse, making it appear as though the sun has set.

When Jayadratha lowers his guard, believing the day to be over, Krishna advises Arjuna to take advantage of the situation. Arjuna uses the opportunity to locate and kill Jayadratha, thereby fulfilling his vow.

This example demonstrates how Krishna prepares for the unexpected by anticipating potential obstacles and devising innovative solutions to overcome them. His strategic foresight and ability to adapt to changing circumstances play a critical role in the Pandavas' success during the war.

Lord Krishna's actions showcase his ability to stay one step ahead of his opponents, using his wisdom and divine powers to navigate the complexities of the battle. His preparation for the unexpected helps the Pandavas achieve victory in several key moments of the epic.

A modern example where the *Mahabharata's* guidance on preparing for the unexpected led to strategic success can be seen in the 2012 landing of the Mars Science Laboratory (MSL) rover, 'Curiosity'. This mission, managed by NASA, exemplifies the importance of planning for unforeseen challenges in achieving a strategic objective. The Mars Science Laboratory mission, featuring the Curiosity rover, was a high-risk, high-reward endeavour aimed at exploring Mars and assessing its habitability. The mission's goal was to land the rover on Mars, explore the planet's surface, and gather data that could provide insights into its potential to support life.

The landing phase was particularly challenging due to the complexities of Mars' thin atmosphere and the need to slow the rover's descent from over 13,000 mph to a gentle landing speed. The MSL team developed a novel system involving a 'skycrane', a technique that had never been used before. This required extensive simulation and testing to anticipate potential problems during the descent and landing.

The team ran thousands of simulations to model different scenarios and potential failures. This included testing in various environments and conditions to ensure that the rover's systems could handle unexpected issues. For instance, they simulated different Martian weather conditions, equipment malfunctions, and communication problems.

The mission was designed with multiple layers of redundancy. Critical systems, such as the rover's landing gear and communication systems, had backup components and procedures to ensure the mission could succeed even if some parts of the plan failed. The team also developed contingency plans for various phases of the mission. For example, they had protocols in place for different landing sites in case the primary site was deemed unsuitable or if the rover's landing trajectory needed to be adjusted. During the landing, the team had to adapt in real-time to unexpected situations. For instance, when the rover made its descent, real-time adjustments were made to ensure a successful landing despite the inherent unpredictability of the Mars environment.

On August 6, 2012, Curiosity successfully landed on Mars, marking one of the most challenging and successful landings in space exploration history. The rover's successful deployment and operation on Mars validated the extensive planning and preparation done by the mission team. The Mars Science Laboratory mission demonstrates how preparing for the unexpected, as advised in the *Mahabharata*, can lead to strategic success. By anticipating potential challenges, implementing innovative solutions, and having contingency plans in place, NASA was able to overcome the many risks associated with landing a rover on Mars. This approach ensured not only the success of the landing but also the continued success of the mission in exploring and analysing the Martian surface.

Step 10: Learn How to Act with Moral Courage

Moral courage is the ability to stand up for one's values, beliefs, and ethical principles, even when faced with fear, adversity, or potential personal loss. It involves acting in accordance with one's convictions, even in challenging or uncomfortable situations. Moral courage is essential for fostering integrity, social justice, and positive change in the world. This step will explore the importance of moral courage, how to develop it, and the impact it can have on individuals and society.

The Importance of Moral Courage

- **Upholding Ethical Standards.** The much sought after tenet of moral courage equips individuals to maintain their ethical standards and act according to their values, even in situations where doing so may not be popular or advantageous.
- **Advocating for Justice.** People with moral courage are more likely to speak out against injustice and advocate for those who are marginalised or oppressed. This can lead to positive change and progress in society.
- **Building Trust and Integrity.** When individuals consistently act with moral courage, they build trust and credibility with others. This integrity fosters strong relationships and a sense of community.
- **Inspiring Others.** Acts of moral courage can inspire others to reflect on their own values and take action. It can create a ripple effect, encouraging more people to stand up for what is right.

Developing Moral Courage

- **Clarify Your Values.** Reflect on your core values and beliefs. Understand what is most important to you and why. Having a clear sense of your principles provides a foundation for moral courage.
- **Practice Self-Reflection.** Regularly assess your thoughts, actions, and decisions. Consider whether they align with your values and where you might need to make adjustments and relevant adaptations.
- **Educate Yourself.** Stay informed about social, ethical, and political issues. Knowledge empowers you to make well-informed decisions and take action when necessary.
- **Cultivate Empathy.** Understanding others' experiences and perspectives can help you develop moral courage by motivating you to advocate for those in need.

- **Surround Yourself with Support.** Build a network of like-minded individuals who share your values and can provide support and encouragement when facing challenges.
- **Start with Small Acts.** Practice moral courage in everyday situations. Speaking up in a meeting, supporting a friend, or making ethical choices can strengthen your resolve for larger challenges.
- **Take Calculated Risks.** Sometimes, acting with moral courage requires taking risks. Evaluate the potential consequences and benefits of your actions to make informed decisions.
- **Prepare for Opposition.** Be aware that acting with moral courage may lead to resistance or criticism. Prepare yourself mentally and emotionally to handle such situations with grace and resilience.

Impact of Moral Courage

- **Personal Growth.** Acting with moral courage can lead to personal growth and self-improvement. It helps you become more confident, resilient, and true to yourself.
- **Positive Influence on Others.** When you act with moral courage, you set an example for others. Your actions can encourage them to reflect on their own values and consider taking similar stands.
- **Social Change.** Individuals with moral courage can drive social change by challenging norms, raising awareness, and advocating for justice and equality.
- **Improved Reputation.** People who consistently act with moral courage earn respect and admiration from others, leading to an improved reputation and stronger relationships.

Moral courage is a powerful and essential quality that enables individuals to stand up for their values and beliefs, even in the face of adversity. By developing this skill through self-reflection, education, empathy, and practice, individuals can make a positive impact on their personal lives and society as a whole. Acting with moral courage fosters integrity, trust, and social change, paving the way for a more just and equitable world.

In the Indian epic *Mahabharata*, an example of a character learning to act with moral courage can be found in the journey of Karna. Karna, the son of Kunti and the sun god Surya, faces numerous challenges and moral dilemmas throughout his life, particularly regarding his loyalty to the Kauravas and his deep-seated conflict with the Pandavas.

One significant moment where Karna learns to act with moral courage occurs in the final days of the Kurukshetra War. Karna is appointed as the commander-in-chief of the Kaurava army after the death of Drona. During this time, he is faced with a moral choice regarding his allegiance to Duryodhana and the Kauravas, who have supported him throughout his life, and his loyalty to his biological brothers, the Pandavas, whom he has long been in conflict with. Karna's phenomenal and epochal moral courage is evident in his actions and decisions during his final battle with Arjuna:

- **Forgiveness and humility:** Before facing Arjuna in battle, Karna reflects on his past actions and decisions. He shows humility and self-awareness by acknowledging the mistakes he has made and his role in the conflict.
- **Fair combat:** Karna demonstrates moral courage by choosing to fight Arjuna fairly, adhering to the rules of combat and not taking advantage of any unfair advantage.
- **Acceptance of fate:** Despite knowing the outcome of the battle could mean his death, Karna accepts his fate and remains steadfast in his principles. He does not seek any special treatment from the gods, even when he faces technical issues with his chariot.

Karna's journey is a testament to his internal struggle with his sense of honour and duty. His moral courage is evident in his decisions during the final battle, where he chooses to uphold his integrity and fight with dignity. Although Karna's life is marked by tragedy and conflict, his journey demonstrates his growth in moral courage, especially in his ability to face difficult decisions with honour and resolve. His character adds depth to the themes of duty, loyalty, and righteousness within the epic.

A modern example where the guidance on acting with moral courage, as reflected in the *Mahabharata*, was notable in certain leaders is the 1994 Rwandan Genocide intervention by the United Nations and international organisations. During the Rwandan Genocide, which lasted from April to July 1994, an estimated 800,000 people were killed in a brutal campaign of ethnic violence orchestrated by the Hutu-led government against the Tutsi minority. The international community faced severe criticism for its slow response to the crisis, but there were notable instances of moral courage that made some small positive impacts.

One prominent example of moral courage in the face of such adversity was the role played by General Roméo Dallaire, the force commander of the United Nations Assistance Mission for Rwanda (UNAMIR). Dallaire, a Canadian, was stationed in Rwanda and witnessed firsthand the unfolding genocide. Despite limited resources and a mandate that severely restricted his ability to intervene, Dallaire made the courageous decision to act against the violence he observed.

Dallaire and his team gathered evidence and repeatedly warned the United Nations and the international community about the impending genocide. He sent urgent cables and reports describing the scale of the violence and urging for immediate intervention. His moral courage lay in his steadfast commitment to his duty and his willingness to speak out despite facing bureaucratic inertia and a lack of support.

Dallaire's actions included overseeing the protection of Tutsi refugees and assisting in evacuations. He managed to rescue thousands of individuals by providing them sanctuary in UN-protected zones, even though his forces were outnumbered and under constant threat. Dallaire faced severe psychological and emotional strain due to the horrors he encountered, and the limitations imposed on him. His commitment to his moral principles and the humanitarian mission exemplified the values of courage and integrity.

Though the international community's response to the genocide was initially inadequate, Dallaire's actions and the efforts of various humanitarian organisations eventually led to the establishment of a more robust intervention force. The genocide ended when the Rwandan Patriotic Front (RPF), a Tutsi-led rebel group, took control of the country. Dallaire's moral courage and persistent efforts contributed to saving lives and setting a precedent for future international humanitarian interventions.

General Roméo Dallaire's moral courage during the Rwandan Genocide aligns with the principles found in the *Mahabharata*, particularly the importance of righteousness and acting with conviction in the face of adversity. His actions, though limited by constraints, showcased how acting with moral courage can lead to significant, albeit partial, success and help in mitigating humanitarian crises. His legacy continues to influence discussions on ethical responsibility and intervention in global conflicts.

The *Mahabharata* – A Summary

The *Mahabharata* is a multifaceted epic that weaves together mythology, philosophy, and history to create a rich tapestry of human experience. It includes several strategic concepts:

- *Dharma* (Righteousness).
- Strategic Planning and Vision.
- Alliance Building.
- Understanding the Enemy
- Adaptability and Flexibility.
- Deception and Diplomacy.
- Leadership and Decision-Making.
- The Role of Wisdom and Counsel.
- The Influence of Fate and Destiny.
- War Ethics and Conduct.

From these concepts a 10-step process to assist with developing a strategic mindset can be developed:

Step 1: Determine Your Personal Values

- Self-Reflection.
- Identify Core Values.
- Assess Priorities.
- Seek Feedback.
- Re-evaluate Over Time.

Step 2: Practice Describing End States in Terms of Feelings and Perceptions.

- Identify Desired Emotions.
- Visualise the Impact.
- Use Descriptive Language.
- Connect to Values and Purpose.
- Engage Stakeholders.

Step 3: Determine the Types of People and Organisations You Will Work With.

- Values Alignment.
- Reputation and Track Record.
- Communication.
- Expertise and Experience.
- Integrity and Trustworthiness.
- Collaborative Approach.
- Cultural Fit.
- Growth and Development.
- Responsiveness and Adaptability.
- Conflict Resolution Skills.
- Financial Stability.
- Shared Vision and Goals.

Step 4: Learn How to Read People and Situations.

- Observe Nonverbal Cues.
- Listen Actively.
- Watch for Patterns.
- Consider Context.
- Pay Attention to Tone.
- Empathise.
- Ask Open-Ended Questions.
- Stay Curious.

Step 5: Demonstrate Cerebral Flexibility.

- Expose Yourself to New Experiences.
- Challenge Your Beliefs.
- Practice Mindfulness.
- Engage in Critical Thinking.
- Read Widely.
- Learn a New Language.
- Collaborate with Others.
- Embrace Uncertainty.
- Practice Perspective-Taking.

Step 6: Practice Deception and Diplomacy.

- Use Deception Sparingly.
- Maintain Ethical Boundaries.
- Consider Alternative Strategies.
- Uphold Transparency.
- Reflect on Long-Term Impact.

Step 7: Show Strong Leadership and Decision-Making Skills.

- Critical Thinking.
- Emotional Intelligence.
- Decisiveness.
- Adaptability.
- Communication Skills.
- Ethical Judgment.

Step 8: Seek Out Wisdom and Counsel.

- Seek Diverse Experiences.
- Reflect on Life Lessons.
- Cultivate Self-Awareness.
- Practice Empathy.
- Embrace Lifelong Learning.

- Practice Patience and Thoughtfulness.
- Develop Critical Thinking Skills.
- Observe and Learn from Others.
- Listen Actively.
- Ask Open-Ended Questions.
- Offer Thoughtful Advice.
- Be Honest and Constructive.
- Respect Autonomy.
- Encourage Reflection.
- Be Humble.

Step 9: Prepare for the Unexpected.

- Assess Risks.
- Create Contingency Plans.
- Build a Support Network.
- Stay Informed.
- Develop a Flexible Mindset.
- Hone Problem-Solving Skills.
- Maintain Physical and Mental Well-Being.
- Practice Financial Preparedness.

Step 10: Learn How to Act with Moral Courage.

- Clarify Your Values.
- Practice Self-Reflection.
- Educate Yourself.
- Cultivate Empathy.
- Surround Yourself with Support.
- Start with Small Acts.
- Take Calculated Risks.
- Prepare for Opposition.

PART 2

ADOPTING A STRATEGIC APPROACH

Part 1 looked at creating a strategic mindset in senior leaders that is so necessary for tackling complex problems. In Part 2, we will explore the next stage of the journey which I call 'adopting a strategic approach.' This section is about the cultural approach adopted within the highest levels or a government or organisation as it is about the 'tradecraft' of strategy rather than how to deal with a specific problem or situation. Chapter 3 looks at the works of Kautilya and specifically his work the *Arthashastra*. This is a large collection of books that covers statecraft, governance and warfare. Chapter 4 looks at the Tamil Sangam poems within the *Purananuru*. This is a rather lovely collection of works that gives advice to kings on how to manage their subjects and lands.

Chapter Three

Kautilya's Arthashastra

"Before you start some work, always ask yourself three questions - Why am I doing it, What the results might be, and Will I be successful?"

—Kautilya

IN THIS CHAPTER

- Who was Kautilya?
- About Kautilya's '*Arthashastra*'.
- The Strategic Leader – *Vijigishu*.
- Strategic Leadership Characteristics – *Svamisampad.*
- The Spiritual End State or *Yogakshema*.
- Diplomatic, Silent, Covert and Open Warfare.
- The Four Approaches – *Upayas*.

- The Tools of Foreign Policy – *Sadgunya.*
- Understanding the Enemy – The *Mandala* Analysis.
- Kautilya's Guide for the Modern Strategist.
- Kautilya – A Summary.

WHO WAS KAUTILYA?

Kautilya, also known as Chanakya or Vishnu Gupta, was an ancient Indian scholar, strategist, and philosopher who is best known for his seminal work on statecraft and political strategy, the *Arthashastra*. He lived during the 4th century BCE and is often considered one of the most influential figures in Indian political thought.

Kautilya played a key role in the establishment of the Maurya Empire, the first major empire in ancient India, and was the principal advisor to its founder, Chandragupta Maurya. His strategic acumen and insights into governance, diplomacy, and warfare were instrumental in the rise of the Maurya Empire.

The *Arthashastra* is a holistic and comprehensive treatise on governance, politics, military strategy, economics, and social organisation. It outlines the principles of statecraft, including the role of the king, the administration of justice, foreign policy, and the management of resources. The text is considered a classic in the field of political science and provides valuable insights into ancient Indian governance and strategy. Kautilya's influence extends beyond his time, and his ideas continue to be studied and respected for their depth and relevance to modern-day strategy and leadership.

ABOUT KAUTILYA'S '*ARTHASHASTRA*'

The *Arthashastra* emerged during a period of political turmoil and transformation in ancient India. As an architect of the Maurya Empire's rise, Kautilya applied his principles of statecraft and strategy to establish a strong and centralised administration. The *Arthashastra* is a detailed treatise divided into 15 books, covering various aspects of governance and administration:

Book I: Concerning Discipline (*Ādhyātmika-kāṇḍa*)

This book addresses the role of the king, the structure of the administration, and the organisation of the state.

Book II: The Duties of Government Superintendents (*Vyāpāra-kāṇḍa*)

This book covers the functions of government officials and superintendents, including their roles in various sectors such as agriculture, trade, and taxation.

Book III: Concerning Law (*Dandanīti-kāṇḍa*)

This book discusses legal matters, including civil, criminal, and family law, as well as the role of judges and the judicial system.

Book IV: The Removal of Thorns (*Tṛṇabheda-kāṇḍa*)

This book addresses internal security and measures to deal with enemies within the state, such as spies and conspirators.

Book V: The Conduct of Courtiers (*Amātya-ācāra-kāṇḍa*)

This book focuses on the conduct and duties of courtiers, including their selection, training, and ethical behaviour.

Book VI: The Source of Sovereign States (*Sāmṛtya-kāṇḍa*)

This book discusses the different types of states, the principles of statecraft, and the qualities of a ruler.

Book VII: The End of the Six-Fold Policy (*Shadgunya-kāṇḍa*)

This book outlines the six-fold foreign policy (peace, war, neutrality, alliance, dual policy, and armed preparations) and its application in international relations.

Book VIII: Concerning Vices and Calamities (*Vyasanādhyāya-kāṇḍa*)

This book explores the challenges faced by the state, including internal and external threats, and how to address them.

Book IX: The Work of an Invader *(Sangrahana-kāṇḍa)*

This book deals with strategies and tactics for military campaigns and invasions.

Book X: Relating to War *(Yuddhānāyaka-kāṇḍa)*

This book covers the conduct of war, including battlefield strategies, formations, and the management of soldiers.

Book XI: The Conduct of Corporations *(Janapada-ācāra-kāṇḍa)*

This book focuses on the administration of different types of groups and communities, such as guilds and corporations.

Book XII: Concerning a Powerful Enemy *(Atyanta-kāṇḍa)*

This book discusses strategies for dealing with a powerful enemy, including diplomacy, alliances, and subversion.

Book XIII: Strategic Means to Capture a Fortress *(Durga-graha-kāṇḍa)*

This book outlines strategies and tactics for besieging and capturing enemy fortresses.

Book XIV: Secret Means *(Utsāhavāda-kāṇḍa)*

This book discusses covert operations, espionage, and other secret methods to achieve strategic objectives.

Book XV: The Plan of a Treatise *(Arthashastra-kāṇḍa)*

This book serves as a conclusion to the treatise, summarising the key concepts and offering a recapitulation of the entire work.

Kautilya's *Arthashastra* is renowned for its pragmatic and realistic approach to statecraft. His insights into themes such as governance, strategy, and diplomacy have influenced generations of scholars and leaders. The treatise's emphasis on strategic foresight, meticulous planning, and adaptability remains relevant today. Kautilya's work also highlights the ethical dimensions of governance. While the *Arthashastra* is often seen as a guide to *realpolitik*, Kautilya stresses the importance of a ruler's moral and ethical obligations to their subjects.

Kautilya's *Arthashastra* is a timeless treatise and classic that offers valuable lessons in governance, strategy, and administration. Its influence extends far beyond ancient India, providing insights that continue to be applicable in modern times. Kautilya's work remains a cornerstone in the study of political science and statecraft, serving as a guide for those seeking to understand the complexities of leadership and the art of governance.

THE STRATEGIC LEADER OR *VIJIGISHU*

Kautilya requires an 'aspiring king' or 'would-be conqueror' known as the *Vijigishu* to formulate and execute the strategy. The concept of *Vijigishu* is an important aspect of ancient Hindu political thought. In the context of the *Arthashastra*, the *Vijigishu* is the ruler who seeks to expand their domain and influence through strategic actions, diplomatic negotiations, and military campaigns. The ultimate goal of the *Vijigishu* is to create a stable and prosperous state that upholds the principles of *dharma* (righteousness) and provides for the welfare of the people.

The *Vijigishu* is expected to possess several qualities and characteristics that make them capable of ruling effectively. These include:

- **Wisdom and Intelligence**: The *Vijigishu* ought to be knowledgeable in various fields, including statecraft, diplomacy, and warfare. They should be able to make informed decisions and navigate complex political situations.
- **Justice and Fairness**: An ideal *Vijigishu* administers justice fairly and equitably, ensuring that all subjects are treated justly and according to the law.
- **Strength and Courage**: The *Vijigishu* must possess physical and moral strength to protect the kingdom and face challenges, whether internal or external.
- **Strategic Thinking**: The *Vijigishu* should be adept at strategic planning, understanding the balance of power, and using various diplomatic and military tactics to achieve their goals.

- **Compassion and Benevolence**: The *Vijigishu* should care for the well-being of their subjects, showing compassion and benevolence in their governance.

While the concept of *Vijigishu* emphasises the expansion of the ruler's domain and influence, there are ethical considerations associated with the pursuit of conquest. These could be described as:

- **Respect for *Dharma***: The *Vijigishu* must uphold *dharma* in their actions, ensuring that their pursuit of expansion does not compromise moral and ethical principles.
- **Welfare of the People**: The expansion of the state should be conducted in a manner that benefits the people, rather than exploiting them for personal gain.
- **Avoidance of Unnecessary Violence**: The *Vijigishu* should avoid unnecessary violence and seek peaceful solutions whenever possible. War and conquest should be a last resort when diplomacy fails.

The concept of *Vijigishu* in Hindu political thought outlines the qualities and responsibilities of an ideal ruler who seeks to expand, fan out and strengthen their kingdom through wise and strategic governance. While the pursuit of conquest and expansion is central to the role of the *Vijigishu*, it must be balanced with ethical considerations, including adherence to *dharma*, concern for the welfare of the people, and a commitment to justice and fairness. By embodying these principles, the *Vijigishu* can achieve success in statecraft while maintaining the stability and prosperity of their kingdom.

In the context of the modern world and in particular hybrid and grey zone conflict situations, this *Vijigishu* is the Senior Responsible Owner (SRO) who coordinates and controls strategic analysis, planning and execution across government and alliances. This could be the Prime Minister in a liberal democracy (or another national equivalent) or an empowered Minister or senior official. However, it cannot be an advisor, committee or council as Kautilya is clear it must be a named and empowered individual. In the time of Kautilya this was easy as in the absolute monarchies of the day the king was both the political and military leader.

When applying the Kautilyan Way to the modern world, a single person with 'skin in the game' is necessary to drive the effective development and execution of strategy. Kautilya was rigid and unwavering in his view that a single accountable person should be placed as the leader (*Vijigishu*) in solving a strategic problem. This is similar to the latest Western Fusion Doctrine where an SRO is appointed by the National Security Council of not less than 3* rank (military or civilian) who has regional and/or thematic expertise. Kautilya also stated that the livelihood and future of the *Vijigishu* should be tied to the success or failure of the strategy. However, this did not remove responsibility for innovation and flair from the lower ranks as a series of 'ministers' and officers were also empowered. The *Arthashastra* is notable for its emphasis on bureaucracies to support the king and the empowered ministers and officials. Kautilya devoted a whole chapter of the *Arthashastra* to state administration.

Kautilya is also clear that selection of the *Vijigishu* and the most senior supporting ministers and officials must be carried out from those with the right character traits for strategic leadership and then they must be trained, too. While in Kautilya's time, noble birth was an important factor, he still ruthlessly weeded out those not up to the task. In many countries, strategic leaders and supporting officials are selected from a very small pool that lacks diversity. This pool is often not conducive to the production of strategic leaders as the hierarchical bureaucracies found in the majority of the world narrow eligibility based on other factors such as political patronage, staff ability, technical skills and previous performance in the tactical and operational disciplines. While some of these personnel will of course have strategic leadership traits, this is due to serendipity rather than any deliberate process or systematic evolution. Therefore, when applying the Kautilyan Way, it is imperative that the *Vijigishu* is selected from the widest possible pool and not just the civil service, the military or political parties. The same applies for supporting ministers and officials.

Once selected, the training for the *Vijigishu* and supporting cast must be intense and the failure criteria ruthless. Kautilya recommended continuous 'secret tests' of ministers and supporting officials to ensure they not only remained loyal, but that they were still up to the job. When applying Kautilya in the modern age, training must be considered as part of the strategy and there must be some form of continual assessment to make sure the *Vijigishu* and supporting officials are not being subverted (by nefarious influence) or producing weak strategy through groupthink, hubris or pathological behaviours.

Groupthink, hubris and pathological behaviours have been shown time-and-time again to seriously undermine strategy development and execution but no serious attempt in the West has been made to address this issue. Kautilya seems to have recognised that this is a severe problem and made provision to prevent it. It is therefore recommended that some form of independent body provides the assessment function recommended by Kautilya noting that this is not to determine whether the strategy is good or bad (only history can judge this), but whether the *Vijigishu* and officials are thinking and behaving sensibly.

STRATEGIC LEADERSHIP CHARACTERISTICS OR *SVAMISAMPAD*

Kautilya is clear that the strategic leader or *Vijigishu* must exhibit certain leadership traits if they are to be effective. In fact, Kautilya had a single word for these strategic leadership traits – *Svamisampad*. Traits included:

- Qualities that inspire confidence in others.
- Approachability.
- Nobility of birth.
- Piety.
- Truthfulness.
- Ability to understand complex issues.
- Ability to think.
- Bravery and moral courage.
- Quickness of decision.
- Strength of mind.
- Eloquence and Charisma.
- Boldness.
- Good memory.

The list was actually much longer and more descriptive than this but, other than nobility of birth, these characteristics are still highly applicable and highly desirable today. Kautilya not only believed these traits to be rare, he also deemed thorough training (*vinaya*) to be essential even when the traits were present. He contended effective strategists and strategic leaders were made not born. In fact, Kautilya dedicated an entire book of the *Arthashastra* to training. This training included the philosophical disciplines (*Anviksiki*), Vedic lore, economics, and political science (*Vartta*). Furthermore, the *Vijigishu* was expected to learn self-control over the senses so he would not be tempted by vices or undermine his reputation and authority through inappropriate behaviour.

Vinaya

The concept of *vinaya* holds a significant place in Hindu philosophy and is commonly associated with humility, discipline, and respect. Although the term originates in Buddhism, where it refers to the rules and guidelines for monastic discipline, it also has broader applications in Hinduism, particularly in the context of ethical and spiritual conduct. *Vinaya* encompasses self-restraint, good behaviour, and the cultivation of moral and ethical virtues.

Vinaya can be applied in various aspects of life, including personal conduct, relationships, and spiritual practice:

- **Personal Conduct**: In personal behaviour, *vinaya* involves self-discipline and restraint, particularly in controlling one's desires and impulses. It includes being mindful of one's actions and their impact on others.
- **Interpersonal Relationships**: *Vinaya* demands respect and humility in relationships with others, including elders, peers, and subordinates. It promotes harmony and mutual understanding in social interactions.
- **Spiritual Practice**: In the context of spiritual practice, *vinaya* involves adhering to ethical and moral guidelines, such as truthfulness, non-violence, and compassion. It also includes showing reverence for spiritual teachers and traditions.

The practice of *vinaya* has a profound impact on both individuals and the community:

- **Moral and Ethical Development**: By practicing *vinaya*, individuals cultivate moral and ethical virtues, such as humility, patience, and self-control. These qualities contribute to personal growth and character development.
- **Social Harmony**: *Vinaya* promotes respect and consideration for others, which fosters harmony and cohesion within the community. It encourages individuals to work together for the common good.
- **Spiritual Progress**: In the context of spiritual practice, *vinaya* supports the development of higher consciousness and self-awareness. It helps individuals align their actions with their spiritual goals.

The concept of *vinaya* is an essential and inalienable aspect of Hindu philosophy, emphasising humility, discipline, and respect in personal and social conduct. By practicing *vinaya*, individuals can cultivate moral and ethical virtues that contribute to their personal growth and the well-being of the community. It fosters harmony in relationships and supports spiritual progress, leading to a more fulfilling and meaningful life. In today's world, the principles of *vinaya* remain relevant and valuable, providing a foundation for ethical conduct and harmonious living.

Anviksiki

Anviksiki is an ancient Indian philosophical discipline that involves critical inquiry, analysis, and logical reasoning. It is considered one of the four traditional sciences (*vidyas*) in Hindu thought, alongside the sciences of statecraft (*arthashastra*), military strategy (*dhanurveda*), and the science of wealth (*varta*). *Anviksiki* is the study of philosophy and the art of rational thinking, encompassing areas such as logic, epistemology, and ethics.

The term *anviksiki* is derived from the Sanskrit word "anvi" (after) and "ksiki" (science or study), and it refers to the pursuit of knowledge through critical inquiry and analytical thinking. It involves questioning, examining, and reasoning about the world, including metaphysical, ethical, and epistemological questions.

Anviksiki has its roots in ancient Indian thought, particularly in the Vedic and Upanishadic traditions. It is closely associated with the development of Indian philosophy and the emergence of various schools of thought, such as Nyaya, Vaisheshika, and Sankhya:

- **Nyaya School**: The Nyaya school of philosophy is closely linked to *anviksiki*, as it focuses on logic and reasoning as a means of attaining knowledge and understanding the world.
- **Vaisheshika School**: The Vaisheshika school complements *anviksiki* by focusing on categorisation and classification, providing a framework for the study of nature and reality.
- **Sankhya School**: The Sankhya school also contributes to *anviksiki* through its analytical approach to understanding the principles of existence and the nature of the self.

Anviksiki has various applications in intellectual and ethical thought:

- **Critical Inquiry**: *Anviksiki* encourages individuals to engage in critical inquiry and questioning, fostering a deeper understanding of complex issues and problems.
- **Logical Reasoning**: The discipline requires the use of logical reasoning to analyse arguments and evaluate evidence, leading to well-reasoned conclusions.
- **Ethical Reflection**: *Anviksiki* promotes ethical reflection and decision-making by encouraging individuals to consider the moral implications of their actions and beliefs.

The practice of *anviksiki* has a significant impact on both intellectual and ethical thought:

- **Intellectual Development**: *Anviksiki* fosters intellectual growth by encouraging curiosity, open-mindedness, and the pursuit of knowledge.
- **Ethical and Moral Insight**: Through critical inquiry and analysis, *anviksiki* helps individuals gain ethical and moral insight, guiding their behaviour and decision-making.
- **Cultural and Philosophical Legacy**: The tradition of *anviksiki*

has contributed to the rich cultural and philosophical legacy of India, influencing subsequent generations of thinkers and scholars.

The concept of *anviksiki* is a foundational aspect of Hindu thought, emphasising critical inquiry, analysis, and logical reasoning. It plays a crucial role in intellectual and ethical development, fostering curiosity and open-mindedness while guiding individuals toward well-reasoned conclusions. As a discipline, *anviksiki* continues to offer valuable insights into the nature of knowledge, reality, and ethical conduct, making it a timeless and enduring aspect of the Indian philosophical tradition.

Vartta

Vartta is an ancient Indian concept that refers to the science of wealth and economic management. It encompasses various aspects of economic activity, including agriculture, trade, industry, and finance. As one of the four traditional sciences (*vidyas*) in Hindu thought—alongside statecraft (*arthashastra*), military strategy (*dhanurveda*), and the science of philosophy and logic (*anviksiki*)—*vartta* plays a central role in ensuring the prosperity and stability of society.

The term *vartta* comes from the Sanskrit word "v[tti," which means occupation or livelihood. It refers to the study and practice of managing resources and wealth to support the well-being of individuals and the community. *Vartta* includes the cultivation of land, production of goods, trade and commerce, and financial management.

The roots of *vartta* can be traced back to ancient Indian texts such as the *Vedas* and the *Arthashastra* by Kautilya, which provide insights into the principles of economic management and wealth creation. The concept evolved over time as part of the broader development of Indian civilisation and culture.

- **Economic Thought**: *Vartta* has been a mainstay of economic thought in India, addressing issues such as resource allocation, production, and distribution.
- **Agriculture**: Agriculture has always been a central focus of *vartta*, as it forms the basis of the economy by providing food and raw materials.

- **Trade and Commerce**: Trade and commerce have played a significant role in the development of *vartta*, contributing to the exchange of goods and wealth within and across regions.
- **Finance**: Financial management, including the use of money and credit, is an important aspect of *vartta* that facilitates economic activity and growth.

Vartta has various applications in economic thought and practice:

- **Resource Management**: *Vartta* emphasises efficient management of resources, including land, labour, and capital, to maximise productivity and wealth.
- **Trade and Exchange**: The discipline promotes trade and exchange as means of distributing goods and wealth, both within and between communities.
- **Financial Management**: *Vartta* includes principles of financial management, such as saving, investment, and credit, to support economic growth and stability.
- **Welfare and Prosperity**: Ultimately, *vartta* aims to enhance the welfare and prosperity of individuals and society by promoting sustainable economic practices.

The practice of *vartta* has a significant impact on economic thought and practice:

- **Economic Development**: By focusing on efficient resource management and trade, *vartta* contributes to economic development and growth.
- **Social Stability**: The principles of *vartta* support social stability by ensuring the equitable distribution of wealth and opportunities for all members of society.
- **Cultural and Philosophical Legacy**: The tradition of *vartta* has influenced the development of Indian economic thought, shaping ideas about wealth, trade, and prosperity.

The concept of *vartta* is a foundational and fundamental element of Hindu thought, emphasising the science of wealth and economic management. It plays a crucial role in supporting the prosperity and stability of society by promoting efficient resource management, trade, and financial practices. As a discipline, *vartta* continues to offer valuable insights into economic thought and practice, making it a timeless and enduring aspect of the Indian philosophical tradition.

Assessment for *Svamisampad*

Assessing individuals for the key leadership traits (*Svamisampad*) is essential if the Kautilyan Way is to be adopted effectively. Let's look at each of the traits below:

1. Qualities that Inspire Confidence in Others

Inspiring confidence in others is a valuable skill that can positively impact personal and professional relationships. Certain qualities and behaviours can help build trust and inspire confidence in those around you. Here are some key qualities that can inspire confidence in others and should be considered as the minimum requirements for the *Vijigishu*:

- **Competence**. The *Vijigishu* ought to demonstrate expertise and knowledge in relevant fields or areas of responsibility. This includes the delivery of quality work and consistently exceeding expectations. The *Vijigishu* must also stay up to date with industry trends and best practices.
- **Integrity**. The *Vijigishu* ought to be honest, open, and transparent in all their interactions. This does not mean they should not undertake deception operations, but within their own organisation they must have the highest levels of integrity. Upholding ethical standards and values is part of this, but perhaps most importantly they must have the moral courage to call out others (particularly senior management) who stray. It goes without saying that they must take responsibility for their actions and admit mistakes.
- **Reliability**. Leaders ought to be completely reliable. This necessitates following through on commitments and promises. The *Vijigishu* must be completely and utterly dependable and consistent with their actions. Simple things like showing up on time and being prepared are critical.

- **Effective Communication**. Senior leaders ideally must be effective communicators. They need to clearly articulate their thoughts and ideas and create compelling strategic narratives. Communication is a two-way process to the *Vijigishu* must listen actively and empathetically to others and be open to feedback and constructive challenge.
- **Emotional Intelligence**. Closely connected to effective communication is emotional intelligence or EQ. This requires the *Vijigishu* to manage their emotions effectively and remain calm under pressure. They must also show empathy and understanding towards others' feelings and perspectives. Ultimately, the *Vijigishu* must build positive relationships and foster a supportive environment.
- **Decisiveness**. Senior leaders must be decisive. Note that this is very different from being impulsive or aggressive. The *Vijigishu* must make decisions confidently and efficiently, even in uncertain and emotional situations. This requires the ability to take calculated risks and consider different perspectives before making decisions.
- **Adaptability**. Being flexible and open to change is a key strategic leadership trait given the dynamic nature of complex problems. Navigating new or challenging situations with a positive attitude is key as is learning from experiences and continuously improving.
- **Confidence**. Confidence is about exuding self-assurance without being arrogant. The *Vijigishu* must have trust in their abilities and judgment. Outwardly they must present themselves confidently through body language, charisma, and tone of voice.
- **Vision and Purpose**. Senior leaders must absolutely have a clear sense of direction and articulate goals that everyone can understand. This is essential for communicating a vision and motivating others to work towards it. Leading by example and inspiring others to achieve shared objectives are key elements of this most critical trait.
- **Respect for Others**. Successful organisations value diverse opinions and perspectives. The *Vijigishu* must therefore treat others

with respect and dignity so as to create an inclusive environment where everyone feels valued.

2. Approachability.

Assessing whether a strategic leader is approachable involves observing their behaviour, communication style, and interactions with others. An approachable leader creates an environment where team members feel comfortable reaching out, sharing ideas, and seeking guidance. Here are several factors to consider when assessing a strategic leader's approachability:

- **Communication Style**. An approachable leader communicates openly and overtly about decisions, changes, and goals, providing clarity and transparency. They listen attentively to others, showing interest in their thoughts and feedback without interrupting or dismissing them. Positive body language is essential. A leader who uses friendly, welcoming gestures and maintains good eye contact conveys approachability.
- **Accessibility**. An approachable leader makes time for team members and is accessible for discussions or feedback. They participate in team activities and engage in informal conversations with team members.
- **Responsiveness**. The *Vijigishu* should respond to questions, concerns, and requests in a timely manner. They should provide constructive feedback and encourage open dialogue.
- **Empathy and Understanding**: Senior leaders must be compassionate and supportive and show empathy for the challenges others face and provide support when needed. An approachable leader recognises and validates the emotions of other team members.
- **Respect for Others**. Strategic leaders treat team members with respect and fairness, regardless of their position or background. An approachable leader acknowledges and values the contributions of others and gives credit where it is due.
- **Conflict Resolution**. Constructive challenge and alternative views are essential for effective strategy, but internal conflict is disastrous.

Therefore, the *Vijigishu* must be open to discussing disagreements and finding solutions through collaboration. An approachable leader remains calm and open to feedback during conflicts.

- **Flexibility and Openness**. Senior leaders must be open to new ideas. They encourage innovation and creativity by being receptive to new perspectives and suggestions. An approachable leader is flexible and willing to adjust plans based on input from others.
- **Fair and Consistent Treatment**. Good leadership requires consistency in decision-making. They make decisions fairly and consistently, which builds trust among team members. An approachable leader treats all team members impartially and avoids favouritism.

3. Piety

Assessing the piety of a strategic leader involves evaluating their moral and ethical values, as well as their adherence to principles such as honesty, integrity, and respect. Piety in a leader can be reflected in their behaviour, decision-making, and interactions with others. Here are some factors to consider when assessing the piety of a strategic leader:

- **Ethical Standards**. A leader who consistently upholds ethical standards and principles demonstrates piety. They act with integrity, being honest and transparent in their dealings.
- **Fairness and Justice**. A pious leader makes decisions fairly and justly, considering the needs and perspectives of all stakeholders. They apply rules and policies consistently, treating everyone equally.
- **Compassion and Empathy**. A leader who shows compassion and empathy for others' needs and challenges is likely to be seen as pious. They provide support and guidance to those who need it.
- **Respect for Others**. A leader who treats others with respect and dignity, regardless of their position, demonstrates piety. They acknowledge and appreciate the efforts and achievements of others.
- **'Serve-to-Lead'**. This is the motto of the UK's Royal Military Academy Sandhurst (RMAS) and expresses the need to focus on

serving others: A pious leader prioritises the well-being of the team, organisation, and community over personal gain, but they are still committed to the mission and goals of the organisation.

- **Accountability**. A leader who takes responsibility for their actions and decisions demonstrates piety. They are open about their decisions and rationale, building trust with others.
- **Spiritual and Moral Guidance**. A pious leader premises their decisions and actions on a strong moral or spiritual foundation. They provide mentorship and moral guidance to others, setting a positive example as a role model of sorts.
- **Humility**. A pious leader demonstrates humility, acknowledging their limitations and being open to learning from others. They express gratitude for the support and contributions of others.

When assessing the piety of a strategic leader, consider these factors in the context of their overall behaviour, interactions, and decision-making processes. A leader's actions and attitudes that align with these qualities can indicate their piety and positive influence on the organisation's culture and success.

4. Truthfulness

Assessing the truthfulness of a strategic leader involves evaluating their communication, behaviour, and interactions with others to determine whether they are honest and transparent in their actions. Here are some key factors to consider when assessing a leader's truthfulness:

- **Consistency in Communication**. A truthful leader's actions consistently match their words, and they follow through on promises and commitments. They communicate openly and clearly, providing accurate and reliable information.
- **Transparency**. A truthful leader is open and transparent about decisions, challenges, and opportunities. They provide clear explanations for their decisions and actions, fostering trust and understanding.
- **Adherence to Ethical Standards**. A truthful leader consistently adheres to ethical principles and values in their decision-making

processes. They maintain confidentiality when necessary and appropriate, demonstrating respect for others' privacy.

- **Responsiveness and Willingness to Address Concerns**. They respond promptly and thoughtfully to questions and concerns, showing respect for others' perspectives. A truthful leader acknowledges and corrects mistakes openly and honestly.
- **Consistency in Messaging**. A truthful leader's messaging remains consistent across different audiences and contexts. They avoid contradictory statements and double standards.
- **Approach to Challenges and Problems**. A truthful leader addresses challenges openly and involves others in finding solutions. They are receptive to feedback and different perspectives, and they use this input constructively.
- **Integrity and Trustworthiness**. A truthful leader earns and maintains the trust of others through consistent honesty and integrity. They set clear boundaries and uphold them, maintaining professional relationships and avoiding conflicts of interest.

By observing a strategic leader's behaviour in these areas, you can assess their truthfulness and determine how their honesty and transparency impact the organisation and its stakeholders. Trustworthy leaders who consistently demonstrate truthfulness foster a positive work environment and contribute to the organisation's overall success.

5. Ability to Understand Complex Issues

Assessing a strategic leader's ability to understand complex issues involves evaluating their critical thinking skills, analytical abilities, and capacity to navigate multifaceted situations. Here are some key factors to consider when assessing a leader's ability to understand complex issues:

- **Analytical Skills**. A leader with strong analytical skills can break down complex problems into manageable parts and identify potential solutions. They use logical reasoning to connect concepts and ideas, drawing meaningful conclusions from data and evidence.
- **Curiosity and Open-Mindedness**. A leader who is open to new perspectives and approaches demonstrates a capacity to understand

complex issues from different angles. They actively seek out knowledge and stay informed about industry trends and developments.

- **Ability to Synthesise Information**. A strategic leader synthesises information from various sources and identifies patterns and relationships. They can determine which aspects of a complex issue are most critical and prioritise their attention accordingly.
- **Decision-Making Under Uncertainty**. A leader who is comfortable making decisions under uncertainty and ambiguity demonstrates an ability to navigate complex issues. They evaluate risks and potential outcomes when making decisions, balancing short-term and long-term considerations.
- **Strategic Thinking**. A strategic leader can see the big picture and understand how complex issues fit into the broader context. They consider the long-term implications of decisions and how they align with the organisation's goals.
- **Effective Communication**. A leader who can clearly explain complex issues to others demonstrates a strong understanding of the subject matter. They can articulate potential solutions and strategies in a way that others can understand and support.
- **Collaboration and Inclusivity**. A strategic leader values input from others and actively seeks diverse perspectives when approaching complex issues. They work well with others to address complex challenges, leveraging the strengths of the team.

By observing these factors in a strategic leader's behaviour and decision-making processes, you can assess their ability to understand and effectively handle complex issues. Leaders with strong critical thinking, strategic insight, and openness to collaboration are well-equipped to manage multifaceted challenges and drive organisational success.

6. Ability to Think

Assessing a strategic leader's ability to think involves evaluating their cognitive and analytical skills, as well as their approach to problem-solving and decision-making. Here are several key factors to consider when assessing a leader's ability to think:

- **Critical Thinking**. A leader who asks probing questions and challenges assumptions demonstrates strong critical thinking skills. They can assess information objectively and identify the strengths and weaknesses of different arguments.
- **Analytical Ability.** A strategic leader can analyse data effectively and draw meaningful insights from it. They can integrate information from various sources to form a comprehensive understanding of complex issues.
- **Strategic Thinking**. A leader who thinks strategically considers the long-term implications of decisions and aligns them with organisational goals. They can connect seemingly unrelated ideas and identify patterns or trends.
- **Creativity and Innovation**. A strategic leader embraces creativity and is open to exploring innovative solutions. They are willing to take calculated risks to achieve better outcomes.
- **Problem-Solving Skills**. A leader who can assess situations quickly and make effective decisions demonstrates strong problem-solving skills. They can adjust their approach as new information emerges and situations evolve.
- **Communication and Persuasion**. A leader who can clearly articulate their thoughts and persuade others of their perspective demonstrates strong thinking abilities. They listen to others' viewpoints and integrate diverse perspectives into their decision-making process.
- **Open-Mindedness**. A leader who is open to different opinions and ideas demonstrates an ability to think critically and objectively. They can adjust their thinking in response to new information or changing circumstances.

By observing these factors in a strategic leader's behaviour and approach to challenges, you can assess their ability to think critically, strategically, and creatively. Strong cognitive and analytical skills enable a leader to navigate complex issues effectively and drive organisational success.

7. Bravery and Moral Courage

Analysing a strategic leader's bravery and moral courage involves evaluating their ability to take principled stands and make difficult decisions in challenging and make or break scenarios and situations. This includes their willingness to uphold ethical standards, even when faced with adversity or opposition. Here are several key factors to consider when assessing a leader's bravery and moral courage:

- **Upholding Ethical Standards**. A leader who consistently upholds ethical principles, even when it is inconvenient or unpopular, demonstrates moral courage. They communicate openly and honestly, providing accurate information and acknowledging mistakes.
- **Willingness to Take Risks**. A brave leader is willing to take calculated risks when necessary for the benefit of the organisation. They take responsibility for their decisions and actions, even when facing criticism or setbacks.
- **Defending Principles and Values**. A leader with moral courage defends their beliefs and principles, even in the face of opposition. They advocate for justice and fairness, even when it requires challenging the status quo.
- **Addressing Difficult Issues**. A brave leader faces difficult issues head-on, rather than avoiding or deflecting them. They handle controversial topics with grace and tact, maintaining a principled stance.
- **Empowering Others**. A leader who encourages open dialogue and supports others in speaking out demonstrates bravery. They protect team members who face adversity for expressing their opinions or ideas.
- **Resilience in Adversity**. A leader with bravery and moral courage perseveres through challenges and setbacks without compromising their values. They learn from failures and use them as opportunities for growth and improvement.
- **Respect for Diversity and Inclusion**. A leader who champions diversity and inclusion demonstrates moral courage by standing

up for equal treatment and opportunities. They create an environment where all team members feel safe and respected.

By observing these factors in a strategic leader's behaviour and decision-making, you can assess their bravery and moral courage. Leaders who demonstrate these qualities can inspire trust, foster a positive organisational culture, and drive long-term success.

8. Quickness of Decision

Assessing whether a strategic leader is able to make quick and effective decisions involves evaluating their decision-making process, ability to handle uncertainty, and responsiveness in dynamic situations. Here are some key factors to consider when assessing a leader's ability to make quick and effective decisions:

- **Decisiveness**. A leader who can make decisions quickly and confidently demonstrates decisiveness. They communicate decisions clearly and directly to their team.
- **Ability to Prioritise**. A leader who can quickly identify and prioritise key issues and opportunities shows strong decision-making abilities. They allocate resources effectively based on priorities and goals.
- **Comfort with Ambiguity**. A leader who can make decisions under uncertainty and ambiguity is comfortable with taking calculated risks. They can adjust decisions as new information emerges and situations evolve.
- **Analytical and Critical Thinking**. A strategic leader who can quickly analyse information and data demonstrates strong analytical skills. They use logical reasoning to assess the situation and make informed decisions.
- **Experience and Expertise**. A leader's depth of knowledge and experience in their field and more widely can help them make more efficient and effective decisions. Review their track record in similar situations to gauge their decision-making abilities.
- **Intuition and Judgement**. A leader who trusts their intuition in combination with data can make quicker decisions in dynamic

situations. They use sound judgment to weigh options and choose the best course of action.

- **Delegation and Empowerment**. A leader who delegates tasks and empowers their team can make quicker decisions without getting bogged down in details. They seek input from experts and trust their team to provide valuable insights.
- **Responsiveness and Adaptability**. A leader who adapts quickly to new information or changes in circumstances can make effective decisions in real-time. They anticipate challenges and opportunities, allowing for quicker decision-making when necessary.

By observing these factors in a strategic leader's behaviour and decision-making process, you can assess their ability to make quick and effective decisions. Leaders who excel in this area can navigate dynamic situations successfully and drive organisational success.

9. Strength of Mind

Assessing a strategic leader's strength of mind involves evaluating their mental resilience, determination, and ability to handle pressure and adversity. Here are several key factors to consider when assessing a leader's strength of mind:

- **Resilience**. A leader with strength of mind can recover quickly from setbacks and challenges, remaining focused on their goals. They persevere through difficulties and obstacles, demonstrating determination and commitment.
- **Emotional Intelligence**. A leader who can manage their emotions and stay calm under pressure demonstrates strong mental resilience. They can understand and manage the emotions of others, fostering positive relationships.
- **Adaptability**. A leader who adapts to changing circumstances and remains flexible shows strength of mind. They embrace new approaches and ideas, even when faced with uncertainty.
- **Decision-Making**. A leader with strength of mind makes clear and confident decisions, even in challenging situations. They stand by their decisions and take responsibility for the outcomes.

- **Stress Management**. A leader who remains composed and focused in high-pressure situations demonstrates mental strength. They prioritise their own well-being and take steps to manage stress effectively.
- **Confidence and Self-Assurance**. A leader who trusts their abilities and decisions exhibits confidence and self-assurance. They remain optimistic and confident in the face of challenges.
- **Vision and Focus**. A leader with a clear vision and focus on their goals shows strength of mind. They inspire others to stay committed to the vision, even during difficult times.
- **Learning from Experience**. A leader who learns from past experiences and continuously improves demonstrates mental resilience. They view challenges as opportunities for growth and development.
- **Feedback and Communication**. A leader who seeks and values feedback demonstrates humility and a willingness to improve. They communicate effectively and transparently, even in tough situations.
- **Supportive Relationships**. A leader with strength of mind builds supportive networks and seeks advice and guidance when needed. They provide support and mentorship to others, helping them navigate challenges.

By observing these factors in a strategic leader's behaviour and approach to challenges, you can assess their strength of mind. Leaders with mental resilience, confidence, and adaptability are better equipped to navigate complex situations and drive organisational success.

10. Eloquence and Charisma

Assessing a strategic leader's eloquence and charisma involves evaluating their communication skills, ability to inspire others, and the potential to build strong relationships. Here are several key factors to consider when assessing a leader's eloquence and charisma:

- **Effective Communication**. A leader who communicates clearly and precisely demonstrates eloquence. They can articulate their ideas persuasively, encouraging others to support their vision.

- **Public Speaking**. A leader who speaks confidently and with poise in public settings exhibits eloquence and charisma. They create engaging and dynamic presentations that captivate their audience.
- **Empathy and Connection**. A charismatic leader empathises with others and builds strong connections by understanding their needs and concerns. They listen actively to others, showing genuine interest and respect.
- **Inspiration and Motivation**. A leader with charisma can inspire others to take action and work toward a common goal. They exude positive energy and enthusiasm, motivating others to excel.
- **Storytelling and Messaging**. A leader who can tell compelling stories to convey their message effectively demonstrates eloquence. They maintain consistent messaging across different platforms and audiences.
- **Emotional Intelligence**. A leader who is aware of their own emotions and those of others can communicate more effectively and build stronger relationships. They manage their emotions in a way that fosters trust and respect.
- **Presence and Body Language**. A leader who maintains confident body language and eye contact demonstrates charisma and self-assurance. They have an approachable demeanour that invites others to engage with them.
- **Adaptability**. A leader who can adjust their communication style to suit different audiences shows eloquence and adaptability. They tailor their messages to resonate with the specific needs and interests of their audience.
- **Feedback and Reflection**. A leader who is open to feedback about their communication style demonstrates humility and a willingness to improve. They continuously seek ways to improve their communication and leadership abilities.

By observing these factors in a strategic leader's behaviour and communication style, you can assess their eloquence and charisma. Leaders who excel in these areas can effectively inspire and motivate others, driving organisational success and fostering a positive work environment.

11. Boldness

Assessing whether a strategic leader is bold involves evaluating their willingness to take risks, innovate, and challenge the status quo. Bold leaders often demonstrate and reflect courage in their decision-making and a readiness to embrace opportunities that others might avoid. Here are several key factors to consider when assessing a leader's boldness:

- **Risk-Taking**. A bold leader is open to taking risks when the potential rewards outweigh the dangers. They are willing to pursue unconventional or novel solutions, even if it involves some level of uncertainty.
- **Challenging the Status Quo**. A leader who challenges traditional practices and seeks improvement demonstrates boldness. They actively work to implement change, even if it requires confronting resistance.
- **Visionary Thinking**. A bold leader sets ambitious goals and strives for transformative outcomes. They have a clear vision for the future and pursue it with determination and courage.
- **Decisiveness**. A bold leader makes decisions confidently and quickly, even in challenging situations. They stand by their decisions and take responsibility for the outcomes.
- **Resilience in the Face of Adversity**. A leader who persists despite challenges and setbacks demonstrates boldness. They are determined to overcome obstacles and learn from failures.
- **Leadership Style**. A bold leader inspires others to take risks and pursue ambitious goals. They empower their team to think creatively and take initiative.
- **Openness to Feedback**. A bold leader is open to feedback and uses it to improve their strategies and approaches. They are willing to adjust their strategies based on new information or feedback.
- **Stakeholder Management**. A bold leader builds support for their vision by communicating its benefits and addressing concerns. They navigate resistance effectively, using persuasion and negotiation.
- **Strategic Insight**. A bold leader identifies opportunities others may

overlook and acts on them. They capitalise on emerging trends and disruptions to gain a competitive edge.

By observing these factors in a strategic leader's behaviour and decision-making process, you can assess their boldness. Bold leaders who take calculated risks, drive innovation, and challenge the status quo can lead their organisations to achieve transformative success.

12. Good Memory

Assessing whether a strategic leader has a good memory involves evaluating their ability to recall and utilise information effectively. A strong memory can help leaders make informed decisions, communicate effectively, and build relationships based on past interactions. Here are some key factors to consider when assessing a leader's memory:

- **Recall of Information**. A leader who can recall key details from meetings, documents, and discussions demonstrates a good memory. They can link past information with current events or decisions, showing a clear understanding of context.
- **Knowledge of History and Background**. A leader with good memory understands the historical context of situations, decisions, and relationships. They can recall relevant precedents and apply them to current situations.
- **Interpersonal Relationships**. A leader who remembers names, faces, and personal details of team members and stakeholders shows attentiveness and good memory. They can recall past conversations and follow up on previous topics, showing respect and understanding.
- **Attention to Detail**. A leader who pays attention to detail and remembers specific points demonstrates strong memory skills. They communicate accurate information and correct any discrepancies.
- **Adaptability and Flexibility**. A leader who can adjust plans and strategies based on past experiences shows memory and adaptability. They learn from past outcomes and use that information to inform future decisions.

- **Information Management**. A leader who takes organised notes and references them when needed demonstrates good information management skills. They may use technology to help manage information, demonstrating an awareness of tools to aid memory.
- **Feedback and Reflection**. A leader who recalls feedback and integrates it into their approach shows attentiveness and a willingness to improve. They reflect on past experiences to enhance their knowledge and understanding.
- **Follow-Through**. A leader who follows through on commitments and keeps track of promises made demonstrates good memory and reliability. They consistently recall and act on prior commitments and decisions.
- **Strategic Insight**. A leader who can synthesise information from different sources and recall it effectively demonstrates good memory. They identify patterns and trends based on past experiences, informing strategic decisions.

By observing these factors in a strategic leader's behaviour and approach to information, you can assess their memory. Leaders with a good memory can leverage past experiences and information to make more effective decisions and strengthen their relationships.

Training for *Vinaya*, *Anviksiki*, and *Vartta*

1. Vinaya

Training a strategic leader in the Hindu philosophy of *Vinaya* involves teaching them the principles of discipline, humility, and respect for others. *Vinaya*, which refers to disciplined conduct and ethical behaviour, is essential for leaders who want to lead with integrity and foster a harmonious and productive work environment. Here are some steps to train a strategic leader in the philosophy of *Vinaya*:

- **Educate on the Concept of *Vinaya***. Provide an overview of *Vinaya*, emphasising its importance in Hindu philosophy and its relevance to leadership. Explain the core principles, including humility, discipline, respect, and self-control.

- **Encourage Self-Reflection**. Encourage the leader to reflect on their behaviour and attitudes, identifying areas for improvement. Teach the leader to acknowledge their limitations and seek feedback from others.
- **Promote Ethical Leadership**. Stress the importance of ethical decision-making and leading by example. Teach the leader to act with integrity in all situations, building trust with their team.
- **Develop Emotional Intelligence**. Train the leader to understand and empathise with others' perspectives and feelings. Teach the leader to listen actively and respectfully to others' opinions and concerns.
- **Encourage Discipline and Consistency**. Teach the leader to establish clear expectations and standards for themselves and their team. Encourage the leader to maintain self-control in challenging situations and avoid impulsive actions.
- **Promote Respect for Diversity**. Teach the leader to appreciate and respect diverse viewpoints and backgrounds. Highlight the importance of inclusive leadership and treating all team members fairly.
- **Foster a Learning Mindset**. Encourage the leader to pursue continuous learning and improvement in their leadership skills. Teach the leader to seek feedback from others and use it constructively to improve.
- **Lead with Compassion.** Encourage the leader to lead with kindness and compassion, promoting a positive and supportive work environment. Teach the leader to support their team members in their personal and professional growth.
- **Provide Mentorship and Guidance**. Pair the leader with a mentor who can provide guidance and support in practicing *Vinaya*. Encourage the leader to learn from the experiences of others who have successfully integrated *Vinaya* into their leadership style.
- **Integrate Vinaya into Leadership Development**. Incorporate the principles of *Vinaya* into leadership training programs and

workshops. Teach the leader mindfulness techniques to enhance self-awareness and discipline.

By training a strategic leader in the principles of *Vinaya*, you help them develop a leadership style that prioritises discipline, humility, and respect for others. This approach can lead to more ethical and effective leadership, fostering a positive and productive organisational culture.

2. Anviksiki

Training a strategic leader in the Hindu philosophy of *Anviksiki* involves teaching them critical thinking, philosophical inquiry, and ethical reasoning. *Anviksiki* is a branch of learning that focuses on intellectual investigation, reflective thinking, and logical analysis. Here are some steps to train a strategic leader in the philosophy of *Anviksiki*:

- **Educate on the Concept of *Anviksiki***. Provide an overview of *Anviksiki*, emphasising its importance in Hindu philosophy and its relevance to leadership. Explain the core principles, including critical thinking, analytical reasoning, and philosophical inquiry.
- **Promote Critical Thinking**. Teach the leader to question assumptions and explore different perspectives. Encourage the leader to critically analyse situations, problems, and decisions.
- **Develop Logical Reasoning**. Teach the leader to apply logical reasoning to draw conclusions from evidence. Provide tools and frameworks for systematic analysis and decision-making.
- **Enhance Problem-Solving Skills**. Train the leader to approach problems using a structured and methodical process. Encourage the leader to generate and evaluate multiple potential solutions to a problem.
- **Cultivate Reflective Thinking**. Teach the leader to reflect on their decisions, actions, and outcomes to learn from experience. Train the leader to view mistakes as opportunities for growth and improvement.
- **Foster Ethical Reasoning**. Underline the importance of ethical decision-making in leadership. Teach the leader to consider the

ethical and societal impact of their decisions.

- **Integrate Philosophy and Ethics**. Encourage the leader to study philosophical texts and concepts, particularly those related to ethics and morality. Teach the leader to apply philosophical concepts to real-world leadership challenges.
- **Encourage Open-Mindedness**. Teach the leader to be open to diverse perspectives and opinions. Encourage the leader to challenge their own biases, prejudices and preconceptions.
- **Practice Mindfulness**. Teach the leader mindfulness techniques to enhance self-awareness and reflective thinking. Encourage the leader to stay present and focused in the moment, fostering clarity of thought.
- **Provide Opportunities for Discussion**. Encourage the leader to engage in debates and discussions to sharpen their reasoning skills. Teach the leader to seek and consider diverse opinions from others in the organisation.

By training a strategic leader in the principles of *Anviksiki*, you help them develop strong critical thinking and ethical reasoning skills. This approach can lead to more thoughtful and well-considered decisions, ultimately benefiting the organisation and its goals.

3. Vartta

Training a strategic leader in the Hindu philosophy of *Vartta* involves teaching them the principles of economic management, resource allocation, and wealth creation. *Vartta* is one of the branches of knowledge in Hindu philosophy that focuses on the practical aspects of managing resources, commerce, and agriculture to ensure the prosperity of individuals and society. Here are some steps to train a strategic leader in the philosophy of *Vartta*:

- **Educate on the Concept of *Vartta***. Provide an overview of *Vartta*, emphasising its importance in Hindu philosophy and its relevance to leadership and economic management. Explain the core principles, including resource management, wealth creation, and economic planning.

- **Teach Economic Management**. Ensure the leader has a strong foundation in financial literacy, including budgeting, accounting, and financial analysis. Train the leader in efficient resource allocation to maximise productivity and returns.
- **Promote Agricultural Knowledge**. Teach the leader the basics of agronomy and sustainable agriculture, as these are key aspects of *Vartta*. Stress the importance of food security and its impact on the stability of an organisation or society.
- **Develop Commerce and Trade Skills**. Train the leader in analysing market trends and understanding supply and demand dynamics. Teach the leader negotiation skills to secure favourable terms in trade and business dealings.
- **Emphasise Strategic Planning**. Teach the leader to develop long-term economic plans that align with organisational goals. Train the leader to prepare for economic uncertainties and market fluctuations.
- **Foster Ethical Business Practices**. Highlight the importance of ethical conduct in business dealings and transactions. Teach the leader the principles of fair trade and the importance of treating business partners equitably.
- **Encourage Entrepreneurship and Innovation**. Train the leader to foster innovation and creative problem-solving in business. Encourage the leader to support entrepreneurship and new ventures within the organisation.
- **Teach Risk Management**. Train the leader to assess and manage financial and business risks effectively. Teach the leader strategies for mitigating risks and protecting assets.
- **Promote Community Engagement**. Articulate the importance of community engagement and corporate social responsibility in business. Teach the leader to integrate sustainable practices into business operations.
- **Provide Opportunities for Continued Learning**. Encourage the leader to stay informed about economic trends and developments. Provide opportunities for the leader to attend workshops and

seminars on effective economic management and *Vartta*.

By training a strategic leader in the principles of *Vartta*, you help them develop strong economic management skills and an understanding of wealth creation. This approach can lead to more effective and sustainable business practices, ultimately benefiting the organisation and its stakeholders.

The Spiritual End State or *Yogakshema*

Yogakshema happens to be a Sanskrit term which encompasses the concept of overall well-being, security, and protection. It is often used in a broader sense to refer to the state of security, stability, prosperity, and welfare of an individual or a community. In Hindu philosophy and thought, the concept of *Yogakshema* is premised in the idea that material and spiritual well-being are interconnected and must be balanced for a harmonious life.

Origins and Meaning

The term "*yogakshema*" is derived from two Sanskrit words: "yoga" and "kshema." "Yoga" refers to the effort or practice required to achieve something, while "kshema" signifies the state of safety, security, and preservation. Together, *yogakshema* implies a sense of security and welfare achieved through disciplined effort and practice.

In ancient Indian texts such as the Vedas and the Upanishads, *yogakshema* is mentioned as a desired state of being. The Rigveda, one of the oldest Hindu scriptures, includes prayers for both yoga and kshema, seeking blessings for success in endeavours and the subsequent preservation and enjoyment of the fruits of one's labour.

Yogakshema in Indian Thought

In the Indian philosophical tradition, *yogakshema* extends beyond material well-being to include spiritual growth and fulfilment. It represents a holistic approach to life that values both worldly success and inner peace. This duality is seen as essential for a well-rounded, fulfilling life.

- **Material and Spiritual Balance**: *Yogakshema* encourages a balance between the pursuit of material goals and spiritual aspirations. It recognises that while material prosperity is important for a secure and comfortable life, spiritual growth and self-realisation are equally crucial for true fulfilment.

- **Ethical and Moral Living**: *Yogakshema* emphasises the importance of ethical and moral conduct in achieving overall well-being. Individuals are encouraged to live according to *dharma* (righteousness) and to cultivate virtues such as compassion, generosity, and honesty.
- **Community Welfare**: The concept of *yogakshema* extends to the well-being of the larger community and society. It promotes social harmony, mutual respect, and cooperation for the common good.

The Concept of Articulating a Strategic Vision via a *Yogakshema*

In contrast to Western strategic schools of thought that zero in upon on hard, physical outcomes, geography and clear delineations of conflict, Kautilya espoused positive spiritual and cognitive conditions focussed on people. This is much more applicable to modern complex crises as the vision is often not a physical end-state but one of a blurred spectrum of deterrence, competition, coercion, partnerships of convenience and one where communities and populations *feel* secure, stable and prosperous.

This *Yogakshema* or spiritual condition can be used to formulate a strategy as much as a traditional physical end-state. However, it should be made clear at this stage that this is not 'Ends' in the Western sense and more of a temporary waypoint in the constant ebb and flow of life and is highly subjective. Kautilya was a realist, and his methodology was very much focussed on delivering pragmatic and practical solutions that were 'good enough' for the moment but always poised to seize further opportunities should they arise. According to Kautilya, this poise requires the ability to recognise and exploit opportunities for strategic advantage as they emerge, and this requires a sense of the strategic direction of travel even if the ends state is blurred.

Kautilya did not differentiate between peace and war in the contemporary Western sense and viewed any period absent of conflict as purely an interlude and preparation period for the next period of confrontation. He also believed in avoiding open physical warfare where there was risk of creating a more negative condition.

A Kautilyan *Yogakshema* based on 'realist' cognitive positive conditions is simple in concept but as the 600-page *Arthashastra* highlights, the methods of achieving a 'good enough' *Yogakshema* is anything but simple. In terms of achieving the *Yogakshema*, the *Arthashastra* has very detailed guidance. Much of the *Arthashastra* is concerned with internal matters of state, but there are two books devoted to foreign affairs and warfare.

How to Articulate a Yogakshema

When articulating a *Yogakshema* the focus should be on how stakeholders and audiences (both internal and external) perceive the outcomes and how they should feel about them. This approach highlights the impact of strategy on the attitudes, beliefs, and emotional responses of the people involved and the target entities. Emotions, perceptions, and feelings could include the following:

Material Prosperity. Describe how the *Yogakshema* encompasses economic growth and stability, including opportunities for wealth creation and equitable distribution of resources. This may involve sustainable development, employment opportunities, and fair wages.

Security and Safety. Emphasise the importance of safety and security for the people. This includes protection from external threats and internal conflicts, as well as safe working and living conditions.

Access to Resources. Discuss how the *Yogakshema* involves ensuring access to essential resources such as food, water, shelter, and healthcare for all individuals.

Social Welfare. Highlight programs and policies that support the vulnerable and marginalised in society, such as education, healthcare, and social services.

Harmony and Justice. Describe how the *Yogakshema* promotes social harmony and justice, including fair and just governance, legal systems, and respect for individual rights.

Quality of Life. Explain how the *Yogakshema* involves a high quality of life, with access to education, culture, and recreational opportunities that enrich the lives of individuals and communities.

Community Well-Being. Emphasise the sense of community well-being and collective responsibility for the common good. This includes collaboration and mutual support among individuals and groups.

Long-Term Sustainability. Describe how the *Yogakshema* focuses on sustainable development and long-term well-being, ensuring that resources and opportunities are preserved for future generations.

Contentment and Happiness. Convey how the *Yogakshema* leads to overall contentment and happiness among the population. This involves a sense of fulfilment and satisfaction with life.

Resilience and Adaptability: Discuss how the *Yogakshema* encourages resilience and adaptability in the face of challenges, allowing individuals and communities to thrive even in difficult times.

By describing the *Yogakshema* in these terms, you can paint a comprehensive picture of the ideal state of well-being and prosperity for your organisation, community, or nation. This vision can guide strategic planning and decision-making to achieve lasting positive outcomes for all stakeholders.

For business strategies, you may also want to articulate wider perceptions, feelings, and emotions such as:

Trust and Confidence. Describe how the strategy will instil trust and confidence in stakeholders, such as customers, employees, partners, and the general public. For example, a successful strategic end state may leave customers feeling secure and confident in certain products or services.

Satisfaction and Loyalty. Explain how the end state will lead to high levels of satisfaction and loyalty among key audiences. For instance, satisfied customers are more likely to remain loyal and recommend your business to others.

Respect and Reputation. Discuss how the strategic end state will build respect and enhance your organisation's reputation. This could include being seen as a leader in your industry or a responsible corporate citizen.

Empowerment and Engagement. Highlight how the strategy will empower and engage stakeholders. This could involve providing employees with opportunities for growth and advancement or giving customers a sense of ownership and involvement.

Safety and Well-being. If applicable, describe how your strategy will create a sense of safety and well-being for those affected. This could involve ensuring safe working conditions for employees or providing products and services that enhance customers' quality of life.

Optimism and Enthusiasm. Convey how your *Yogakshema* will generate optimism and enthusiasm among stakeholders. This may include fostering a positive organisational culture or creating excitement about future possibilities.

Recognition and Value. Discuss how your strategy will make stakeholders feel recognised and valued. For example, employees may feel appreciated for their contributions, or customers may feel valued through personalised experiences.

Alignment with Values and Purpose. Explain how your strategic end state aligns with the values and purpose of your organisation and its stakeholders. This alignment can lead to a sense of pride and fulfilment for those involved.

Clarity and Transparency. Describe how your strategy will promote clarity and transparency in communication and decision-making. This can lead to a feeling of trust and openness among stakeholders.

By focusing on how people perceive and feel about the *Yogakshema*, you create a more holistic and impactful vision of success. This approach helps ensure that your strategy resonates with stakeholders on an emotional level, fostering stronger relationships and long-term success.

Diplomatic Methodologies, Silent and Covert Operations, and Open Warfare

Kautilya's insights and idioms into diplomacy and warfare are particularly noteworthy, offering guidance on various forms of engagement with adversaries and allies. Kautilya's approach includes diplomatic methodologies, silent and covert operations, and open warfare.

Diplomatic Methodologies

Kautilya emphasised the importance of diplomacy as a primary means of managing relationships with other states and achieving strategic objectives. His approach to diplomacy is multifaceted and includes:

- **Forming Alliances**. Kautilya outlined the significance of building alliances with other states to strengthen one's position and counter potential threats. These alliances could be formed through marriage, trade agreements, or mutual defence pacts.
- **Negotiations and Treaties**. He advocated for negotiations and treaties as tools to resolve conflicts and maintain stability. Diplomacy allowed for peaceful coexistence with neighbours and minimised the need for direct confrontation.
- **Intelligence**. Kautilya stressed the role of information in diplomacy. By gathering intelligence on allies and adversaries, one could make informed decisions and identify opportunities for negotiation.

Silent Operations

Kautilya recognised the value of silent operations as methods of achieving strategic objectives without direct confrontation. Silent operations are loosely described by Kautilya as "...secret practices and instigations through secret agents is the mark of silent war." However, in order to truly understand Kautilya's approach to strategy we must dig deeper into the concept of silent warfare precisely because it is so alien to Western minds and ethics. Firstly, he stated that the kings and entities that are the focus of silent warfare should never know they have been targeted. In fact, Kautilya suggests that in diplomatic and other circles friendly relationships should be maintained while secret agents work undercover to subvert and undermine key leaders, exploit divisions within a country and sow dissension within an alliance. He also suggests a number of techniques from poisonings to the use of women to create jealousy between pivotal leaders. Kautilya also wrote extensively about breaking alliances and agreements. He stated that a king should only abide by a treaty for as long as it is advantageous. If all this sounds familiar, then it may be because this is exactly the type of activity undertaken by Russia against the West to great effect. Just look at their use of poisonings (novichok against Skripal and Navalny), the use of women (*compromat* operations) and the breaking of alliances and treaties (Ukraine, Crimea and various weapons treaties). Note that the targets of all these silent warfare operations by Russia were pivotal leaders.

These tactics include:

- **Espionage**. Espionage plays a central role in Kautilya's strategy. He advocated for the use of spies to gather information on enemies, allies, and internal affairs. This intelligence could be used to identify weaknesses and opportunities for battlefield and political advantages.
- **Sabotage and Subversion**. Kautilya recommended sabotaging enemy resources and infrastructure to weaken their ability to wage war. He also advised subverting enemy leadership and sowing discord within enemy ranks.
- **Deception and Propaganda**. Kautilya encouraged the use of deception and propaganda to mislead and manipulate adversaries. This could involve spreading false information or creating confusion among enemy forces.

Covert Operations

Covert operations are probably what we would describe as guerrilla warfare today or perhaps a 'conventional' insurgency. Kautilya defines it as "...creating fright [terrorism?], sudden assault [raids, hit and run, bombings?], striking when there is error or calamity [infiltration, ambush?], giving way [not attempting to hold ground?] and striking in one place..." While the West views this type of activity as the purview of weak adversaries and insurgencies, Russia, China, Iran and North Korea in particular see it as one of the preferred ways of operating (often through proxies and private military companies) precisely because it reduces the risk of escalation and overwhelming response characterised by open warfare

Open Warfare

While diplomacy, silent actions and covert operations were preferred methods of achieving objectives, Kautilya acknowledged that open warfare was sometimes unavoidable. Open Warfare is as the name suggests the highly recognisable conventional war where all parties know they are in conflict and the combatants are clearly identifiable. This is the type of conflict where the West excels in and therefore is not the preferred option of most adversaries today who do their utmost to avoid conventional confrontation. Kautilya described it as "...fighting at the time and place indicated." Rather sensibly, Kautilya only advised open warfare "...when superior in troops...when the weather is suitable...when on favourable terrain...and when secret instigations have been made [shaping the enemy through the manipulation of key individuals]..." In our modern context, open warfare has its place but with nuclear armed rivals, complex alliance and treaty systems and renewed Great Power competition, there are huge risks in adopting open warfare. This is a similar situation to that which existed in Kautilya's time, and he was very wary about using open warfare. He is also very clear about the futility of using force against internal populations or for suppressing uprisings. His approach to open warfare includes:

- **Preparation and Planning**: Kautilya emphasised the importance of thorough preparation and planning for warfare. This includes organising and training the military, fortifying defences, and ensuring adequate supplies and logistics.
- **Tactics**: Kautilya offered guidance on various military tactics, including manoeuvres, formations, and siege warfare. He stressed the need for adaptability and the ability to respond to changing circumstances.
- **Victory and Aftermath**: Kautilya also provided insights into the aftermath of warfare, including managing conquered territories and integrating them into one's state. He emphasised the importance of maintaining stability and order.

Kautilya's approach to diplomacy, silent and covert operations, and open warfare is a comprehensive guide to statecraft and strategy. His insights into managing relationships with allies and adversaries, gathering intelligence, and waging war efficiently have stood the test of time and continue to be relevant today. By combining diplomacy, covert tactics, silent operations, and open warfare, Kautilya provided a nuanced framework for achieving strategic success and maintaining power in the complex world of politics and conflict.

THE FOUR APPROACHES OR *UPAYAS*.

Kautilya describes four *Upayas* or approaches, idioms and ideas. These were not the original work of Kautilya and appear to have an even more ancient origin and are sometimes described as Hindu diplomacy or a Hindu problem-solving system. They were intended for use in all walks of life from individual interactions to foreign policy. The four *Upayas* are:

- *Sama* (conciliation).
- *Dana* (gifts).
- *Bheda* (disruption or dissension).
- *Danda* (force).

These at first glance could be equated to the Diplomatic, Information, Military and Economic levers of power articulated in Western military doctrine but that oversimplifies the subtlety and complexity of Kautilya's *Upayas*. They could be applied individually, sequentially in order to severity, or in combination and 'out of order.'

1. *Sama* (conciliation)

The Hindu concept of *sama* refers to a sense of harmony, equanimity, and tranquillity in one's life and relationships. The term "*sama*" can be interpreted in various contexts within Hindu philosophy and spiritual thought, emphasising the importance of balance and peace in personal conduct, relationships, and one's approach to life.

Individual Well-Being

In the context of individual well-being, *sama* refers to a state of mental and emotional balance. This includes:

- **Mental Equanimity**: Achieving mental calmness and stability allows individuals to navigate life's challenges with composure and clarity. In the *Bhagavad Gita*, Lord Krishna emphasises the importance of equanimity (*samatva*) in facing both success and failure.

- **Emotional Harmony**: Emotional stability and control are integral to *sama*. By cultivating self-awareness and self-regulation, individuals can maintain inner peace and avoid being swayed by external circumstances.
- **Detachment**: The ability to remain detached from the outcomes of actions is a key aspect of *sama*. This does not mean indifference, but rather the ability to perform one's duties without attachment to specific results.

Interpersonal Relationships

In interpersonal relationships, *sama* signifies harmony, fairness, and respect for others. This includes:

- **Equal Treatment**: *Sama* encourages treating others with fairness and respect, regardless of their background, status, or beliefs. This principle is rooted in the concept of *sama-drishti* (equal vision) and is emphasised in Hindu teachings on ethical conduct.
- **Conflict Resolution**: By promoting understanding and compassion, *sama* helps facilitate the resolution of conflicts and fosters peaceful relationships. This involves listening to different perspectives and seeking common ground.
- **Empathy and Compassion**: Cultivating empathy and compassion towards others is a manifestation of *sama* in relationships. This includes being mindful of others' needs and experiences.

Broader Spiritual Practice

In the context of broader spiritual practice, *sama* encompasses a state of inner harmony and alignment with the divine. This includes:

- **Yoga and Meditation**: Practices such as yoga and meditation help individuals achieve *sama* by calming the mind and fostering a sense of connection with the self and the universe.
- **Spiritual Discipline**: Adhering to spiritual disciplines such as self-study, prayer, and selfless service helps cultivate *sama* by promoting

inner peace and self-mastery.

- **Self-Realisation**: The ultimate goal of Hindu spiritual practice is self-realisation—recognising one's true nature as part of the divine. *Sama* plays a crucial role in this journey by helping individuals transcend the fluctuations of the mind and ego.

The Hindu concept of *sama* encompasses a holistic approach to life that values harmony, equanimity, and tranquillity in various aspects of existence. Whether in individual well-being, interpersonal relationships, or broader spiritual practice, *sama* encourages balance and peace as a means of achieving a fulfilling and meaningful life. By cultivating *sama*, individuals can navigate life's challenges with grace and maintain a deep connection to themselves and the world around them.

2. *Dana* (gifts)

The Hindu concept of *dâna* refers to the practice of giving and generosity, a fundamental tenet of Hinduism that promotes compassion, selflessness, and social harmony. *Dâna* can take many forms, including the giving of material wealth, food, knowledge, time, and service. It is considered an essential aspect of ethical and spiritual living, fostering a sense of interconnectedness and mutual support within the community. Let's explore the significance of *dâna* in Hindu philosophy, its various forms, and its impact on individuals and society.

Philosophical and Ethical Foundations

Dâna is rooted in the Hindu principles of *ahimsa* (non-violence) and *karma* (action and its consequences). The practice of *dâna* embodies the virtues of compassion and detachment—compassion in giving to those in need and detachment from the material rewards of one's actions. The *Bhagavad Gita* emphasises the importance of performing good deeds without attachment to the fruits of those actions, and *dâna* aligns with this teaching.

The practice of *dâna* also upholds the concept of *dharma* (righteousness), as it promotes ethical conduct and moral responsibility towards others. By giving selflessly, individuals fulfil their duty to support the well-being of their community and society at large.

Forms of Dâna

Dâna can take various forms, reflecting the diversity of ways individuals can give and contribute to the welfare of others:

- **Material Giving**: This involves giving money, food, clothing, or other tangible resources to those in need. Material giving is one of the most common forms of *dâna* and is often practiced during religious ceremonies and festivals.
- **Knowledge Sharing**: Sharing knowledge, wisdom, and skills is another important form of *dâna*. This includes teaching, mentoring, and providing guidance to others, especially the younger generation.
- **Time and Service**: Offering one's time and service to help others is a valuable form of *dâna*. Volunteering for community service, assisting those in need, and providing emotional support are examples of this form of giving.
- **Spiritual Giving**: This includes offering prayers, rituals, and blessings on behalf of others. It may also involve supporting religious institutions and activities.

Impact on Individuals and Society

The practice of *dâna* has a profound impact on both individuals and society as a whole:

- **Spiritual Growth**: By practicing *dâna*, individuals cultivate detachment, compassion, and humility, which are essential qualities for spiritual growth and self-realisation.
- **Social Cohesion**: *Dâna* and generosity, fosters a sense of interconnectedness and solidarity within the community. It encourages individuals to support one another and work towards the common good.
- **Reducing Inequality**: By redistributing resources and providing support to those in need, *dâna* helps reduce social and economic inequality. This amounts to a grand philanthropy.
- **Promoting Karma Yoga**: The practice of selfless giving aligns with the concept of karma yoga, or the path of selfless action, which

is a means of attaining spiritual liberation.

The Hindu concept of *dâna* is a cornerstone of ethical and spiritual living. It emphasises the virtues of generosity, compassion, and selflessness, promoting individual spiritual growth and social harmony. By practicing *dâna*, individuals contribute to the well-being of their community and cultivate a deeper sense of connection to the world around them. The tradition of giving continues to play a significant role in Hindu culture and serves as a guiding principle for leading a meaningful and fulfilling life

3. *Bheda* (disruption or dissension)

In Hindu philosophy and political thought, the concept of *bheda* refers to division or differentiation, and it is often associated with strategy and diplomacy in the context of statecraft. While *bheda* can have different meanings depending on the context, it is most commonly understood as a tactical approach that involves creating divisions or exploiting existing differences to achieve specific objectives.

Context and Interpretation

The term *bheda* can be interpreted in multiple ways within Hindu thought:

- **Division and Differentiation**: At its core, *bheda* involves creating or emphasising divisions between groups or individuals. This can be used strategically in statecraft to weaken opponents or strengthen alliances.
- **Strategy and Diplomacy**: In the context of strategy, *bheda* is often associated with tactics such as divide and conquer, where existing divisions are exploited to achieve political or military objectives.
- **Distinguishing and Discriminating**: In a broader sense, *bheda* can refer to distinguishing between different elements or aspects of a situation to gain clarity or insight.

Bheda in Statecraft

In the realm of statecraft, *bheda* is one of the key strategies outlined in Hindu treatises such as Kautilya's *Arthashastra*. It involves using division and differentiation as a means of achieving political goals:

- **Divide and Conquer**: One of the primary applications of *bheda* is the divide and conquer strategy. By creating divisions within opposing groups or alliances, a ruler can weaken their adversaries and gain a strategic advantage.
- **Exploiting Differences**: *Bheda* can involve exploiting existing differences between individuals or groups, such as ideological, social, or economic disparities, to achieve specific objectives.
- **Creating Alliances**: In some cases, *bheda* may involve creating alliances with certain groups or individuals to counterbalance opposing forces or gain leverage.

Ethical Considerations

While *bheda* can be an effective strategic tool, its use raises ethical questions:

- **Manipulation and Exploitation**: The use of *bheda* can sometimes involve manipulating or exploiting divisions for personal or political gain, which may lead to ethical dilemmas.
- **Long-Term Consequences**: Creating divisions can have long-term consequences, such as increased conflict and instability. Ethical statecraft requires considering the broader impact of such strategies on society.

The Hindu concept of *bheda* is a complex and multifaceted approach that plays a significant role in statecraft and strategy. While it can be an effective tool for achieving political objectives, it must be used with caution and ethical consideration. As with any strategy, the long-term consequences of creating divisions must be weighed against the immediate benefits. By understanding the nuances of *bheda*, individuals and leaders can make informed decisions that balance strategic interests with ethical considerations and the well-being of society.

4. *Danda* (force)

The Hindu concept of *danda* reflects an amalgam of authority, governance, and the exercise of power through discipline, punishment, and justice. Derived from the Sanskrit word meaning "staff" or "rod," *danda* symbolises the authority of the ruler and the state's power to enforce laws and maintain order. It is an essential component of statecraft and governance, as described in ancient Hindu texts such as the *Arthashastra*.

Context and Interpretation

Danda is a multifaceted concept that encompasses various aspects of governance and authority:

- **Authority and Governance**: *Danda* represents the authority of the ruler to govern and enforce laws. It is the power to administer justice and maintain order within the state.
- **Discipline and Punishment**: In the context of governance, *danda* involves the use of discipline and punishment to correct wrongdoing and deter criminal behaviour.
- **Justice and Protection**: *Danda* also encompasses the idea and idiom of justice, ensuring that individuals are treated fairly and that their rights and property are protected.

Danda in Statecraft

In the realm of statecraft, *danda* is a key principle that guides the exercise of power and governance:

- **Rule of Law**: *Danda* emphasises the importance of the rule of law and the consistent enforcement of laws to maintain order and stability.
- **Punishment and Deterrence**: The use of punishment as a deterrent is central to *danda*. This includes imposing penalties for crimes and misconduct to prevent future violations.
- **Protection and Security**: *Danda* involves the protection of the state and its citizens from external threats and internal disorder. This includes maintaining a strong defence and security apparatus.

Ethical Considerations

The exercise of *danda* comes with ethical considerations that must be balanced with the need to maintain order:

- **Fairness and Proportionality**: The use of punishment should be fair and proportional to the offense committed. Excessive or arbitrary use of *danda* can lead to injustice and abuse of power. Thus, a modicum of balance in execution has to be attained.
- **Compassion and Mercy**: While *danda* involves the enforcement of laws, it should also be tempered with compassion and mercy, allowing for rehabilitation and reform.
- **Accountability and Transparency**: Rulers and officials who exercise *danda* must be accountable for their actions and transparent in their decision-making to maintain public trust.

The Hindu concept of *danda* is a fundamental aspect of governance and statecraft, emphasising the authority to govern, administer justice, and maintain order. It is essential for ensuring the rule of law and protecting the well-being of citizens. However, the exercise of *danda* must be guided by ethical principles, including fairness, proportionality, compassion, and accountability. By balancing the need for discipline and order with ethical considerations, rulers and leaders can effectively govern and uphold the principles of justice and righteousness.

THE TOOLS OF FOREIGN POLICY OR *SADGUNYA*

The *Upayas* have to be integrated with the six tools of foreign policy called *Sadgunya*: The six *Sadgunya* are:

- *Samdhi* (Peace)
- *Vigraha* (War)
- *Asana* (Staying Quiet or Neutrality)
- *Yana* (Marching or Armed Preparations)
- *Samsraya* (Seeking Shelter or Alliance)
- *Dvaidhibhava* (Dual Policy)

All six are derived from ancient Hindu philosophy and are complex, multi-faceted concepts. Let is look at each in turn:

1. *Samdhi* (Peace). "*Samdhi*" in Kautilya's *Arthashastra* refers to the strategic approach of making a treaty or alliance. It is one of the six-fold strategies used in diplomacy and statecraft. *Samdhi* is employed when it is advantageous to form a treaty or agreement with another state or power. The aim of *Samdhi* is to secure peace, stability, and mutual benefits through cooperation and agreement. Here are some key aspects of *Samdhi* in the *Arthashastra*:

- **Making Alliances**: *Samdhi* engages nations in forming alliances or agreements with other states or rulers to achieve specific objectives. These alliances can provide mutual support, shared resources, and joint military action if needed.
- **Negotiation and Diplomacy**: *Samdhi* is based on negotiation and diplomacy, allowing parties to resolve conflicts and disputes without resorting to warfare.
- **Balance of Power**: By forming alliances, a ruler can balance power and prevent potential threats from adversaries. This can help maintain stability and security within the state.
- **Flexible Agreements**: *Samdhi* allows for flexible agreements that can be adapted to changing circumstances. Treaties can be revised or dissolved as needed to suit the interests of the parties involved.
- **Avoiding War**: *Samdhi* is a peaceful approach to resolving disputes, which can help avoid the costs and risks associated with warfare.
- **Establishing Clear Terms**: In negotiating a treaty, it is important and significant to establish clear terms and conditions that both parties agree upon. This can include mutual defence clauses, trade agreements, and other forms of cooperation.

Overall, *Samdhi* is a strategic approach that allows rulers to navigate complex diplomatic situations, forge alliances, and achieve objectives through negotiation and cooperation. It is one of the six key strategies outlined in Kautilya's *Arthashastra* for managing foreign relations and ensuring the stability and security of the state,

In the context of Kautilya's *Arthashastra*, *Samdhi* could be described as working constructively with states, groups, tribes, clans, factions, key individuals, opinion formers and organisations in a consensual manner. Compromise, shared interests, negotiations, alliances, etc. This was always viewed by Kautilya as a temporary state of affairs for use when the state was weak.

2. *Vigraha* (War). In Kautilya's *Arthashastra,* "*Vigraha*" refers to the strategic approach of waging war or engaging in hostility. *Vigraha* is one of the methods, which a ruler can employ in the process of foreign policy when other options such as *Samdhi* (alliance), *Asana* (neutrality), *Dana* (gifting or bribery), and *Bheda* (division or sowing discord) are not viable or have been exhausted. Here are some key aspects of *Vigraha* in Kautilya's *Arthashastra*:

- **Engaging in War**: *Vigraha* involves actively waging war against an enemy or adversary. This may include direct military conflict, sieges, and other forms of combat.
- **Timing and Justification**: In employing *Vigraha*, the ruler must carefully assess the timing and justification for going to war. It is essential to consider the potential benefits and risks of conflict.
- **Strategic Objectives**: The purpose of engaging in war is to achieve specific strategic objectives such as acquiring territory, securing resources, or eliminating a threat.
- **Preparation and Planning**: *Vigraha* requires thorough preparation and planning, including assembling an army, securing supplies, and developing strategies for both offensive and defensive operations.
- **Resource Management**: Waging war can be resource-intensive, so careful management of financial and material resources is essential to sustain the war effort.
- **Assessing Strengths and Weaknesses**: A ruler must evaluate the strengths and weaknesses of their own forces as well as those of the enemy. This includes assessing military capabilities, terrain, and potential allies.
- **Use of Intelligence**: Gathering intelligence on the enemy's movements, plans, and capabilities is crucial for effective execution of *Vigraha*. This can provide a strategic advantage in planning and conducting military operations.
- **Negotiation and Peace**: While *Vigraha* involves waging war, it

may also include the possibility of negotiation and seeking peace under favourable terms if the objectives of the conflict are met or if continued fighting becomes too costly.

In summary, *Vigraha* in Kautilya's *Arthashastra* is the strategic approach of engaging in war or hostility to achieve specific political and territorial goals. It is a complex method that requires careful planning, resource management, and intelligence gathering to be executed effectively. It is one of the six key strategies that rulers can use to navigate the complexities of statecraft and diplomacy.

For Kautilya, *Vigraha* meant forcing change upon entities. This is within the context of competition where an entity is actively resisting change and also themselves trying to force change upon the system and other entities. It may include the use of targeted force, but many other tools were used by Kautilya from blackmail to kidnap and hostage taking.

3. *Asana* (Staying Quiet). In the context of Kautilya's *Arthashastra*, "*Asana*" refers to a strategic conceptualisation rather than a physical posture as in yoga. Kautilya took *Asana* to mean maintaining or accepting the *status quo*. This tool is used for when a cost/benefit analysis shows that the resources to engineer the required change are not available at a reasonable cost or when the current situation does not have a significant negative effect on delivering the *Yogakshema*. This again highlights Kautilya's realistic and pragmatic mindset.

Asana, as a strategic concept, involves remaining in a state of neutrality or inactivity in certain situations. This strategy is employed when it is more advantageous to maintain a stable position rather than engaging in active diplomacy, forming alliances, or going to war. The goal is to conserve resources, avoid unnecessary conflicts, and wait for a more favourable opportunity to arise.

By choosing *Asana*, a ruler or leader can assess the changing dynamics of the situation and adapt their strategy accordingly. This approach can be a way to maintain balance and stability while preserving the potential for future action when circumstances change.

Overall, *Asana* in Kautilya's *Arthashastra* is a strategic choice for a state or leader to remain neutral or inactive in a given situation, using patience and observation to navigate the complexities of statecraft and diplomacy.

4. *Yana* (Marching). In Kautilya's *Arthashastra*, "*Yana*" refers to the strategic approach of preparing for war or mobilisation against an adversary. Here are the key aspects of *Yana* in Kautilya's *Arthashastra*:

- **Mobilisation**: *Yana* involves mobilising military forces and resources in preparation for engaging an enemy in battle.
- **Advance or March**: The term can also imply the advance or march of an army towards an enemy's territory.
- **Timing and Strategy**: The decision to employ *Yana* requires careful consideration of timing and strategic planning. A ruler must assess the best time and method to launch an attack.
- **Gathering Intelligence**: To effectively prepare for war, intelligence on the enemy's capabilities, strengths, and weaknesses must be gathered and analysed.
- **Logistics**: Managing logistics such as the supply of food, weapons, and other necessary resources for the army is crucial for a successful military campaign.
- **Types of *Yana***: Kautilya also discusses different types of *Yana*, including land-based, water-based, and even air-based advances (kites?). These approaches may be used based on the terrain and the capabilities of the enemy.
- **Assessing Allies and Adversaries**: A ruler must evaluate potential allies and adversaries in the context of *Yana*. This includes considering whether to seek support from other states or to engage in conflict independently.
- **Objective Setting**: *Yana* should have clear objectives, such as capturing enemy territory, securing resources, or neutralising threats.
- **Flexibility and Adaptation**: A successful *Yana* requires the ability to adapt to changing circumstances on the battlefield and make quick decisions as needed.

- **Negotiation**: While *Yana* primarily focuses on preparing for and engaging in war, it does not preclude negotiation. A ruler may choose to negotiate peace or alliance if it serves strategic interests.

Yana in Kautilya's *Arthashastra* emphasises the importance of thorough preparation and strategic planning for war. By carefully considering timing, objectives, and available resources, a ruler can increase the chances of success in military endeavours. In the original context of the *Arthashastra* this was largely about military expeditions but in order to contemporise this tool for the modern era we need to expand its use. It could be confrontational or coercive in nature, but it may also be a 'hearts and minds' campaign or an aid programme. The underpinning concept of this tool is that it is a deliberate, intentional, long-term and an eminently costly undertaking.

5. *Samsraya* (Seeking Shelter). This tool is concerned with utilising external support and protection. In Kautilya's *Arthashastra*, "*Samsraya*" refers to the strategic approach of seeking protection, refuge, or support from a stronger power. *Samsraya* is a method a ruler may use when faced with a powerful adversary or when other strategies, such as *Samdhi* (alliance), *Vigraha* (war), *Yana* (preparation for war), *Asana* (neutrality), and *Dvaidhibhava* (division), are not feasible or advantageous. Here are some key aspects of Samsraya in Kautilya's *Arthashastra*:

- **Seeking Protection**. *Samsraya* involves seeking protection, refuge, or support from a stronger or more powerful state or ruler. This can provide safety and security when facing a powerful enemy.
- **Establishing an Alliance**. A weaker state may align itself with a stronger state through treaties or agreements, gaining military support or political protection.
- **Balance of Power**. By seeking the protection of a stronger power, a ruler can maintain a balance of power and counteract potential threats from adversaries.
- **Consideration of Mutual Interests**. When seeking protection, it is essential to consider mutual interests and benefits for both parties involved. The stronger power may require certain concessions or cooperation in return for protection.

- **Assessing Trustworthiness**. It is crucial to assess the trustworthiness and reliability of the stronger power when seeking protection. A dependable ally can provide stability and security.
- **Long-Term Implications**. Seeking protection from a stronger power may have long-term implications for the state's sovereignty and autonomy. Careful consideration is needed to ensure that the terms of the agreement are favourable.
- **Timing and Circumstances**. *Samsraya* may be employed under specific circumstances, such as when a state is under imminent threat or faces a powerful adversary.
- **Negotiation and Diplomacy**. Establishing protection or refuge may involve negotiation and diplomacy to ensure that the terms of the agreement are beneficial and acceptable to both parties.
- **Leveraging Strength**. While seeking protection from a stronger power, a ruler may leverage the strength and resources of the ally to achieve their strategic objectives.

In summary, *Samsraya* in Kautilya's *Arthashastra* is a strategic approach that involves seeking protection or refuge from a stronger power when faced with a powerful enemy or challenging circumstances. It is a method that allows a state to maintain security and stability by aligning with a more powerful ally

6. *Dvaidhibhava* (Dual Policy). This tool considers information, propaganda and media campaigns as part of a dual policy of playing one entity off against another or adopting different *Sadgunya* for different entities. *Dvaidhibhava* is a method a ruler can use to weaken an enemy by creating internal divisions or conflicts within the enemy's ranks. Here are some key aspects of *Dvaidhibhava* in Kautilya's *Arthashastra*:

- **Sowing Discord**. *Dvaidhibhava* involves creating disagreements, distrust, or conflict within an enemy's ranks, such as among their leaders, officials, or factions.
- **Exploiting Existing Divisions**. A ruler can take advantage of existing divisions or rivalries within the enemy's organisation and use them to their advantage.

- **Creating New Divisions**. When internal divisions are not apparent, a ruler may employ tactics to create new divisions or rivalries within the enemy's ranks.
- **Disrupting Unity**. By causing internal divisions, the enemy's unity and coherence are disrupted, weakening their ability to respond effectively to challenges.
- **Manipulating Information**. Spreading misinformation or rumours can be used to create divisions or exacerbate existing conflicts within the enemy's ranks.
- **Targeting Key Individuals**. Identifying and targeting key individuals within the enemy's organisation can lead to divisions, especially if these individuals hold opposing views or interests.
- **Offering Incentives**. Offering incentives such as rewards or privileges to certain factions or individuals within the enemy's ranks can help in creating divisions.
- **Timing and Discretion**. The successful use of *Dvaidhibhava* requires careful and meticulous timing and discretion to avoid exposing the ruler's involvement and to maximise the impact of sowing discord.
- **Collaborating with Disgruntled Groups**. Collaborating and conniving with disgruntled or dissenting groups within the enemy's organisation can amplify divisions and further weaken the enemy.

Dvaidhibhava in Kautilya's *Arthashastra* is a strategic approach that aims to weaken the enemy by causing internal divisions and conflicts. This can lead to a decrease in the enemy's effectiveness, cohesion, and overall strength, providing the ruler with a strategic advantage.

UNDERSTANDING ENTITIES AND ACTORS VIA THE *MANDALA* ANALYSIS

Kautilya also advises the development of a *Mandala* that identifies all the entities and actors within the context to be changed by the strategy and dynamically measures their relative strengths, motivations and levers of power. This is a key feature of Kautilyan strategy and the concept for which he is perhaps most well-known. It is important to stress that this is a continuous and ongoing process and not the static one-off assessment that seems to dominate Western strategies. This analysis and continuous dynamic measurement are a major undertaking in its own right, but is absolutely essential for a successful strategy outcome.

The elements of the *Mandala* are as given below but it is important to bear in mind that these are just a handrail for a deep analysis and every crisis, situation or environment will require a unique *Mandala*. In addition, they must be contemporised for the modern era and expanded beyond their traditional focus of foreign kings. The original text of the *Arthashastra* is very much focussed on kings and their territories as this was where power emanated from in ancient times. In the modern age, territory is not the only focus of power and so I have attempted to move away from this and include other factors while staying broadly true to Kautilya's concept of a *Mandala*.

1. ***Ari***. In simple terms these are states opposed to the *Yogakshema* and/or the *Vijigishu*. These are normally considered to be the external 'hostile' states closest to the crisis or issue. In the modern context this should not be considered in just physical or geographical terms but also look at history, economic concepts, politic models and values. For example, China's attempts to revise the International System in its favour would make it an *Ari* to the US regardless of the geography.
2. ***Mitra***. Loosely speaking, *Mitra* refers to states that are allies or champions of the *Yogakshema* and/or the *Vijigishu*. These are normally considered to be external 'friendly' states closest to the crisis or issuc. Again, this should not be limited to geography. In the China example above, the UK would be a *Mitra* as it is a close ally to the US and supports the current International System.
3. ***Arimitra***. Arimitra are allies of those *Ari* states opposed to the *Yogakshema* and/or *Vijigishu*. So, in the China example this might include North Korea and Iran as state supporters and allies to China in its confrontation with the US over reforming the International System.
4. ***Mitramitra*** (non-state supporters of those champions of the strategy). This is the category where supportive and formally

organised and legal non-state actors and NGOs would get placed. In the China example, certain Western financial and economic bodies such as the World Bank would be in this category. While these bodies may not be under the direct overt control of the *Vijigishu's* state, there is some form of influence brought to bear that allows *de facto* control.

5. ***Arimitramitra*** (non-state supporters of those states opposed to the strategy). This is the opposition non-state actors and NGOs. Continuing with our China example, this is where the Asian Infrastructure Investment Bank would feature.
6. ***Parashanigraha*** (overt internal opposition). This is where many of the hybrid and grey zone entities would feature. It could include opposition groups, opinion formers, hostile media, charities, private schools, protesters and money raisers. The key point is that they are linked to the *Ari* in some way. It may be cultural identity, money or simply shared interests.
7. ***Aakranda*** (overt internal champions). This could include supportive media, opinion formers, charities, etc.
8. ***Parashanigrahasara*** (covert internal opposition). These are non-attributable, covert or low-profile supporters of internal opposition. This is a large and complex grouping but absolutely vital for analysis in the contemporary era. It could include social media trolls, funding routes, spies, saboteurs, insurgents and dissidents. The key point is that they try to remain undetected and receive moral and physical support from the *Ari*.
9. ***Akrandasara*** (covert supporters of overt internal champions). This could include financiers, errand runners, undercover agents and the like.

The *Mandala* must be global in outlook as in our modern, interconnected world virtually everyone on the planet can bring influence to bear within the system through social media. While a physical conflict or a crisis may have a defined geographic footprint, the cognitive arena is all-pervasive. The Russians and Chinese understand this very well and are masters at using a crisis in another part of the world to further their aims or to aggravate a situation elsewhere in the world in order to divert attention away from something at home. Consider also their use of social media trolls, 'bots', charities and funding for dissident and opposition groups.

Kautilya also stated that there was no such thing as a permanent ally or foe. This is a remarkably similar position to British thinking at the end of the 19th Century:

> "*...we have no eternal allies, and we have no perpetual enemies. [Only] our interests are eternal and perpetual, and those interests it is our duty to follow.*"
>
> ***—Lord Palmerston***

KAUTILYA'S GUIDE FOR THE MODERN STRATEGIST

Step 1: Understand The Strategic Context. In this opening stage, it is necessary to describe the situation that needs to be transformed and why the current cognitive state is not good enough. This is an essential precursor to any Kautilyan strategy and must be brutally honest. Kautilya was a master of evidence-based decision-making, and this depends on removing any propaganda, hubris, cultural stereotypes, political bias or wishful thinking. There is no set format for the strategic context, but it is likely to contain mixture of reminders of the national interests, the latest government policy objectives, descriptive prose, diagrams, bullet points, maps and cultural analysis. It is also a continuous and ongoing process and must be constantly updated as new information is gleaned or old information found to be inaccurate. The key question to answer is 'why does all this matter?' A series of questions and deductions can help develop the strategic narrative. Some examples are presented below:

- What is at stake and why does it matter?
- How does it affect our national interests?
- Who is opposed to our national interests and why?
- Is it a priority for us to change the situation, if so, where does it sit?
- What are the government's current policy objectives over this issue?
- Is there a critical timeline associated with the issue?

- What needs to change?
- What does 'good enough' look like?
- What is the general sense of direction on this issue? Will it get worse if we do nothing? Will it negatively affect other areas? Will inaction damage our reputation or future options?
- Where are our knowledge gaps? What don't we know about the issue?

Step 2: Select the *Vijigishu* and Supporting Officials to Build the Strategy Team. Once the strategic narrative has started to articulate the issue it is necessary to identify, name and empower the strategic leader (*Vijigishu*) who will be responsible for analysing the problem, producing the plan, coordinating the execution, controlling activity and leading the strategic communication. Firstly, and most importantly the *Vijigishu* must be an expert on strategy. Secondly, they must have good knowledge of the issue at hand. Finally, they must receive further specific training for the task ahead. Their reward for success and punishment for failure should also be articulated. However, it is important to ensure that alternative views, constructive challenge and 'red-teaming' are still permitted so this stage also selects the officials that will support the *Vijigishu*. The officials should be diverse, with a range of experiences and must also be experts in strategy. They will join the *Vijigishu* for specific training, including how to 'red-team' and offer constructive challenge. This stage is absolutely critical as a poor *Vijigishu* and poor supporting officials will lead to poor results. The composition of the 'council of advice' should be treated as dynamic to take due account of the volatility, unpredictability and flux of the operative context. New issues and considerations might emerge (and the priority of existing ones change), demanding different perspectives, experience and expertise.

Step 3: Define the *Yogakshema*. This is a critical but difficult stage. The cognitive condition or change required (*Yogakshema*) is derived from the government's policy objectives but is very much a two-way dynamic feedback process with the *Vijigishu* working closely with the NSC/Cabinet to develop a realistic and 'good enough' *Yogakshema*. The *Yogakshema* is amply described in written prose and may have several themes. To be purely

Kautilyan, it should focus on behaviours, feelings and perceptions rather than physical goals.

Step 4: The *Mandala* Analysis. This is a continuous and ongoing process throughout life regardless of whether there is peace, war or crisis. There should be a separate and independent *Mandala* Development Team that is continually analysing the world. The *Vijigishu* will work closely with the *Mandala* development team to keep a dynamic version available at all times. The *Mandala* Development Team will be resource intensive and make use of intelligence agencies, open-source reporting, diplomatic networks and any other source of reliable information. The *Mandala* will be largely focussed on people but also take into account other factors like technology, environmental issues and legal concerns but only in the context of how they affect people, behaviours and cognitive states.

Step 5: Identify Entity Weak Points. It is critical to identify weak points (and strengths) for each entity within the *Mandala*. Wherever possible, named individuals within the *Mandala* should be analysed as Kautilyan strategy requires levers to be applied to people and not things. For example, an insurgent group may be one of the entities within the *Mandala,* but this is not good enough for the Kautilyan strategy. The *Vijigishu* needs the names of key leaders and opinion formers within the insurgency, their cognitive state (fanatic, profiteer, reluctant, etc) and then critically their individual and collective weaknesses. Perhaps one of the leaders is an alcoholic, perhaps a couple of others detest each other, or maybe communications are difficult between the group. This may sound more tactical rather than strategic, but Kautilya was clear that changing the behaviours and cognitive states of pivotal leaders was the key to success.

Step 6: Determine the Approaches. Kautilya requires determination on whether to adopt Diplomatic Warfare, Open Warfare, Covert Warfare or Silent Warfare or a combination of these. Furthermore, different approaches may be taken against different elements of the Mandala and in different phases of a strategy. This is a treacherous phase to get right and Kautilya advised to err on the side of caution and adopt covert and/or silent approaches rather than risk 'declaration of open war', unless success was virtually guaranteed.

Step 7: Consider the *Upayas* and *Sadgunyas* and How They Could be Applied Against the Weak Points of the *Mandala*. This is a complex, detailed and intense step where the various *Upayas* and *Sadgunyas* are considered for each entity in the Mandala and how they could shift the behaviour, cognitive state, feeling or perception of the entity in order to move closer to the *Yogakshema*. Nothing should be discounted at this stage, but some will clearly be more realistic than others. If time is short, only the more realistic considerations should be pursued. However, it is important to give every opportunity for the 'moment of genius' to occur.

Step 8: Determine the Resources Available. Resources will always be constrained so it is important at this stage to make a realistic assessment of what could be made available and for how long. This should be a dynamic process with the consideration of *Upayas* and *Sadgunyas*.

Step 9: Develop Options. Broad options should be considered at this stage. These must be focussed on the cognitive change of key entities and preferably named pivotal leaders using approaches, ways and methods that are feasible, acceptable, adaptable, sustainable and affordable.

Step 10: Consider Calamities (Risks). Each of the options must be assessed for risk but wider calamities must also be considered. Part of this process is also studying what calamities might befall adversaries or other entities so these can be exploited should they occur.

Step 11: Decide on an Option, Refine and Take Action. The process of deciding which option to adopt is a critical step and will be preceded by a significant amount of red-teaming, discussion and challenge. There is likely to be a requirement for the *Vijigishu* to get political sign-off for the option chosen. It is important to note that the strategy must be continually refined and the *Vijigishu* must be given significant leeway to make changes in nature and scale and with timing of their choice.

Step 12: Test and Adjust. Good strategy must be tested and adjusted while it is being implemented. The *Vijigishu* will need to integrate, control, coordinate, communicate, assess, feedback and adjust on a continual basis and not be afraid to terminate activity if it is failing to deliver the cognitive results required or even worse it is undermining the strategy. During this stage, it is critical that the *Vijigishu* has some form of executive command or control over the levers being used. Measuring whether cognitive end-states have been achieved is notoriously difficult, but it is essential in not only determining the success of any Kautilyan strategy, but for informing the vital dynamic feedback loops.

KAUTILYA – A SUMMARY

Kautilya was an ancient Indian scholar, strategist, and philosopher who is best known for his seminal work on statecraft and political strategy, the *Arthashastra*. He one of the most influential figures in Indian political thought. His philosophy on adopting a strategic approach consisted of:

- The Strategic Leader – *Vijigishu*.
- Strategic Leadership Characteristics – *Svamisampad*.
- The Spiritual End State or *Yogakshema*.
- Diplomatic, Silent, Covert and Open Warfare.
- The Four Approaches – *Upayas*.
- The Tools of Foreign Policy – *Sadgunya*.
- Understanding the Enemy – The *Mandala* Analysis.

From his teachings in the Arthashastra, it is possible to develop a Kautilyan guide for adopting a strategic approach:

Step 1: Understand The Strategic Context. Ask the following questions:

- What is at stake and why does it matter?
- How does it affect our national interests?
- Who is opposed to our national interests and why?
- Is it a priority for us to change the situation, if so where does it sit?
- What are the government's current policy objectives over this issue?
- Is there a critical timeline associated with the issue?
- What needs to change?
- What does 'good enough' look like?
- What is the general sense of direction on this issue? Will it get worse if we do nothing? Will it negatively affect other areas? Will inaction damage our reputation or future options?

- Where are our knowledge gaps? What don't we know about the issue?

Step 2: Select the *Vijigishu* and Supporting Officials to Build the Strategy Team. Look for the following:

- Qualities that Inspire Confidence in Others.
- Approachability.
- Piety.
- Truthfulness.
- Ability to Understand Complex Issues.
- Ability to Think.
- Bravery and Moral Courage.
- Quickness of Decision.
- Strength of Mind.
- Eloquence and Charisma.
- Boldness.
- Good Memory.

Step 3: Define the *Yogakshema*. Consider feelings and perceptions such as:

- Material Prosperity.
- Security and Safety.
- Access to Resources.
- Social Welfare.
- Harmony and Justice.
- Quality of Life.
- Community Well-Being.
- Long-Term Sustainability.
- Contentment and Happiness.
- Resilience and Adaptability.
- Trust and Confidence.

- Satisfaction and Loyalty.
- Respect and Reputation.
- Empowerment and Engagement.
- Safety and Well-being.
- Optimism and Enthusiasm.
- Recognition and Value.
- Alignment with Values and Purpose.
- Clarity and Transparency.

Step 4: The *Mandala* Analysis. Identify and analyse stakeholders and entities:

- *Ari*. These are external 'hostile' states closest to the crisis or issue.
- *Mitra*. These are external 'friendly' states closest to the crisis or issue.
- *Arimitra*. Allies of external hostile states.
- *Mitramitra*. Non-state friendly supporters.
- *Arimitramitra*. Non-state supporters of hostile states.
- *Parashanigraha*. Overt internal opposition.
- *Aakranda*. Overt internal champions.
- *Parashanigrahasara*. Covert internal opposition.
- *Akrandasara*. Covert supporters of overt internal champions.

Step 5: Identify Entity Weak Points. Some areas to analyse.

- Internal divisions.
- Financial position.
- Capability gaps.
- Unfavourable terrain.
- Poor logistics.
- Inexperience and poor training.
- Toxic leadership.

- Over-centralised decision making.
- Low morale.
- Intelligence gathering and analytical deficiencies.
- Inferior equipment.

Step 6: Determine the Approaches. Consider the four warfare methodologies:

- Diplomatic.
- Silent.
- Covert.
- Open.

Step 7: Consider the *Upayas* and *Sadgunyas* and How They Could be Applied Against the Weak Points of the *Mandala*.

- *Sama* (conciliation).
- *Dana* (gifts).
- *Bheda* (disruption or dissension).
- *Danda* (force).
- *Samdhi* (peace).
- *Vigraha* (war).
- *Asana* (neutrality or staying quiet).
- *Yana* (marching or armed preparation).
- *Samsraya* (alliance or seeking shelter).
- *Dvaidhibhava* (dual policy).

Step 8: Determine the Resources Available. Some common considerations.

- Money.
- Personnel.
- Equipment.
- Time.
- Supplies.

- Infrastructure.
- Communication systems.
- Industrial capacity.

Step 9: Develop Options.

- High risk.
- Medium risk.
- Low risk.
- Cheap.
- Expensive.

Step 10: Consider Calamities (Risks). Some points to consider:

- Weather and natural disasters.
- Political instability.
- Loss of key personnel.
- Cyber-attack.
- Scandal or PR disaster.
- Supply chain disruption.
- Market collapse or economic downturn.
- Unexpected legal action.
- Public disorder or insecurity.

Step 11: Decide on an Option, Refine and Take Action.

- Wargame.
- Scenario planning.
- Simulation.
- Pilot schemes and small-scale tests.
- Issue clear direction and commit.

Step 12: Test and Adjust. Adaptation will be essential.

Chapter Four

The Purananuru

"The greatest enemy is one's own ego."

—Thiruvalluvar

IN THIS CHAPTER

- About the Tamil Sangam literature and the *Purananuru*.
- The Strategic Concepts of the *Purananuru*.
- Adopting a Strategic Approach – *Purananuru* Guidance for the Modern Strategist.
- The *Purananuru* – A Summary.

The Saga of Tamil Sangam Literature and *Purananuru*

The *Purananuru* is a classical Tamil poetic anthology that forms a part of the *Sangam* literature, a body of work produced between 300 BCE and 300 CE in the Tamil-speaking regions of southern India. The *Purananuru*, translated as "Four Hundred Poems," is one of the eight anthologies (known as *Ettuthokai*) in the *Sangam* literature corpus. It is considered one of the oldest poetic works in Tamil literature and provides a valuable window into the history, culture, and values of ancient Tamil society. The *Purananuru* is divided into two main sections. These are *Agam* and *Puram*.

Agam poetry primarily deals with the intimate and internal aspects of human life, particularly romantic relationships, and emotions. The poets capture the various stages of love and domestic life, including:

- **Union and Separation**. *Agam* poetry delves into the experiences of lovers, ranging from the joys of union to the pain of separation. It portrays the longing, passion, and anticipation that lovers experience.
- **Different Types of Love**. The poems address different types of love relationships, including courtship, marriage, and the emotional connections between partners.
- **Symbolism and Metaphor**. *Agam* poetry is known for its use of symbolism and metaphor to convey complex emotions. The poems often draw on nature—such as flowers, rivers, and mountains—as metaphors for the moods and experiences of the characters.
- **Five Landscapes**. The poems are categorised into five landscapes or "tinai" based on the geography and associated themes of love: *kurinji* (mountainous regions, representing union), *mullai* (pastoral regions, representing waiting and patience), *marutham* (fertile plains, representing quarrel and separation), *neythal* (coastal regions, representing longing and separation), and *paalai* (arid regions, representing hardship and separation).

The major themes in *agam* poetry include:

- **Love and Romance**. The central focus of *agam* poetry is the exploration of romantic relationships between men and women. The poems depict the emotions and challenges faced by lovers, as well as their joys and sorrows.

- **Social Expectations**. The poetry often reflects the social norms and expectations surrounding love and marriage in ancient Tamil society. It portrays the struggles of individuals navigating the boundaries of tradition and personal desires.
- **Nature and Landscape**. The poets utilise the natural landscape as a backdrop for the emotional experiences of the characters. The environment often mirrors the internal states of the lovers, providing a vivid and symbolic context for their stories.
- **Gender Roles**. The poems provide insights into traditional gender roles and dynamics within romantic relationships. They depict the experiences of both men and women, highlighting their different perspectives and challenges.

Agam poetry is a testament to the depth and richness of Tamil literary tradition. Through its exploration of love, emotions, and relationships, it captures the universal human experiences that resonate across time and cultures. Its enduring legacy continues to shape and influence Tamil literature and remains a cherished part of the cultural heritage of Tamil Nadu.

Puram poetry, in contrast to the intimate and personal focus of *agam* (love and domestic life) poetry, centres on the public and external aspects of life. It encompasses themes such as war, heroism, governance, philanthropy, and the role of individuals within society. These poems provide a rich depiction of the values, customs, and societal structures of ancient Tamil culture. *Puram* poetry primarily addresses the external world, focusing on the interactions between individuals and society at large. Key themes include:

Heroism and Valour. Many poems in the *Purananuru* celebrate the bravery and valour of warriors. The anthology paints a vivid picture of the martial culture of the time, highlighting the significance of honour, courage, and sacrifice in battle.

Kingship and Governance. The anthology emphasises the role of the king as a just and righteous ruler. It presents the ideal of a king who governs with fairness, wisdom, and compassion, and who protects his subjects.

Ethics and Morality. The *Purananuru* addresses ethical and moral questions, such as the nature of duty, loyalty, and the responsibilities of individuals within society. It also explores themes of charity, hospitality, and respect for elders.

Social Hierarchy and Customs. The poems provide insights into the social structure and customs of ancient Tamil society, including the importance of family, community, and caste.

Nature and Environment. The anthology also contains descriptions of the natural landscape, including rivers, mountains, and forests, reflecting the close relationship between the people and their environment.

The *Purananuru* holds significant literary and cultural importance. The poems in the exhibit a range of literary styles, from praise and elegy to satire and reflection. The language is rich in metaphor and imagery, and the poems often employ various poetic devices such as alliteration and rhyme. The anthology serves as a historical record of ancient Tamil society, providing details about the customs, traditions, and beliefs of the time. The *Purananuru* has influenced subsequent Tamil literature and continues to be celebrated as a cornerstone of Tamil culture and heritage.

The Strategic Concepts of The *Purananuru*

The *Purananuru* is a remarkable work that offers a unique glimpse into the lives, values, and beliefs of ancient Tamil society. Through its exploration of heroism, governance, ethics, and social customs, the anthology provides a rich tapestry of Tamil culture and continues to be a source of inspiration for scholars, poets, and readers around the world. Its enduring legacy is a testament to the depth and richness of Tamil literary tradition. While not explicitly focused on strategic concepts in the way military texts might be, the *Purananuru* does contain themes and principles that can be interpreted in strategic terms and used to adopt a strategic approach. Let's explore some of the key ideas:

Leadership and Governance. The poems often praise and critique the rulers of the time, highlighting the qualities of effective leadership. Just and wise governance is recommended, suggesting that successful rulers should be attuned to the needs and aspirations of their people.

Diplomacy and Alliances. Some poems touch upon diplomatic relationships and alliances between different rulers and kingdoms. The importance of maintaining peaceful relations, engaging in alliances, and negotiating conflicts diplomatically is hinted at in various verses.

Economic Strategies. The *Purananuru* reflects on the economic prosperity of the Tamil people. The importance of fostering economic growth through agriculture, trade, and other means is implicit in the poems. Economic strength is often depicted as a source of power and stability.

Ethics and Virtue. Moral and ethical considerations are prevalent in the Sangam literature. The poems often extol the virtues of righteousness, justice, and ethical behaviour. These values can be interpreted as foundational elements for societal and personal success, aligning with strategic principles.

Adaptability and Resilience. The Sangam literature frequently portrays the resilience of individuals and communities in the face of challenges. The ability to adapt to changing circumstances and persevere through difficulties is celebrated, suggesting the importance of flexibility in strategic thinking.

Cultural Soft Power. The poems showcase the cultural richness of the Tamil society. The promotion of cultural values, art, and literature is implicitly strategic, as it contributes to the soft power of a community. Cultural strength is presented as an asset that enhances the reputation and influence of a society.

Social Cohesion and Unity. Unity among people and communities is a recurring theme. The importance of social cohesion and collective action is implied as a strategic approach to addressing challenges and maintaining stability.

Environmental Awareness. Some poems highlight the connection between nature and human life. The understanding of environmental factors and the importance of sustainable practices are embedded in the verses, suggesting an awareness of the strategic implications of ecological balance.

Innovation and Creativity. The Sangam literature often celebrates innovation in various fields, including agriculture, trade, and warfare. The encouragement of creativity and the pursuit of new ideas can be seen as strategic elements contributing to progress and success.

Courage and Bravery. The valour and bravery of individuals, particularly warriors, are frequently praised in the poems. While not explicitly strategic, these qualities align with the importance of courage in facing challenges and conflict.

In summation, while the Sangam *Purananuru* poems may not provide a systematic treatise on military strategy, they offer a nuanced portrayal of the values, virtues, and dynamics that contribute to the strategic success of individuals and communities in ancient Tamil society. The principles of effective leadership, diplomacy, ethical conduct, and adaptability are interwoven into the fabric of the Sangam literature, providing a cultural and historical perspective on strategic thinking.

ADOPTING A STRATEGIC APPROACH – INPUTS FROM THE *PURANANURU*

Before developing a strategy to tackle a complex problem, it is essential to determine the strategic approach that will be adopted. In this regard, the *Purananuru* is superb as it clearly describes an effective strategic approach that has been successful for millennia. The 10 steps below provide a structure to help shape the planning phase of a strategy.

Step 1: Ensure Your Strategy Focuses on People

According to the *Purananuru*, if one is to adopt a strategic approach to complex problems then the focus must be on people, their needs, and their behaviours and not terrain or physical outcomes.

A successful strategy is one that prioritises people at its core. Whether in business, politics, or community projects, focusing on people is essential for long-term success and sustainability. This step will discuss key approaches and principles to ensure a strategy focuses on people.

Understand the Needs and Goals of People. The first step in creating a people-focused strategy is understanding the needs, goals, and aspirations of the individuals and groups involved. Engage in dialogue with stakeholders and conduct research to identify their challenges and expectations. This understanding forms the basis for developing a strategy that resonates with the people it serves.

Promote Inclusivity and Diversity. A strategy that focuses on people should embrace inclusivity and diversity. This means considering the perspectives and experiences of a wide range of individuals, including those from different backgrounds, cultures, and demographics forming a larger substratum. An inclusive approach leads to more innovative solutions and stronger relationships.

Align Strategy with Values and Culture. Aligning the strategy with the values and culture of the people involved creates a sense of ownership and commitment. A strategy that reflects the core beliefs of the organisation or community fosters trust and loyalty among stakeholders.

Encourage Collaboration and Participation. A people-focused strategy encourages collaboration and participation from those it affects. By involving individuals in the decision-making process, you empower them and gain valuable insights. This collaborative approach also promotes buy-in and ownership, leading to smoother implementation and stronger results.

Focus on Employee and Stakeholder Well-being. In a business context, a strategy that prioritises the well-being of employees and stakeholders leads to higher productivity, job satisfaction, and loyalty. Providing opportunities for growth and development, offering support for work-life balance, and recognising achievements contribute to a positive work environment.

Create Clear Communication Channels. Clear communication is essential for ensuring that everyone understands the strategy and their role in its execution. Keep stakeholders informed and engaged through regular updates and provide opportunities for feedback and dialogue.

Adaptability and Flexibility. A people-focused strategy should be adaptable and flexible to accommodate changing needs and circumstances.

Regularly review the strategy's progress and be open to making adjustments based on feedback and new insights.

Empowerment and Autonomy. Empowering individuals with autonomy and decision-making authority within their areas of responsibility encourages ownership and accountability. This leads to a more engaged and motivated workforce or community.

Consider Ethical and Social Responsibility. Ethical considerations and social responsibility should be integral to a people-focused strategy. This includes ensuring fair treatment, promoting equality, and contributing positively to society and the environment.

Measure Success and Impact. Establishing metrics to measure the success and impact of the strategy on people is crucial. Regular assessments help track progress, identify areas for improvement, and ensure that the strategy remains aligned with people's needs and goals.

A people-focused strategy prioritises understanding and addressing the needs and aspirations of individuals and groups. By promoting inclusivity, collaboration, well-being, and ethical considerations, such a strategy fosters trust, engagement, and long-term success. Continuously reviewing and adapting the strategy based on feedback and changing circumstances ensures that it remains relevant and impactful.

One instance from the *Purananuru* that focuses on people is found in the poem 192, attributed to the poet Kabilar. In this poem, the poet communicates to the ruler Paari about the significance of taking care of his people. The ruler is encouraged to provide for his subjects and ensure their well-being, as they are the foundation of his kingdom.

The poem brings to the fore how the prosperity of the people is intertwined with the prosperity of the ruler and the state. By prioritising the needs and welfare of his people, the ruler can create a strong and stable kingdom. The poem advises the ruler to pay attention to the needs of his subjects and provide for them. This strategic focus on people helps ensure the loyalty and support of the populace. By nurturing relationships with the people and ensuring their well-being, the ruler creates a supportive environment for his reign. A kingdom with content and prosperous subjects is more likely to thrive in the long term. The ruler's focus on people builds a solid foundation for his governance.

This example illustrates the importance of prioritising the welfare of the people in strategy and governance, as advised in the *Purananuru*. By focusing on the well-being of the subjects, a ruler can strengthen their rule and maintain a stable and prosperous kingdom.

A notable modern example of a strategy focused on people leading to success is Starbucks' employee-centric approach that has been integral to its global growth and brand loyalty. Founded in 1971, Starbucks grew from a single coffee shop in Seattle to become one of the world's largest coffeehouse chains. While Starbucks is known for its high-quality coffee, its remarkable success is also deeply rooted in its commitment to its employees, whom it refers to as "partners."

From the early stages of its expansion, Starbucks prioritised providing comprehensive benefits to its employees. In the U.S., the company offers health insurance, stock options, and even tuition reimbursement for online degrees through the Starbucks College Achievement Plan. This focus on education and well-being has fostered loyalty and reduced turnover.

Starbucks has also built an inclusive work environment where diversity is celebrated, and all employees are encouraged to bring their authentic selves to work. This emphasis on inclusion has strengthened the company's internal culture and appeal as an employer. Starbucks invests heavily in employee training, ensuring that every barista not only masters the technical skills needed for the job, but also understands the company's culture and values. This training empowers employees to deliver consistently high customer service, enhancing the overall Starbucks experience.

Store managers and employees are given a degree of autonomy to make decisions that best serve their customers and communities. This empowerment fosters a sense of ownership and responsibility, leading to better service and stronger connections with customers. Starbucks regularly seeks feedback from its employees through surveys and meetings, ensuring that their voices are heard in decision-making processes. This engagement helps the company continuously improve working conditions and employee satisfaction. The company has also implemented policies that allow for flexible scheduling, acknowledging the importance of work-life balance, which further enhances job satisfaction.

Starbucks' people-focused strategy has resulted in several key successes. The company's comprehensive benefits and inclusive culture have led to significantly lower turnover rates compared to the industry average, which in turn reduces recruitment and training costs. Happy and motivated employees translate into better customer service, which has played a crucial role in building strong customer loyalty. Customers often associate their positive in-store experiences with the brand itself, reinforcing Starbucks' position in the market. By focusing on its employees, Starbucks has been able to maintain consistency in its service and culture across its thousands of locations worldwide. This consistency has been critical to its global expansion and the creation of a uniform brand experience.

Starbucks' core and key strategy of focusing on its people—ensuring their well-being, empowering them, and creating a positive work environment—has been a key driver of its long-term success. This approach not only fosters employee satisfaction and loyalty, but, also enhances the overall customer experience, contributing to the company's growth and a strong market position. This example illustrates how a people-centric strategy can be a powerful foundation for sustained success in a competitive industry.

Step 2: Always Attempt Diplomacy First and Reach Out to Potential Partners or Allies

Diplomacy is the art of managing international relations and fostering peaceful cooperation between different entities, such as nations, organisations, or individuals. It plays a crucial role in addressing global challenges, promoting stability, and facilitating constructive dialogue. The fundamentals of diplomacy encompass a range of skills, principles, and practices that enable diplomats and negotiators to navigate complex situations effectively. This step will discuss the key elements of diplomacy and their importance in international relations.

Effective Communication. Clear and respectful communication is at the heart of diplomacy. Diplomats must be skilled in active listening, articulate expression, and non-verbal cues. They need to convey messages persuasively while maintaining a courteous and professional demeanour.

Negotiation and Mediation. Diplomats often engage in negotiation and mediation to resolve disputes or reach mutually beneficial agreements. This requires a deep understanding of the interests and perspectives of all parties involved. Diplomats must find common ground and develop creative solutions.

Cultural Awareness and Sensitivity. Understanding and respecting cultural differences is essential for successful diplomacy. Diplomats must be aware of local customs, traditions, and social norms to build rapport and avoid misunderstandings. Cultural sensitivity fosters trust and cooperation.

Conflict Resolution and Peacebuilding. Diplomats play a key role in preventing and resolving conflicts. They work to de-escalate tensions and facilitate peaceful resolutions through dialogue and compromise. Diplomats also contribute to post-conflict peacebuilding efforts.

Confidentiality and Discretion. Diplomacy often involves sensitive and confidential information. Diplomats must exercise discretion and maintain the confidentiality of negotiations and discussions. Trustworthiness and integrity are essential qualities in diplomacy.

Strategic Thinking and Analysis. Diplomats must be strategic thinkers, capable of analysing complex situations and anticipating future developments. They assess potential risks and opportunities, considering both short-term and long-term implications of decisions.

Relationship Building. Establishing and maintaining strong relationships with key stakeholders is a cornerstone of diplomacy. Diplomats cultivate connections with government officials, community leaders, business representatives, and other influencers to advance their objectives.

Adherence to International Law and Norms. Diplomacy subsists within the framework of international law and norms. Diplomats must be knowledgeable about treaties, agreements, and customary practices governing international relations.

Patience and Persistence. Diplomatic processes often take time and require patience. Diplomats must be persistent in pursuing their objectives while remaining flexible and open to compromise.

Adaptability and Resilience. The international landscape is constantly evolving, with new challenges and opportunities emerging regularly. Diplomats must adapt to changing circumstances and be resilient in the face of setbacks.

Ethical Conduct. Ethical conduct is fundamental to diplomacy. Diplomats must uphold principles such as honesty, integrity, and respect for human rights in their interactions and decisions.

Public Diplomacy. In addition to traditional diplomacy, public diplomacy involves engaging with the general public and other non-governmental actors. Diplomats use various communication tools and platforms to shape public opinion and promote mutual understanding.

The fundamentals of diplomacy encompass effective communication, negotiation, cultural awareness, and strategic thinking. Diplomats must build strong relationships, uphold ethical standards, and navigate complex situations with patience and resilience. By adhering to these principles, diplomacy can contribute to the peaceful resolution of conflicts, the promotion of international cooperation, and the advancement of common goals across borders.

One notable example from the *Purananuru* that highlights the use of diplomacy first can be found in poem 145, attributed to the poet Ulochanar. In this poem, the poet advises the Chera king on the importance of employing diplomacy and wise counsel when dealing with canny and arch adversaries.

The poem highlights the importance of seeking peaceful solutions and avoiding unnecessary conflict. It suggests that the ruler should strive to negotiate and resolve disputes through dialogue and mutual understanding before resorting to war. The poem advises the king to seek the advice of knowledgeable counsellors and wise individuals to guide his decisions and strategies. The poem also suggests using negotiation and compromise to resolve disputes and maintain peaceful relationships with other rulers and states. By choosing diplomacy first, the king can avoid the destruction and resource drain that often accompanies war. This approach allows the king to preserve his kingdom's strength and stability.

This example illustrates how the *Purananuru* values the use of diplomacy and wise counsel as a means of resolving conflicts and managing relationships. By prioritising diplomatic solutions, a ruler can maintain peace, stability, and prosperity within the kingdom.

A prime example of a strategy that put diplomacy and alliances first is the creation and expansion of the European Union (EU), particularly the role it has played in ensuring peace and stability in Europe after World War II. After the annihilation and devastation of World War II, European nations faced the enormous challenge of rebuilding their economies, addressing deep-seated animosities, and preventing future conflicts. The idea of European integration emerged as a way to foster cooperation, promote economic recovery, and ensure lasting peace. This was a significant shift from a history of repeated conflicts to one where diplomacy and alliances were prioritised.

The European Coal and Steel Community (ECSC) was established by the Treaty of Paris in 1951, signed by six nations: France, West Germany, Italy, Belgium, the Netherlands, and Luxembourg. The idea, spearheaded by French Foreign Minister Robert Schuman and Jean Monnet, was to create a common market for coal and steel, industries critical to military power. By tying these industries together under a supranational authority, the ECSC aimed to make war between member states "not merely unthinkable but materially impossible."

Building on the success of the ECSC, the Treaty of Rome in 1957 established the European Economic Community (EEC), which aimed to create a common market and customs union among its members. This further deepened economic ties and promoted political cooperation, laying the groundwork for broader European integration.

Over the decades, the EU expanded to include more member states, bringing in countries from Southern Europe (like Spain, Portugal, and Greece) after they transitioned from dictatorships to democracies, and later, Central and Eastern European countries after the fall of the Soviet Union. This expansion was rooted in the belief that economic integration and political cooperation would ensure stability and prosperity across the continent. The EU also deepened its integration through the creation of institutions like the European Parliament, the European Court of Justice, and the introduction of the Euro as a common currency for many member states.

The EU has consistently stressed diplomacy, dialogue, and cooperation both within its borders and in its external relations. It has been a key actor in promoting democratic values, human rights, and the rule of law, both in Europe and globally. The EU's enlargement policy, which offers the prospect of membership to countries that meet specific political and economic criteria, has been a powerful tool for promoting reform and stability in neighbouring regions.

The most significant and important success of prioritising diplomacy and alliances has been the maintenance of peace among EU member states. Since the EU's inception, Western Europe has experienced an unprecedented period of peace, with no major conflicts between member states—a remarkable achievement given Europe's history.

The EU has created one of the largest single markets in the world, facilitating trade, investment, and economic growth. Member states have benefited from the free movement of goods, services, capital, and people, which has contributed to increased prosperity and living standards. The EU, as a unified bloc, has become a major global player in trade, diplomacy, and environmental policy. It has a significant voice in international organisations and negotiations, such as the United Nations, the World Trade Organisation, and climate change agreements. The prospect of EU membership has also been a powerful incentive for political and economic reform in candidate countries. This has led to the spread of democracy and the strengthening of institutions in many parts of Europe, particularly in countries that were once under authoritarian rule.

The strategy of prioritising diplomacy and alliances in the formation and expansion of the European Union has been an extraordinary success. By fostering cooperation, economic integration, and political dialogue, the EU has transformed Europe from a continent plagued by wars and divisions into one characterised by peace, stability, and prosperity. This example highlights the power of diplomacy and alliances as a strategy for achieving long-term success.

Step 3: Power and Strength Flow from Prosperity. Prioritise Economic Issues in your Strategy

Prioritising economic issues in a strategy is essential for ensuring long-term growth, stability, and success in business, government, or community projects. Economic considerations play a central role in shaping strategic decisions and influencing outcomes. This step will discuss key approaches to prioritising economic issues in a strategy.

Assess the Economic Landscape. Begin by conducting a thorough assessment of the economic environment in which you operate. This includes analysing market trends, industry dynamics, regulatory changes, and global economic factors. Understanding the broader economic context will help you identify opportunities and risks.

Identify Key Economic Objectives. Clearly define your economic objectives, such as increasing revenue, reducing costs, or achieving specific financial targets. These objectives should align with the overall mission and vision of the organisation or project.

Allocate Resources Effectively. Prioritise economic issues by strategically allocating resources, such as capital, personnel, and technology. Focus on initiatives that offer the highest return on investment and align with your economic objectives.

Monitor Cash Flow and Profit Margins. Cash flow and profit margins are critical indicators of financial health. Regularly monitor these metrics to ensure your strategy is on track and identify areas for improvement. Managing cash flow effectively allows for agility in responding to economic changes.

Optimise Operational Efficiency. Streamlining operations and reducing waste can lead to significant cost savings and improved profitability. Implement continuous improvement processes and leverage technology to enhance efficiency and productivity.

Invest in Innovation and Growth. Prioritising economic issues doesn't mean neglecting innovation and growth opportunities. Allocate resources to research and development, new markets, and product diversification to stay competitive and sustain long-term success.

Mitigate Economic Risks. Assess potential economic risks, such as market volatility, changes in interest rates, or shifts in consumer behaviour. Develop contingency plans and risk management strategies to navigate uncertainties and protect your economic interests.

Establish Partnerships and Collaborations. Forming strategic partnerships can help leverage resources, reduce costs, and access new markets. Collaborate with other organisations or stakeholders to achieve shared economic goals.

Stay Informed and Adapt. Continuously monitor economic trends and changes in your industry. Stay informed about new regulations, emerging markets, and shifts in consumer preferences. Be prepared to adapt your strategy as needed to stay ahead of economic challenges.

Measure Economic Impact and Outcomes. Define key performance indicators (KPIs) to measure the economic impact of your strategy. Track metrics such as revenue growth, cost savings, and market share to evaluate success and make data-driven decisions.

Prioritising economic issues in a strategy requires a clear understanding of the economic landscape, a focus on key objectives, and the ability to allocate resources effectively. By monitoring financial health, optimising efficiency, investing in growth, and mitigating risks, you can develop a strategy that leads to sustainable economic success. Regularly assessing and adapting your strategy based on changing economic conditions ensures continued relevance and resilience.

One poem from the Purananuru that demonstrates how power and strength flow from prosperity is poem 361, attributed to the poet Maturai Maruthana Ilanakanar. In this poem, the poet praises the Pandya king, highlighting how the prosperity of his kingdom leads to his power and strength.

The poet innovatively elaborates upon the land of the king as abundant with natural resources such as fertile fields, thriving agriculture, and rich waters. This prosperity provides the foundation for the king's power. The prosperity of the land leads to wealth, which in turn enables the king to maintain a strong army and a stable government. This strength is necessary for defending the kingdom and expanding its influence. A prosperous and well-cared-for population supports the king's rule. The people contribute to the kingdom's success through their work and loyalty. Prosperity allows the king to focus on good governance, ensuring peace and stability within the kingdom.

The poem illustrates how the prosperity of the land and its people directly contributes to the power and strength of the ruler. By fostering a prosperous environment, the king can maintain control over his domain and achieve lasting success.

A compelling example of where prioritising the economy has delivered strategic success is China's economic reforms and opening-up policies that began in 1978 under the leadership of Deng Xiaoping. By the late 1970s, China was struggling with widespread poverty, economic stagnation, and the lingering effects of the Cultural Revolution. The country's economy was largely agrarian and centrally planned, with limited interaction with the global economy. Recognising the need for change, Deng Xiaoping initiated a series of economic reforms that would transform China into a global economic powerhouse.

The first major reform was the de-collectivisation of agriculture, allowing farmers to cultivate land under the household responsibility system. This shift from collective farming to individual incentives led to a significant increase in agricultural productivity and rural incomes.

Deng then established Special Economic Zones in coastal cities like Shenzhen, Zhuhai, and Xiamen, where foreign investment was encouraged, and market-oriented policies were implemented. These zones became testing grounds for economic liberalisation, attracting foreign capital, technology, and management expertise. China gradually moved away from a purely planned economy towards a mixed economy, introducing market mechanisms while maintaining state control over key sectors. This included allowing private businesses to operate, reforming state-owned enterprises, and encouraging entrepreneurship.

China went on to open its economy to the world, attracting significant foreign direct investment (FDI). The government implemented policies that promoted exports, which became a driving force of China's economic growth. China's accession to the WTO in 2001 was a pivotal moment in its economic strategy. It marked China's full integration into the global trading system, leading to an unprecedented expansion of its exports and access to international markets.

Massive investments were made in the realm of infrastructure, including roads, railways, ports, and energy, which supported quick industrialisation and urbanisation. The construction of the high-speed rail network and modernisation of cities transformed China's economic landscape. China also prioritised education and the development of its human capital, which laid the foundation for its rapid growth in technology, manufacturing, and innovation sectors. This investment has driven China's transition from a low-cost manufacturing hub to a leader in high-tech industries.

Over the past four decades, China has experienced one of the fastest and most sustained periods of economic growth in history. It lifted over 800 million people out of poverty, according to the World Bank, and became the world's second-largest economy by nominal GDP. China's prioritisation of the economy has transformed it into a central player in the global economy. It is now a major trading partner for countries around the world, a leading exporter, and a significant source of global investment.

China's focus on economic development has enabled it to emerge as a leader in various high-tech industries, including telecommunications, renewable energy, and artificial intelligence. Companies like Huawei, Alibaba, and Tencent are now global giants. The economic success of China has also bolstered its geopolitical influence. China's Belt and Road Initiative (BRI) is a prime example of how it uses economic power to build alliances, influence global trade routes, and extend its reach across Asia, Africa, and beyond.

China's strategic focus on prioritising the economy has delivered extraordinary success, transforming it from an impoverished, isolated nation into a global superpower. This economic success has not only improved the standard of living for hundreds of millions of people but also significantly altered the global balance of power. The Chinese burgeoning instance illustrates how an unwavering focus on economic development can achieve strategic dominance on the world stage.

Step 4: Ensure your Strategy Aligns with your Values

Creating a strategy that aligns with one's values and standards is essential for ensuring that personal and professional goals are met in a meaningful and ethical manner. When a strategy aligns with one's values, it promotes integrity, consistency, and fulfilment. Here are some key points to ensure a strategy aligns with one's values and standards:

Identify Core Values. Begin by clarifying your personal or organisational core values. These values serve as guiding principles that reflect your beliefs and priorities. Examples include integrity, honesty, creativity, collaboration, and respect for others. Comprehending your core values is crucial for developing a strategy that is meaningful and authentic.

Assess Current Practices. Evaluate existing practices, both personal and professional, to identify areas of alignment and misalignment with your values. This process may involve examining current goals, projects, and behaviours to understand how they contribute to or detract from your values.

Set Clear Objectives. Define clear and measurable objectives that reflect your values. These objectives should provide direction for your strategy and act as benchmarks for evaluating success. Aligning your goals with your values ensures that your efforts are purposeful and contribute to your overarching principles.

Incorporate Values into Decision-Making. Integrate your values into every decision-making process. Consider how each choice, big or small, aligns with your values and long-term objectives. This can help guide your actions and ensure that your strategy remains consistent with your values.

Communicate and Collaborate. Share your values and strategy with others involved in your work or personal life, such as team members, family, or peers. Open communication ensures that everyone understands the underlying principles guiding your decisions and actions. Collaboration can also bring different perspectives that may enhance your strategy.

Evaluate and Adjust. Continuously monitor your strategy to ensure it remains aligned with your values and standards. Regularly review your progress and outcomes and be open to making adjustments if necessary. Flexibility and adaptability are essential for maintaining alignment over time.

Lead by Example. Demonstrate your commitment to your values through your actions. Leading by example reinforces your dedication to your principles and sets a standard for others to follow. It also helps build trust and credibility with those around you.

Seek Feedback and Reflection. Encourage feedback from others on your strategy and its alignment with your values. This can provide valuable insights and help you stay accountable. Additionally, take time for personal reflection to ensure your strategy is true to your principles.

Stay Informed and Adaptable. Stay updated on industry trends, new information, and best practices. Adapt your strategy as needed to maintain alignment with your values in changing circumstances.

Be Consistent. Consistency is key to ensuring your strategy aligns with your values and standards. Maintain a steady approach to your goals and avoid compromising your values for short-term gains.

Aligning a strategy with one's values and standards is an ongoing process that requires self-awareness, reflection, and commitment. By following these steps, individuals and organisations can create strategies that not only achieve their goals but also uphold their core values and principles. This alignment leads to greater satisfaction, integrity, and success in both personal and professional endeavours.

In poem 67 of the *Purananuru*, attributed to the poet Mamulanar, the poet praises the Chola king for his just and ethical rule. The king's strategy aligns with the values of righteousness, justice, and compassion. The poem praises the king for his commitment to righteous governance. He follows a strategy that aligns with the values of fairness and justice. The king's strategy is centred around the well-being of his people. He is compassionate and ensures that his subjects are treated fairly and with respect. The king is described as a protector of the oppressed and a defender of justice. His strategy includes safeguarding the rights and welfare of those who are vulnerable. The king is portrayed as a wise and ethical leader whose strategy is informed by moral principles. He uses his power to maintain order and promote prosperity.

This poem illustrates how a ruler's strategy aligns with values such as justice, righteousness, and compassion. By prioritising these values, the king is able to establish a just and prosperous kingdom that earns the loyalty and respect of his people. This alignment of strategy with values leads to effective and ethical governance.

A powerful and telling instance of a values-based strategy delivering success is the Civil Rights Movement in the United States, particularly under the leadership of Dr. Martin Luther King Jr. The movement was rooted in the values of justice, equality, nonviolence, and the belief in the fundamental rights of all human beings. By the mid-20th century, racial segregation and discrimination against African Americans were entrenched in many parts of the United States, particularly in the South. The Civil Rights Movement sought to end these injustices and secure equal rights for African Americans through a strategy deeply rooted in moral and ethical values.

Inspired by Mahatma Gandhi's principles of nonviolent resistance, Dr. King and other civil rights leaders adopted nonviolence as a core strategy. They believed that nonviolent protest would demonstrate the moral superiority of their cause and expose the brutality and injustice of the segregationist system. This approach was grounded in the value of nonviolence, aiming to bring about change through peaceful means.

The movement framed its demands for equality in terms of universal human rights, appealing to the fundamental American values of liberty, justice, and the belief that "all men are created equal." By grounding their strategy in these shared values, civil rights leaders sought to unite people across racial and regional lines.

Dr. King's leadership exemplified a values-based approach. His speeches, most notably the "I Have a Dream" speech, articulated a vision of a just society where individuals were judged "not by the colour of their skin, but by the content of their character." This vision was deeply rooted in the ethical and moral values of equality and justice.

The Civil Rights Movement employed civil disobedience, such as the Montgomery Bus Boycott, sit-ins, freedom rides, and the March on Washington, to challenge unjust laws and practices. These actions were based on the value of standing up against injustice in a way that maintained the dignity and humanity of all involved, including the oppressors.

The values-based strategy of the Civil Rights Movement led to significant legislative successes. The Civil Rights Act of 1964, which ended segregation in public places and banned employment discrimination, and the Voting Rights Act of 1965, which protected voting rights for African Americans, were landmark victories that fundamentally changed American society.

The movement's emphasis on values of the order of justice, equality, and nonviolence helped to shift public opinion. Over time, more Americans came to see segregation and racial discrimination as morally unacceptable. This cultural shift was as crucial as the legal victories in achieving the movement's long-term goals.

The success of the Civil Rights Movement inspired other movements for social justice around the world. It demonstrated the power of a values-based strategy in achieving profound social change, influencing movements in South Africa, India, and other nations struggling for freedom and equality. The Civil Rights Movement is a quintessential example of how a values-based strategy can deliver success. By grounding their struggle in the universal values of justice, equality, and nonviolence, civil rights leaders were able to achieve profound and lasting change. This strategy not only transformed American society but also provided a powerful model for other social justice movements globally.

Step 5: Stay Flexible and be Prepared to Adapt and Improvise

Adaptability and improvisation are essential skills for navigating unexpected challenges and uncertainties. Whether in personal life, business, or any other realm, the ability to adjust plans and think on one's feet, can make a significant difference in successfully overcoming obstacles. This step will discuss some key methods for adapting and improvising when encountering the unexpected.

Cultivate a Flexible Mindset. Developing a flexible mindset is the foundation of adaptability. Embrace change and uncertainty as opportunities for growth and learning. Stay open to new ideas and be willing to adjust your perspective when needed.

Stay Calm and Focused. When faced with unexpected challenges, remaining calm and focused is crucial. Take a moment to assess the situation and prioritise your actions. Panicking can cloud judgment and lead to impulsive decisions.

Gather Information and Assess the Situation. Quickly gather information about the unexpected challenge to understand its scope and potential impact. Analyse available data and resources to assess the situation and identify possible courses of action.

Leverage Previous Experience. Drawing on past experiences and lessons learned can provide valuable insights and guidance when improvising. Consider how you have handled similar situations in the past and apply relevant methodologies.

Break Down the Problem. Breaking down the unexpected challenge into smaller, manageable parts can help clarify the situation and identify potential solutions. This approach also makes the challenge feel less overwhelming.

Be Resourceful and Creative. Improvisation often requires resourcefulness and creativity. Explore unconventional solutions and think outside the box. Utilise available resources and skills in innovative ways to address the challenge.

Communicate Effectively. Clear communication is essential when adapting to unexpected situations. Keep stakeholders informed about the situation and your plan of action. Seek input and collaboration from others to generate new ideas and solutions.

Embrace Collaboration and Teamwork. Working with others can lead to more effective problem-solving and adaptation. Collaborate with team members, colleagues, or other stakeholders to pool knowledge and resources.

Be Willing to Experiment. Improvisation involves a degree of trial and error. Be willing to experiment with different approaches and strategies. Learn from both successes and failures to refine your course of action.

Stay Positive and Resilient. Maintaining a positive attitude and resilience is essential when facing unexpected challenges. Focus on the potential opportunities that may arise from the situation and stay determined to find a solution.

Reassess and Adjust as Needed. Continuously reassess the situation and the effectiveness of your response. Be prepared to adjust your strategy based on new information or changing circumstances.

Learn from the Experience. After navigating the unexpected challenge, take time to reflect on the experience. Identify what worked well and what could be improved. Use these lessons to enhance your adaptability and improvisation skills for future challenges.

Adapting and improvising when encountering the unexpected requires a flexible mindset, resourcefulness, and effective communication. By staying calm, assessing the situation, and collaborating with others, individuals can navigate challenges more effectively. Continuous learning and reflection help build resilience and prepare for future unexpected situations. Embracing change as an opportunity for growth can lead to innovative solutions and long-term success.

One poem from the Purananuru that highlights the need for flexibility and adaptation is poem 223, attributed to the poet Perunkunrur Perukidattayar. In this poem, the poet praises the Chera king Yanaikkatsei for his ability to adapt and improvise in the face of changing circumstances. The poem describes how the Chera king can adjust his strategies and decisions according to the situation. This ability to stay flexible allows him to handle different challenges effectively. The king is praised for employing a variety of tactics to suit different scenarios. He is able to switch between offensive and defensive strategies as needed. The poem mentions the king's adaptability in warfare, where he is skilled at changing his approach based on the opponent's moves and the battlefield conditions. The king combines his strength with wisdom and insight, which allows him to make quick decisions and adjust his plans as circumstances evolve.

This poem enunciates how a character's ability to stay flexible and adapt to changing situations can lead to successful outcomes. By being open to new approaches and adjusting his strategies as needed, the king demonstrates effective leadership and the ability to handle unforeseen challenges.

A modern example where flexibility, adaptability, and improvisation in strategy delivered success is Franklin D. Roosevelt's leadership during the Great Depression and World War II. Franklin D. Roosevelt (FDR) became the President of the United States in 1933, at a time when the country was grappling with the Great Depression, the worst economic crisis in its history. Later, he led the nation through World War II, a period of immense global turmoil. His leadership during these crises demonstrated remarkable flexibility, adaptability, and improvisation.

When FDR occupied his White House office, he did not have a fixed, detailed plan to combat the Great Depression. Instead, he adopted a flexible approach, willing to experiment with different policies and programs to see what worked. This led to the development of the New Deal, a series of economic programs designed to provide relief, recovery, and reform.

Roosevelt adapted his strategies as he encountered new challenges. For example, when the initial wave of New Deal programs faced legal challenges or did not achieve the desired results, FDR was willing to revise them or try new approaches. This adaptability was critical in sustaining public support and addressing the evolving economic crisis.

FDR used "Fireside Chats," his series of radio broadcasts, to speak directly to the American people. This was an improvisational approach to build public trust and maintain morale, explaining complex issues in simple terms and ensuring that the public was engaged and supportive of his policies.

Before the U.S. entered World War II, FDR had to navigate a complex international landscape with a strong isolationist sentiment at home. He adapted his foreign policy to support the Allies while preparing the U.S. for potential involvement, gradually shifting public opinion without provoking backlash. Programs like Lend-Lease allowed the U.S. to provide crucial support to Britain and other allies before officially entering the war.

Once the U.S. joined the war, Roosevelt worked closely with military leaders to adapt strategies to changing circumstances. The U.S. faced challenges on multiple fronts—Europe, Africa, and the Pacific—requiring a flexible approach to resource allocation, alliances, and military tactics. The successful execution of D-Day and the overall Allied strategy reflected an adaptive and coordinated effort.

Roosevelt demonstrated improvisation in diplomacy by forging and maintaining the "Big Three" alliance with Winston Churchill and Joseph Stalin, despite their differing political ideologies and goals. FDR's ability to navigate these complex relationships was crucial to maintaining the Allied coalition and achieving victory.

The New Deal did not end the Great Depression on its own, but it provided critical relief and reforms that stabilised the economy, restored public confidence, and laid the groundwork for future prosperity. FDR's flexible approach allowed him to respond effectively to the economic crisis and adapt to changing conditions.

Roosevelt's adaptive and improvisational leadership was key to the Allied victory in World War II. His ability to adjust strategies, manage diverse alliances, and keep the American public engaged and supportive were crucial to overcoming the challenges of a global war.

FDR's leadership left a lasting legacy, both in terms of the economic reforms that reshaped American society and in the post-war international order, including the creation of the United Nations, which reflected his vision of a cooperative global community.

Franklin D. Roosevelt's presidency is a prime instance of how flexibility, adaptability, and improvisation in strategy can lead to success. Faced with unprecedented challenges, FDR's willingness to experiment with new ideas, adapt to changing circumstances, and improvise solutions allowed him to guide the United States through two of the most significant crises of the 20th century. His leadership not only secured economic recovery and victory in war but also reshaped the global political landscape for decades to come.

Step 6: Make your Vision or Offer Attractive to Stakeholders. Carrots Work Better than Sticks

A strategic vision serves as a roadmap for an organisation, outlining its long-term goals and direction. For a strategic vision to be effective, it must resonate with stakeholders, individuals or groups who have a vested interest in the organisation's success. An attractive strategic vision can inspire commitment, support, and collaboration from stakeholders. This step will elaborate upon key strategies for making a strategic vision attractive to stakeholders.

Craft a Compelling Narrative. An attractive strategic vision begins with a compelling narrative that captures stakeholders' attention and imagination. Use clear, concise, and relatable language to communicate the vision's purpose and objectives. Tell a story that resonates with stakeholders' values and aspirations.

Align with Stakeholders' Interests. A strategic vision should align with the interests and goals of key stakeholders. Understand their needs and priorities and demonstrate how the vision addresses these concerns. Show how the vision benefits stakeholders directly and indirectly.

Involve Stakeholders in the Development Process. Involving stakeholders in the vision's development creates a sense of ownership and buy-in. Seek their input and feedback during the planning stage to ensure their perspectives are considered. Collaborative vision-building strengthens commitment and trust.

Set Clear, Achievable Goals. Stakeholders are more likely to support a vision that includes clear, measurable, and achievable goals. Outline specific milestones and objectives that lead to the overall vision. This gives stakeholders confidence in the vision's feasibility and the organisation's ability to deliver.

Demonstrate a Path to Success. Stakeholders want to see a clear path to achieving the strategic vision. Present a well-thought-out plan that outlines the steps and resources needed to reach the vision. Highlight key strategies and initiatives that will drive progress.

Showcase Tangible Benefits and Impact. Highlight the tangible benefits and impact of achieving the strategic vision. Explain how the vision will improve the organisation, its stakeholders, and the broader community. Emphasise the long-term value and positive change the vision will bring.

Communicate Regularly and Transparently. Maintain open and transparent communication with stakeholders throughout the process. Provide regular updates on progress, challenges, and successes. Transparency builds trust and keeps stakeholders engaged and informed.

Demonstrate Leadership Commitment. Stakeholders look to leadership for assurance and direction. Leaders should demonstrate commitment to the vision through their actions and decisions. Strong leadership buy-in signals to stakeholders that the vision is a top priority.

Be Adaptive and Responsive. While a strategic vision provides long-term direction, it should also be adaptable to changing circumstances. Be open to stakeholder feedback and willing to adjust the vision as needed. Demonstrating flexibility and responsiveness shows stakeholders that their input is valued.

Celebrate Milestones and Achievements. Recognising and celebrating progress toward the strategic vision boosts morale and reinforces commitment. Share achievements with stakeholders and acknowledge their contributions. This builds a sense of shared success.

Making a strategic vision attractive to stakeholders requires crafting a compelling narrative, aligning the vision with stakeholders' interests, and involving them in the development process. Clear goals, transparent communication, and tangible benefits enhance the vision's appeal. By demonstrating leadership commitment, adaptability, and celebrating milestones, organisations can inspire stakeholders to support and engage with the strategic vision.

In poem 70, attributed to the poet Mamulanar, the poet praises the Chera king for his strategic vision that is made attractive to his people. This is reflected in the king's approach to ruling his kingdom and his focus on creating prosperity and stability for his subjects. The king's strategic vision centres on ensuring the prosperity and well-being of his people. By focusing on creating abundance and economic stability, he gains the support and loyalty of his subjects. The king is praised for his commitment to fairness and justice in his rule. This approach appeals to his people, who see him as a just and righteous leader. The king's strategic vision includes protecting the vulnerable and upholding their rights. This commitment to social justice garners support from a wide range of stakeholders. The king's vision of maintaining peace and order in the kingdom is made attractive to his people, as it ensures a safe and secure environment for them to thrive.

This poem demonstrates how the king's strategic vision aligns with the values and interests of his stakeholders, making it attractive and compellingly attractive to them. By focusing on prosperity, fairness, protection of the vulnerable, and peace, the king inspires loyalty and commitment from his people. This approach leads to a stable and successful reign.

A modern political example where a strategy with a compelling vision attractive to stakeholders has delivered success is Justin Trudeau's 2015 Canadian federal election campaign. In the 2015 federal election, Justin Trudeau, leader of the Liberal Party of Canada, presented a vision that resonated deeply with various stakeholders, leading to a significant political victory. His campaign focused on progressive policies and a positive, inclusive vision for Canada's future.

Trudeau's campaign was built around the promise of "real change" and a vision of a more inclusive and progressive Canada. His messaging was optimistic and aimed at rejuvenating the Canadian political landscape, which had become marred by scandals and perceived stagnation under the Conservative government of Stephen Harper. Trudeau's vision emphasised diversity and inclusion, appealing to a broad spectrum of voters. He highlighted issues such as gender equality, indigenous rights, and refugee resettlement. This approach was particularly attractive to younger voters, minorities, and those seeking a departure from previous administration policies.

Trudeau proposed specific policies designed to benefit the middle class, such as tax cuts for middle-income earners and increased investments in infrastructure and education. These policies addressed the concerns of key voter demographics and demonstrated a commitment to tangible enhancements in their lives. The Liberal platform included ambitious plans to address climate change, such as investing in clean energy and introducing a carbon pricing system. This vision aligned with the values of environmentally conscious voters and positioned the Liberals as forward-thinking on a global issue.

Trudeau and his campaign team effectively used social media and other communication channels to engage with voters directly. His personal charisma and ability to connect with people played a significant role in shaping a positive public perception. The campaign successfully built a broad coalition of support by addressing the concerns of various stakeholder groups, including urban voters, younger Canadians, and progressive constituencies. This coalition was crucial in winning the election.

In the 2015 federal election, the Liberal Party won a majority of the seats in the House of Commons, defeating the incumbent Conservative Party and ending nearly a decade of Conservative rule. Trudeau's vision and campaign strategy were key to this resounding victory. Once in power, Trudeau's government proceeded with many of the policies proposed during the campaign. This included implementing middle-class tax cuts, advancing gender equality initiatives, and taking steps to address climate change. The government also focused on improving relations with indigenous communities and enhancing Canada's role on the global stage. Trudeau's successful campaign and subsequent leadership helped rebrand the Liberal Party as a modern, progressive, and inclusive political force. This rebranding contributed to the party's long-term appeal and its subsequent electoral success in subsequent years.

Justin Trudeau's 2015 election campaign exemplifies how a strategy with a compelling vision is often found attractive to stakeholders which can lead to significant political success. By presenting a positive, inclusive vision that resonated with a diverse array of voters, Trudeau was able to secure a decisive victory and implement a range of progressive policies. This approach not only won the election but also reshaped the political landscape in Canada, demonstrating the power of an appealing and well-articulated vision in modern politics.

Step 7: Ensuring Solidarity and Cohesion at Home

Enhancing solidarity and cohesion within an organisation is essential for building a strong, collaborative, and productive work environment. When individuals work together harmoniously and share common goals, the organisation can achieve higher levels of performance and success. This step will discuss key strategies for fostering solidarity and cohesion within an organisation.

Establish a Clear Vision and Shared Goals. A clear and compelling vision provides a sense of purpose and direction for the organisation. Communicate the organisation's mission and goals to all members, and ensure they understand how their work contributes to the bigger picture. Shared goals unite individuals and encourage collaboration.

Promote Open Communication. Effective communication is the foundation of cohesion. Encourage open and transparent dialogue at all levels of the organisation. Provide multiple channels for communication, such as meetings, emails, and feedback sessions. Listen actively to employees and address their concerns and ideas.

Foster a Positive Organisational Culture. A positive culture promotes trust, respect, and collaboration. Encourage teamwork, recognition, and appreciation for employees' contributions. Cultivate an inclusive and diverse environment where everyone feels valued and empowered.

Encourage Collaboration and Teamwork. Promote collaborative work across departments and teams. Offer opportunities for cross-functional projects and encourage knowledge sharing. Team-building activities and workshops can strengthen relationships and improve cooperation.

Provide Opportunities for Professional Growth. Supporting employees' professional development fosters a sense of loyalty and commitment. Offer training, mentorship, and opportunities for advancement. When employees feel invested in and supported, they are more likely to work cohesively with others.

Set Clear Expectations and Accountability. Clearly define roles, responsibilities, and performance expectations. When individuals understand their contributions and are held accountable, they are more likely to work together toward common goals.

Celebrate Achievements and Milestones. Recognising and celebrating achievements boosts morale and reinforces a sense of unity. Celebrate team successes and individual milestones, whether through formal events or informal acknowledgments.

Address Conflicts Promptly and Fairly. Conflicts can disrupt cohesion if not addressed promptly. Implement conflict resolution strategies and provide training on effective communication and mediation. A fair and transparent approach to conflict resolution helps maintain trust and solidarity.

Encourage Employee Involvement in Decision-Making. Involving employees in decision-making processes fosters a sense of ownership and engagement. Seek input from employees on important matters and consider their perspectives when making decisions.

Lead by Example: Leadership plays a critical role in fostering solidarity and cohesion. Leaders should model the values and behaviours they expect from their team. By demonstrating trust, respect, and collaboration, leaders set the tone for the rest of the organisation.

Enhancing and amplifying solidarity and cohesion within an organisation requires clear communication, a positive culture, and opportunities for collaboration and growth. By fostering trust, recognising achievements, and addressing conflicts fairly, organisations can create an environment where individuals work together harmoniously and achieve shared success. Leadership support and a commitment to open dialogue contribute to a cohesive and productive work environment.

In poem 79, attributed to the poet Kambiyan Maran, the poet describes the Chola king and his approach to ruling his kingdom with unmatched solidarity and cohesion. The king emphasises maintaining harmony within his kingdom by promoting justice and fairness. The king's focus on ensuring justice and fairness within his kingdom helps to maintain cohesion and solidarity among his subjects. The king respects the traditions and customs of his people, which fosters a sense of unity and common identity. By being attentive to the needs and concerns of his subjects, the king helps to create an environment where people feel valued and heard. The king promotes a sense of community and mutual support among his subjects, which strengthens solidarity and cohesion at home. The king's efforts to maintain peace and security within his kingdom help to create a stable environment where his people can thrive.

This poem illustrates how the Chola king's approach to ruling his kingdom focuses on ensuring solidarity and cohesion at home by promoting justice, respecting traditions, and providing safety and security. By fostering a sense of unity and common purpose among his subjects, the king is able to create a harmonious and prosperous kingdom.

A notable example where a strategy ensuring solidarity and cohesion at home delivered success abroad, happens to be Germany's approach to the European Union's handling of the Eurozone crisis during the late 2000s and early 2010s. During the Eurozone crisis, which began around 2009, several European countries, notably Greece, faced severe debt crises. The crisis posed a significant threat to the stability of the Eurozone and the broader European Union. Germany, as Europe's largest economy and a key player in the Eurozone, played a crucial role in addressing the crisis.

Germany's strategy during the Eurozone crisis involved building broad-based political support at home for its approach to managing the crisis. Chancellor Angela Merkel and her government worked to secure consensus across party lines on measures to address the crisis, which helped to present a unified front in international negotiations. Domestically, Germany adhered to strict economic policies and fiscal discipline, which reinforced its credibility and leadership in the EU. This commitment to economic stability at home ensured that Germany could advocate effectively for similar reforms and fiscal responsibility among its European partners.

Germany supported bailout packages for troubled Eurozone countries, including Greece, Ireland, and Portugal. This support, however, was conditional on the implementation of stringent austerity measures and economic reforms by the recipient countries. Germany's strategy emphasised that financial assistance was paired with a commitment to reform, promoting stability in the Eurozone.

Germany played a key role in advocating for and supporting reforms to strengthen EU institutions and mechanisms for financial stability. This included supporting the establishment of the European Stability Mechanism (ESM) and the European Financial Stability Facility (EFSF), which were designed to provide financial assistance and ensure the stability of the Eurozone.

The German government worked to maintain domestic public support for its role in managing the crisis. This involved transparent communication about the necessity of measures like austerity and bailouts, as well as highlighting the benefits of a stable Eurozone for Germany's own economic interests. The German strategy included promoting deeper European integration as a means of ensuring long-term stability. This vision was aimed at solidifying Germany's position within a more cohesive and resilient Eurozone, which was crucial for both domestic and international success, stability and prosperity.

Germany's strategy largely led to stabilising the Eurozone and preventing a complete collapse of the single currency. The financial assistance and reforms helped to restore economic stability in several Eurozone countries and rebuild investor confidence. By successfully managing the crisis and leading efforts to stabilise the Eurozone, Germany reinforced its position as a central economic and political leader in Europe. This enhanced its influence in European and global affairs, solidifying its role as a key player in shaping European economic policy. The crisis led to important reforms in EU governance and financial oversight mechanisms. Germany's leadership and commitment to European integration played a significant role in these developments, contributing to a more robust and integrated EU.

Germany's strategy of ensuring domestic solidarity and cohesion while addressing the Eurozone crisis was instrumental in delivering success overseas. By fostering bipartisan support, maintaining economic discipline at home, and advocating for financial stability and integration in Europe, Germany played a pivotal role in managing the crisis and enhancing its own position within the EU. This approach demonstrates how internal cohesion and strategic leadership can effectively address complex international challenges.

Step 8: Protect the Environment

Ensuring a strategy includes protection of the environment, which is crucial in today's world, where the health of the planet and the well-being of future generations are at stake. By integrating environmental considerations into strategic planning, individuals and organisations can contribute to sustainability, reduce their ecological footprint, and promote a healthier future. Here are some key points to ensure a strategy which includes the protection of the environment.

Understand the Environmental Impact. Begin by assessing the potential environmental impact of your strategy. Identify areas where your actions may harm or benefit the environment, such as resource consumption, waste production, emissions, and land use. This assessment will help you identify priorities and set targets for environmental protection.

Set Clear Environmental Goals. Define clear, measurable, and achievable environmental goals that align with your strategy. These goals should focus on reducing negative impacts and enhancing positive contributions to the environment. Examples include reducing carbon emissions, conserving water, or increasing the use of renewable energy sources.

Incorporate Sustainable Practices. Integrate sustainable practices into your operations and decision-making processes. This may include adopting energy-efficient technologies, sourcing materials responsibly, and implementing waste reduction strategies. Sustainable practices can improve your strategy's overall efficiency and long-term viability.

Follow Environmental Regulations and Standards. Ensure your strategy complies with all relevant environmental laws, regulations, and standards. Staying informed about current legal requirements and industry best practices helps avoid potential legal and reputational issues and demonstrates your commitment to environmental protection.

Promote a Culture of Environmental Awareness. Foster a culture of environmental awareness among your team members or peers. Educate them about the importance of sustainability and encourage them to adopt eco-friendly practices in their daily activities. This collective effort can have a significant impact on the success of your environmental strategy.

Engage Stakeholders. Involve key stakeholders, such as employees, customers, suppliers, and community members, in your environmental strategy. Solicit their input and feedback to identify opportunities for improvement and build support for your initiatives. Collaborating with stakeholders can also lead to innovative solutions and stronger partnerships.

Monitor and Measure Progress. Continuously monitor and measure your progress toward achieving your environmental goals. Use key performance indicators (KPIs) to track your performance and identify areas where adjustments may be needed. Regular assessment helps ensure your strategy remains on track and aligned with your environmental objectives.

Adopt Green Innovation and Technology. Explore and invest in green innovations and technologies that can enhance your environmental strategy. Examples include renewable energy sources, energy-efficient systems, and waste recycling technologies. These innovations can help reduce your ecological footprint and improve your overall sustainability.

Communicate and Report. Transparently communicate your environmental goals, actions, and progress to stakeholders and the public. Regular reporting demonstrates accountability and builds trust in your commitment to environmental protection. It can also inspire and deftly instil others to take recourse to similar practices.

Be Adaptable and Open to Change. Stay informed about emerging environmental challenges and opportunities. Be willing to adjust your strategy as new information becomes available or as circumstances change. Flexibility allows you to remain responsive to evolving environmental needs.

Incorporating environmental protection into your strategy requires a proactive and holistic approach. By prioritising sustainability, setting clear goals, and involving stakeholders, you can create a strategy that benefits both the environment and your long-term success. Taking these steps will not only contribute to a healthier planet but also enhance your reputation and relationships with others who share your commitment to environmental stewardship.

In poem 356 of the *Purananuru*, attributed to the poet Velli Veethiyar, there is a focus on the harmony between people and nature. The poet speaks about the natural abundance in the kingdom of the Pandya king, highlighting the richness of the land and its ability to sustain life. The poem describes the fertility of the land, the lush fields, and the plentiful resources available to the people. This natural abundance is seen as a gift that sustains the kingdom. The poet acknowledges the importance of nature and its role in providing for the needs of the people. There is an implicit respect for the environment and its ability to nurture life. The poem suggests that the people of the kingdom live in harmony with nature, using its resources wisely and sustainably. This approach helps to ensure the continued prosperity of the land. The poet highlights the link between the richness of the environment and the prosperity of the kingdom. The king's rule is seen as successful because it aligns with the natural abundance of the land.

This poem illustrates an early recognition of the value of protecting and respecting the environment. While the *Purananuru* may not explicitly discuss modern environmental concerns, it does underline the importance of living in harmony with nature and using its resources responsibly to ensure long-term prosperity.

A notable instance where protecting the environment has delivered strategic success, is Denmark's transition to renewable energy. Denmark, a country with a relatively small land area and a high standard of living, faced challenges related to energy security and environmental sustainability. Recognising the risks associated with reliance on fossil fuels and the impact of climate change, Denmark embarked on a strategic transition to renewable energy starting in the late 20th century.

Denmark invested early in wind power, which began in the 1970s with the creation of the Danish Wind Industry Association. The country was committed to developing wind turbine technology and scaling up production. This early investment positioned Denmark as a global leader in wind energy technology. The Danish government provided substantial support through subsidies, research funding, and favourable policies to promote wind energy. This included setting ambitious renewable energy targets and creating a stable regulatory environment for investors.

Denmark set clear and ambitious targets for reducing greenhouse gas emissions and increased the share of renewable energy. The Danish government's energy policies included goals for achieving 50% of electricity from wind power by 2020 and transitioning to a carbon-neutral energy system by 2050. Denmark focused on integrating renewable energy into the national grid and investing in energy storage and grid management technologies. The country developed innovative solutions for balancing supply and demand with high levels of intermittent renewable energy.

The growth of Denmark's wind energy sector led to the development of a robust wind turbine manufacturing industry, with companies like Vestas and Siemens Gamesa becoming global leaders in the field. This created economic opportunities and positioned Denmark as a key player in the global renewable energy market. The renewable energy sector became a significant source of employment and economic growth. Denmark's focus on green technology and sustainability contributed to a strong and resilient economy, even as it addressed environmental concerns.

Denmark's early and sustained investment in wind power established it as a global leader in renewable energy. The country's expertise and technology have been widely adopted around the world, enhancing Denmark's reputation and influence in international environmental and in the realm of energy policy. The success of Danish wind turbine manufacturers, has, contributed to significant export revenues and strengthened Denmark's economy. The renewable energy sector has become a major economic driver, with Danish companies exporting technology and services globally.

Denmark's commitment to renewable energy has led to a significant reduction in greenhouse gas emissions. The country is on track to meet its climate targets and has demonstrated that it is possible to achieve substantial environmental benefits while maintaining economic growth. By investing in renewable energy, Denmark has reduced its reliance on imported fossil fuels. This has enhanced national energy security and reduced exposure to global energy price fluctuations.

Denmark's strategic focus on protecting the environment through the development of renewable energy has delivered substantial success. The country has become a global leader in wind power, achieved significant economic benefits, and made meaningful progress toward its environmental goals. This example illustrates how environmental protection can drive innovation, economic growth, and strategic success on the global stage.

Step 9: Be Innovative and Creative

Innovation and creativity are essential drivers of progress and success in various fields, including business, science, technology, and the arts. By fostering a culture that encourages fresh ideas and novel solutions, individuals and organisations can stay competitive, solve complex problems, and unlock new opportunities. This step will discuss key strategies for improving innovation and creativity.

Encourage Open-Mindedness. An open-minded approach is key to fostering innovation and creativity. Encourage individuals to explore new perspectives, challenge assumptions, and consider alternative solutions. Embrace diverse viewpoints and be open to unconventional ideas.

Create a Safe Environment for Experimentation. A supportive environment where individuals can experiment without fear of failure is essential for nurturing creativity. Encourage risk-taking and learn from setbacks. Celebrate efforts, even if they do not lead to immediate success.

Promote Cross-Disciplinary Collaboration. Collaboration across different disciplines can spark innovative ideas and creative solutions. Encourage teams to work together and share insights from their respective fields. Diverse expertise can lead to unexpected breakthroughs.

Provide Time and Resources for Exploration. Allocate dedicated time and resources for creative exploration and experimentation. Whether it's through innovation labs, hackathons, or dedicated project time, providing space for creativity can yield valuable results.

Encourage Continuous Learning. Foster a culture of continuous learning and curiosity. Encourage individuals to stay informed about industry trends, emerging technologies, and new methodologies. Ongoing learning can inspire fresh ideas and enhance problem-solving skills.

Foster a Culture of Feedback and Reflection. Constructive feedback and reflection are essential for growth and improvement. Encourage individuals to seek feedback from peers, mentors, and other sources. Reflecting on successes and failures can lead to new insights and learning.

Embrace Iterative Processes. Adopting an iterative approach to projects allows for continuous improvement and refinement. Encourage prototyping, testing, and iterating based on feedback. This approach enables experimentation and fosters creativity.

Provide Opportunities for Networking. Facilitating networking opportunities can expose individuals to new ideas and perspectives. Attend conferences, workshops, and industry events to connect with others and stay inspired.

Set Clear Goals and Challenges. While creativity often thrives in unstructured environments, setting clear goals and challenges can provide direction and motivation. Define specific problems or objectives for individuals and teams to tackle creatively.

Lead by Example. Leadership plays a critical role in fostering a culture of innovation and creativity. Leaders should model open-mindedness, risk-taking, and curiosity. By encouraging and supporting creative endeavours, leaders set the tone for the entire organisation.

Improving innovation and creativity requires a supportive environment that encourages open-mindedness, experimentation, and collaboration. By providing time and resources for exploration, fostering continuous learning, and embracing iterative processes, individuals and organisations can unlock their creative potential and drive innovation. Leadership support and a culture that celebrates creativity contribute to long-term success and sustainable growth.

In poem 40, attributed to the poet Kabilar, the poet praises the leadership of Pari, a renowned king of the Parambu country. The poem highlights Pari's innovative approach to the idiom and praxis of deft governance and his creative strategies for protecting his people and kingdom. Pari is known for his creative defence strategies, particularly his ability to use the natural landscape to his advantage. He leverages the hills and terrain around his fortress to provide additional protection and to stage strategic counterattacks. Pari's resourcefulness is evident in his ability to use available resources in unique ways. For instance, he is praised for being able to navigate difficult situations and find novel solutions to challenges. Pari's innovative approach to leadership extends to his relationships with others. He is known for his generosity and support of poets, scholars, and artists, which fosters a rich cultural environment. Pari creatively builds alliances with other rulers and tribes, which strengthens his position and contributes to his reputation as a wise and innovative leader.

In this example, Pari's innovative and creative approaches to governance and leadership are highlighted amply. His ability to use the natural environment for strategic purposes and his resourcefulness in building alliances and supporting culture contribute to his reputation as a forward-thinking and visionary monarch.

A modern example where innovation and creativity have delivered strategic success in warfare is the Israeli use of Iron Dome. The Iron Dome is an advanced missile defence system developed by Israel to intercept and destroy short-range threats such as rockets and artillery shells. Its development and deployment have been a significant factor in Israel's military strategy, particularly given the country's security environment with frequent rocket attacks from neighbouring regions.

The Iron Dome system uses radar to detect and track incoming projectiles. Once a threat is identified, the system calculates its trajectory and determines whether it poses a risk to a populated area. If the threat is deemed significant, it launches an interceptor missile to destroy the incoming projectile mid-air. This capability represents a significant leap in missile defence technology, combining rapid detection, tracking, and interception.

The system is designed to be highly cost-effective. Interceptors are only launched against incoming threats that are projected to hit populated areas or critical infrastructure. This selective targeting ensures that resources are used efficiently, reducing the overall cost of defence compared to traditional, more indiscriminate systems.

The Iron Dome can be rapidly deployed and moved to different locations as needed. This flexibility allows it to be positioned where threats are most likely, enhancing its effectiveness in various operational scenarios. The system's adaptability to different environments and its ability to work in tandem with other defence systems have been critical to its success.

The Iron Dome is part of a multi-layered defence strategy that includes other systems such as the Arrow and David's Sling, which target different types of threats. This layered approach ensures comprehensive protection against a range of missile and rocket threats, with Iron Dome specifically addressing short-range threats from regional adversaries.

The effectiveness of the Iron Dome has had a significant psychological impact on both the Israeli public and its adversaries. By successfully intercepting a high percentage of incoming rockets, the system has reduced civilian casualties and damage, bolstering public confidence in the government's ability to protect its citizens. The Iron Dome's success in intercepting rockets has also contributed to a strategic deterrent effect. Adversaries may be less inclined to launch attacks if they perceive a high probability of interception and failure.

The Iron Dome has demonstrated an impressive success rate in intercepting and destroying incoming rockets, with reports suggesting interception rates above 90% during various conflicts. This effectiveness has significantly reduced the impact of rocket attacks on Israeli cities and infrastructure. By intercepting rockets before they can reach their targets, the Iron Dome has played a crucial role in protecting Israeli civilians from harm. This has been particularly evident during periods of heightened conflict, such as the Gaza conflicts. The success of the Iron Dome has led to international interest and sales. Countries facing similar threats have sought to acquire the system or collaborate with Israel to develop similar technologies. The system has thus become a significant export item and a symbol of Israeli military innovation.

The Iron Dome is a prime example of how innovation and creativity in modern warfare can deliver strategic success. Its advanced technology, cost-effective defence strategy, operational flexibility, and integration with a broader defence framework have made it a highly effective tool in protecting Israel from short-range rocket attacks. This success highlights the importance of technological innovation and strategic creativity in achieving military and security objectives in the contemporary world.

Step 10: Be Prepared for Extreme Hardship and Sacrifice

Preparing for extreme hardship and sacrifice is a crucial aspect of building resilience and endurance in both the personal and professional spheres. While such challenges may be difficult to predict or avoid, a well-thought-out approach can help mitigate their impact and enable individuals or organisations to navigate through adversity more effectively. This step will discuss key strategies for preparing for extreme hardship and sacrifice.

Cultivate a Resilient Mindset. Developing a resilient mindset is fundamental to enduring hardship. This involves cultivating mental toughness, emotional stability, and the ability to adapt to change. Practice positive thinking, self-reflection, and mindfulness to strengthen your mental resilience.

Establish a Support Network. Having a strong support network can make a significant difference during times of extreme hardship. Build relationships with friends, family, colleagues, and mentors who can provide emotional support, practical assistance, and advice when needed.

Create a Contingency Plan. Anticipate potential challenges and develop contingency plans to address them. Identify possible risks and scenarios, and outline steps to take in response to each situation. Having a plan in place can reduce panic and help you stay focused when adversity strikes.

Develop Financial Reserves. Financial preparedness is critical for navigating economic hardship. Build an emergency fund and manage your finances prudently to provide a safety net during challenging times. Consider diversifying your income streams to increase financial stability.

Build Skills and Knowledge. Continuously invest in developing your skills and knowledge. Being versatile and adaptable can help you tackle new challenges and find creative solutions during times of hardship. Stay informed about industry trends and emerging opportunities.

Prioritise Health and Well-being. Maintaining physical and mental health is essential for enduring hardship. Prioritise self-care, including exercise, healthy eating, sleep, and stress management. A healthy body and mind provide the strength and resilience needed to face challenges.

Set Realistic Expectations. Extreme hardship often requires significant adjustments and sacrifices. Set realistic expectations for yourself and others and be prepared for setbacks. Focus on what you can control and take one step at a time.

Embrace Change and Uncertainty. Accept that change and uncertainty are inevitable, especially during challenging times. Embrace the opportunity to learn and grow from adversity. Flexibility and openness to new possibilities can lead to unexpected solutions and opportunities.

Stay Committed to Your Values. During times of hardship and sacrifice, staying true to your values can provide a sense of purpose and direction. Reflect on your core principles and let them guide your decisions and actions.

Seek Professional Help if Needed. In some cases, extreme hardship may require professional support, such as counselling, therapy, or financial advice. Do not hesitate to seek help if you need it, as professional guidance can provide clarity and support during challenging times.

Preparing for extreme hardship and sacrifice involves cultivating resilience, building a support network, creating contingency plans, and prioritising health and well-being. By staying committed to your values, embracing change, and setting realistic expectations, you can navigate through adversity with strength and determination. While hardship is never easy, preparation and resilience can help you emerge stronger and more capable of facing future challenges.

In poem 192, attributed to the poet Pisiranthaiyar, there is a focus on the character Pisiranthaiyar himself and his dedication to preparing for extreme hardship and sacrifice for the sake of his values and beliefs. Pisiranthaiyar is described as someone who lives a simple and austere life, demonstrating his willingness to sacrifice material comforts in favour of a life devoted to wisdom and virtue. Pisiranthaiyar's commitment to his values, particularly his pursuit of knowledge and wisdom, is evident in his readiness to endure hardships. He prioritises his quest for truth over personal comfort. Despite his simple lifestyle, Pisiranthaiyar takes on the responsibility of guiding and teaching others. He shares his knowledge and wisdom with those who seek it, demonstrating his dedication to a greater cause. Pisiranthaiyar's life serves as an example of someone who prepares for extreme hardship and sacrifice. His actions inspire others to follow a similar path of dedication and resilience.

This example illustrates how Pisiranthaiyar's preparation for extreme hardship and sacrifice is rooted in his commitment to values such as wisdom and virtue. His life serves as a model for others who seek to prioritise higher ideals and navigate challenges with resilience and determination.

A modern example where enduring extreme hardship and sacrifice delivered strategic success is the Ukrainian resistance and resilience during the 2022 Russian invasion of Ukraine. In February 2022, Russia launched a large-scale invasion of Ukraine, marking the beginning of one of the most significant conflicts in Europe since World War II. Ukraine faced overwhelming military aggression, with significant challenges including a larger and better-equipped opponent, widespread destruction, and severe economic strain.

The Ukrainian military faced extreme hardship, including intense combat, limited resources, and the initial surprise of the invasion. Ukrainian forces engaged in fierce resistance, utilising innovative tactics and making significant sacrifices to defend key positions and cities. Ukrainian civilians also played a crucial role. Many volunteered for territorial defence units or provided support through various means, including logistical assistance, intelligence gathering, and maintaining morale. Cities like Kyiv, Mariupol, and Kharkiv experienced heavy bombardment, and the civilian population endured substantial hardships.

The invasion led to severe economic disruptions, including damage to infrastructure, a significant drop in economic activity, and displacement of millions of people. Despite these hardships, the Ukrainian government worked to maintain economic stability and ensure the continuity of essential services. Key infrastructure such as power plants, transportation networks, and communication systems were targeted by Russian attacks. Ukrainians, both military and civilian, endured significant hardships to repair and maintain these critical systems under constant threat.

Ukraine leveraged its resilience to gain international sympathy and support. The Ukrainian government and President Volodymyr Zelenskyy effectively communicated their struggle to the global community, leading to widespread international support, sanctions against Russia, and military and humanitarian aid from numerous countries. The persistence of the Ukrainian people and their ability to withstand extreme hardship garnered substantial international backing, including military aid, financial support, and political pressure on Russia.

The extreme hardships faced by Ukrainians fostered a strong sense of national unity and determination. The resolve to defend their country and sovereignty became a driving force for both military and civilian efforts, contributing to their ability to withstand prolonged conflict. The enduring sacrifice and resilience of the Ukrainian people have been widely recognised and praised internationally. This has bolstered global support and solidarity, further isolating Russia diplomatically and economically.

Ukrainian forces successfully defended key cities and launched counteroffensives, retaking territories previously occupied by Russian forces. The resistance contributed to significant strategic setbacks for Russia and prevented a swift victory. The ability to endure hardship and continue resisting prolonged the conflict, disrupting Russian plans and strategy. The war became more costly and challenging for Russia, both militarily and economically.

The strategic success of Ukrainian resilience led to an increased and augmented international military and humanitarian aid, strengthening Ukraine's ability to continue the fight. The unity and resolve displayed by Ukraine helped secure vital support from Western allies. The international community imposed severe economic sanctions on Russia in response to its invasion, contributing to significant economic challenges for Russia and altering its strategic calculations.

Ukraine's ability to endure extreme hardship and sacrifice helped preserve its sovereignty and national identity. The resistance efforts have solidified Ukraine's position as a resilient and sovereign state in the face of aggression.

The Ukrainian resistance during the 2022 Russian invasion exemplifies how enduring extreme hardship and sacrifice can deliver strategic success. The resilience of the Ukrainian military and civilian population, combined with effective international diplomacy and support, played a crucial role in withstanding aggression, gaining global backing, and achieving significant military and political outcomes. This example highlights the profound impact that perseverance and sacrifice can have in modern warfare and international conflict.

THE *PURANANURU* – A SUMMARY

The *Purananuru* is a remarkable work that offers a unique glimpse into the lives, values, and beliefs of ancient Tamil society. It covers key subjects such as:

- Leadership and Governance.
- Diplomacy and Alliances.
- Ethics and Virtue.
- Adaptability and Resilience.
- Cultural Soft Power.
- Social Cohesion and Unity.
- Environmental Awareness.
- Innovation and Creativity.
- Courage and Bravery.

It is possible to derive a 10-step process from the *Purananuru* that can assist with adopting a strategic approach within one's personal life or an organisation. Most readers will probably think that these 10 steps to adopting a strategic approach are just common sense. However, a cursory study of failed historic strategies shows that most were missing one or more of the steps listed above. While the steps are easy to articulate, they are incredibly tricky to implement and measure. The steps are:

Step 1: Ensure Your Strategy Focuses on People

- Understand the Needs and Goals of People.
- Promote Inclusivity and Diversity.
- Align Strategy with Values and Culture.
- Encourage Collaboration and Participation.

- Focus on Employee and Stakeholder Well-being.
- Create Clear Communication Channels.
- Adaptability and Flexibility.
- Empowerment and Autonomy.
- Consider Ethical and Social Responsibility.
- Measure Success and Impact.

Step 2: Always Attempt Diplomacy First and Reach Out to Potential Partners or Allies

- Effective Communication.
- Negotiation and Mediation.
- Cultural Awareness and Sensitivity.
- Conflict Resolution and Peacebuilding.
- Confidentiality and Discretion.
- Strategic Thinking and Analysis.
- Relationship Building.
- Adherence to International Law and Norms.
- Patience and Persistence.
- Adaptability and Resilience.
- Ethical Conduct.
- Public Diplomacy.

Step 3: Power and Strength Flow from Prosperity. Prioritise Economic Issues in your Strategy

- Assess the Economic Landscape.
- Identify Key Economic Objectives.
- Allocate Resources Effectively.
- Monitor Cash Flow and Profit Margins.
- Optimise Operational Efficiency.
- Invest in Innovation and Growth.

- Mitigate Economic Risks.
- Establish Partnerships and Collaborations.
- Stay Informed and Adapt.
- Measure Economic Impact and Outcomes.

Step 4: Ensure your Strategy Aligns with your Values

- Identify Core Values.
- Assess Current Practices.
- Set Clear Objectives.
- Incorporate Values into Decision-Making.
- Communicate and Collaborate.
- Evaluate and Adjust.
- Lead by Example.
- Seek Feedback and Reflection.
- Stay Informed and Adaptable.
- Be Consistent.

Step 5: Stay Flexible and be Prepared to Adapt and Improvise

- Cultivate a Flexible Mindset.
- Stay Calm and Focused.
- Gather Information and Assess the Situation.
- Leverage Previous Experience.
- Break Down the Problem.
- Be Resourceful and Creative.
- Communicate Effectively.
- Embrace Collaboration and Teamwork.
- Be Willing to Experiment.
- Stay Positive and Resilient.
- Reassess and Adjust as Needed.
- Learn from the Experience.

Step 6: Make your Vision or Offer Attractive to Stakeholders. Carrots Work Better than Sticks

- Craft a Compelling Narrative.
- Align with Stakeholders' Interests.
- Involve Stakeholders in the Development Process.
- Set Clear, Achievable Goals.
- Demonstrate a Path to Success.
- Showcase Tangible Benefits and Impact.
- Communicate Regularly and Transparently.
- Demonstrate Leadership Commitment.
- Be Adaptive and Responsive.
- Celebrate Milestones and Achievements.

Step 7: Ensure Solidarity and Cohesion at Home

- Establish a Clear Vision and Shared Goals.
- Promote Open Communication.
- Foster a Positive Organisational Culture.
- Encourage Collaboration and Teamwork.
- Provide Opportunities for Professional Growth.
- Set Clear Expectations and Accountability.
- Celebrate Achievements and Milestones.
- Address Conflicts Promptly and Fairly.
- Encourage Employee Involvement in Decision-Making.
- Lead by Example.

Step 8: Protect the Environment

- Understand the Environmental Impact.
- Set Clear Environmental Goals.
- Incorporate Sustainable Practices.
- Follow Environmental Regulations and Standards.

- Promote a Culture of Environmental Awareness.
- Engage Stakeholders.
- Monitor and Measure Progress.
- Adopt Green Innovation and Technology.
- Communicate and Report.
- Be Adaptable and Open to Change.

Step 9: Be Innovative and Creative

- Encourage Open-Mindedness.
- Create a Safe Environment for Experimentation.
- Promote Cross-Disciplinary Collaboration.
- Provide Time and Resources for Exploration.
- Encourage Continuous Learning.
- Foster a Culture of Feedback and Reflection.
- Embrace Iterative Processes.
- Provide Opportunities for Networking.
- Set Clear Goals and Challenges.
- Lead by Example.

Step 10: Be Prepared for Extreme Hardship and Sacrifice.

- Cultivate a Resilient Mindset.
- Establish a Support Network.
- Create a Contingency Plan.
- Develop Financial Reserves.
- Build Skills and Knowledge.
- Prioritise Health and Well-being.
- Set Realistic Expectations.
- Embrace Change and Uncertainty.
- Stay Committed to Your Values.
- Seek Professional Help if Needed.

PART 3

STRATEGIC TOOLSETS

In Part 3, we look at strategic toolsets that can help a leader to actually 'do strategy.' Strategy is very different to simple plans and tactics. The complexity and dynamic nature of 'wicked' problems make them tough to deal with and linear 'Standard Operating Procedures' can make matters worse as they lack creativity and flexibility. However, Sun Tzu (Chapter 5) and Julius Caesar (Chapter 6) give us some useful toolsets that can help senior leaders and their teams devise successful strategy to deal with a specific problem set. Please note, these toolsets should not be followed slavishly. They are designed more as a checklist and prompt rather than a rigid set of rules.

Chapter Five

Sun Tzu

"If you know the enemy and know yourself, you need not fear the result of a hundred battles. If you know yourself but not the enemy, for every victory gained you will also suffer a defeat. If you know neither the enemy nor yourself, you will succumb in every battle."

—***Sun Tzu***

In This Chapter

- Who was Sun Tzu?
- The Fundamentals of Sun Tzu's Teachings:
  * Preparation and Planning.
  * Adaptability and Flexibility.
  * Deception and Indirect Approach.
  * Know Yourself and Know the Enemy.
  * The Importance of Timing.

    * Winning Without Fighting.
    * Leadership and Discipline.
- The Five Factors:
    * The Way.
    * Heaven.
    * Earth.
    * The Commander.
    * Method and Discipline.
- A Strategic Toolset Based on Sun Tzu's Art of War.
- Sun Tzu – A Summary.

Who was Sun Tzu?

Sun Tzu was an ancient and classical Chinese military strategist, general, and philosopher. He is traditionally believed to have lived during the Eastern Zhou period in China, around the 6th century BCE, though his exact dates of birth and death are uncertain. Sun Tzu is best known as the author of *The Art of War* (*Sunzi Bingfa* in Chinese), a classic treatise on military strategy and tactics that has had a profound influence on military thought and practice throughout history.

The Art of War is a comprehensive guide to warfare and strategy, covering topics such as planning, tactics, leadership, and the conduct of battle. It highlights the importance of flexibility, deception, and understanding both oneself and the enemy in achieving victory. The work is notable for its insights into the psychology of warfare and the importance of careful planning and adaptability. Sun Tzu's teachings have been studied and applied not only in military contexts but also in business, politics, and other fields. His strategic principles have stood the test of time and remain relevant in modern strategic thinking.

The Fundamentals of Sun Tzu's Teachings

Sun Tzu's approach to strategy is holistic and articulates the importance of understanding the fundamental principles of warfare. His philosophy encourages strategic thinking as a means of avoiding conflict when possible and achieving victory with minimal confrontation. The fundamental principles of his philosophy are:

Preparation and Planning. Sun Tzu emphasises the importance of thorough preparation and planning before engaging in battle. He advocates for understanding both one's own strengths and weaknesses, as well as those of the enemy. This includes gathering intelligence, assessing terrain, and evaluating logistical support.

A prime example of a strategy that utilised Sun Tzu's fundamentals of planning and preparation is the operation to kill Osama bin Laden, known as Operation Neptune Spear, conducted by the United States in May 2011. Osama bin Laden, the leader of al-Qaeda, was responsible for orchestrating the September 11, 2001, terrorist attacks on the United States. He had evaded capture for nearly a decade, hiding in various locations across the Middle East and South Asia. After years of intelligence gathering, the CIA located bin Laden's compound in Abbottabad, Pakistan, in August 2010.

Once Bin Laden's location was confirmed, the U.S. government, under President Barack Obama, began a highly secretive and meticulous planning process for a mission to either capture or kill him. The operation was led by the CIA and involved elite Navy SEALs from SEAL Team 6.

The CIA and other intelligence agencies gathered extensive information about the compound, including its layout, security measures, and the daily routines of its inhabitants. This intelligence was critical in formulating a precise plan. The planners considered multiple scenarios, including potential Pakistani military intervention, the possibility of Bin Laden escaping, and the risk to U.S. forces. Various contingencies were developed to address these risks.

The SEALs conducted many rehearsals on a full-scale replica of the compound constructed in the U.S. These rehearsals helped the team to familiarise themselves with the layout, practice their assault, and refine their approach to minimise risks and increase the likelihood of success.

The operation was kept highly confidential to prevent any leaks that could compromise its success. The U.S. also carefully managed diplomatic relations with Pakistan to avoid alerting the Pakistani government and military, which might have inadvertently tipped off Bin Laden. The timing of the operation was critical. It was conducted at night to minimise the risk of detection and to take advantage of the SEALs' night-fighting capabilities.

On May 2, 2011, Navy SEALs executed the operation with precision. They infiltrated Pakistan via helicopters, breached the compound, and conducted a 40-minute raid that resulted in the death of Osama bin Laden. The SEALs then exfiltrated, taking Bin Laden's body with them for verification.

The success of Operation Neptune Spear is a testament to Sun Tzu's advice on the importance of meticulous planning and thorough preparation. By gathering intelligence, assessing risks, rehearsing extensively, and executing with precision, the U.S. was able to achieve a strategic victory with minimal casualties and without escalating tensions in the region. The operation not only eliminated a key terrorist leader but also dealt a significant psychological blow to al-Qaeda.

Adaptability and Flexibility. A core aspect of Sun Tzu's philosophy is the ability to adapt strategies based on the changing circumstances of a situation. He believes that no plan should be rigid, and that commanders must be willing to adjust their tactics as new information becomes available.

An example of a strategy that showcases Sun Tzu's fundamental of adaptability and flexibility delivering victory is the Battle of Marathon, fought in 490 BCE between the Greek city-state of Athens and the Persian Empire. The Persian Empire, under King Darius I, invaded Greece and landed their forces near the plains of Marathon. The Persians had a significant advantage in terms of numbers and resources. The Athenians, aware of the threat, quickly assembled an army to confront the Persians.

The Athenian general Miltiades assessed the situation and recognised that the Persians had a larger army but lacked familiarity with the terrain. He decided to engage the Persians in battle despite the numerical disparity. Miltiades adapted his battle formations to suit the conditions. He arranged his forces in a wide line, thinning out the centre and strengthening the wings. This strategy aimed to surround the Persian forces from both sides.

The Athenians moderated their tactics by launching a surprise attack at a run, catching the Persians off guard. This swift and unexpected assault disrupted the Persian formations. Once the Athenians' centre was under pressure from the Persians, Miltiades adapted his strategy by pushing his stronger wings forward. This manoeuvre allowed the Athenians to surround the Persians and exploit the enemy's vulnerabilities. The Athenian forces, through their flexible tactics and rapid manoeuvres, were able to overcome the larger Persian army. The Battle of Marathon ended in a decisive victory for Athens, demonstrating the effectiveness of adaptability and flexibility in strategy.

The Battle of Marathon serves adroitly as a classic example of how Sun Tzu's fundamental of adaptability and flexibility can lead to victory in challenging situations. General Miltiades' ability to assess the situation, adapt his strategies, and exploit the enemy's weaknesses allowed the Athenians to triumph against a larger and well-equipped Persian force. This battle is a testament to the value of being flexible and responsive in the face of uncertainty and change, aligning with Sun Tzu's teachings on the importance of adaptability in warfare.

Deception and Indirect Approach. Sun Tzu is known for his focus on using deception, guile, deceit and misdirection to gain an advantage over the enemy. By making the enemy believe one thing while executing another, a commander can exploit weaknesses and create opportunities for victory. The Battle of Chibi, fought in 208 CE, is a famous battle from Chinese history that demonstrates the use of deception and indirect strategy, in line with Sun Tzu's teachings.

The battle took place during the late Eastern Han Dynasty, involving a conflict between the warlords Cao Cao and a coalition of Sun Quan and Liu Bei. Cao Cao had a significant advantage in terms of troop numbers, with over 200,000 soldiers, while Sun Quan and Liu Bei had a much smaller force of around 50,000.

To confront Cao Cao's massive army, the coalition forces used the tactic of a feigned retreat. This manoeuvre involved pretending to withdraw from battle, thereby luring Cao Cao's forces into a vulnerable position. Once Cao Cao's forces were drawn into the trap, the coalition used the geography of the area to launch an ambush. By using the river and surrounding terrain, they were able to surround and attack Cao Cao's forces from multiple angles. The coalition took advantage of the strong winds blowing in their favour. They set fire to Cao Cao's fleet of ships, causing chaos and devastation within Cao Cao's ranks. The coalition's strategy not only physically outmanoeuvred Cao Cao's forces, but also had a psychological impact. Cao Cao's troops, facing a surprise attack and their fleet in flames, quickly lost morale.

The strategy led to a decisive victory for Sun Quan and Liu Bei, despite their smaller force. Cao Cao's army suffered significant losses, and he was forced to retreat. This example from the Battle of Chibi showcases the successful application of Sun Tzu's principles, particularly the use of deception, surprise, and exploiting the environment for strategic advantage. By employing Sun Tzu's philosophy, the coalition forces were able to overcome a larger enemy and secure a significant victory. This strategy serves as a classic example of how Sun Tzu's teachings can be effectively used in real-world situations to achieve success through clever and innovative tactics.

Know Yourself and Know the Enemy. One of Sun Tzu's most famous maxims is the importance of knowing both oneself and the enemy. This deep understanding allows for more precise and effective planning and execution of strategy. One famous example is the Battle of Midway during World War II, where the United States Navy achieved a decisive victory against the Imperial Japanese Navy. The Battle of Midway took place in June 1942, six months after Japan's attack on Pearl Harbor. The Japanese, seeking to eliminate the United States as a strategic power in the Pacific, planned to lure the U.S. fleet into a trap at Midway Island. The goal was to destroy the U.S. aircraft carriers that had escaped the attack on Pearl Harbor.

The U.S. Navy had a significant advantage in this battle due to superior intelligence. American codebreakers had successfully deciphered Japanese communications, giving the U.S. a deft insight into Japan's plans. They knew the time, location, and strength of the Japanese attack. This intelligence allowed Admiral Chester W. Nimitz, the U.S. Pacific Fleet commander, to prepare and position his forces effectively.

Nimitz also understood the strengths and limitations of his own forces. The U.S. fleet was outnumbered, but Nimitz knew his aircraft carriers and airmen were highly capable. He used this knowledge to devise a strategy that maximised the U.S. advantages. By carefully positioning his forces and timing their engagement, he ensured that the U.S. Navy could strike first and decisively.

When the Japanese launched their attack on Midway, they were met with an unexpected and overwhelming American response. U.S. carrier-based aircraft managed to surprise and sink four Japanese aircraft carriers, turning the tide of the war in the Pacific. The Japanese Navy, which had been on the offensive, was forced into a defensive posture for the remainder of the war.

The Battle of Midway is a classic example of how knowing both yourself and the enemy can deliver a strategic victory. The U.S. Navy's understanding of Japanese plans, combined with an honest assessment of its own capabilities, allowed it to outmanoeuvre and outfight a numerically superior enemy. This victory was a turning point in the Pacific War and showcased the enduring relevance of Sun Tzu's wisdom.

The Importance of Timing. Sun Tzu emphasises the significance of timing in warfare. Knowing when to strike, when to retreat, and when to exploit openings can be decisive factors in achieving victory. A strategic example of where Sun Tzu's fundamental of the importance of timing led to victory is the Battle of Trenton, fought on December 26, 1776, during the American Revolutionary War. This battle demonstrates how George Washington's precise timing of the attack played a crucial role in securing a decisive victory.

The Continental Army, led by General George Washington, was facing a difficult situation in late 1776. After a series of defeats, Washington's forces had retreated across the Delaware River into Pennsylvania. The British and Hessian troops, under the command of Colonel Johann Rall, were stationed in Trenton, New Jersey, on the other side of the river. Washington knew that a victory was necessary to boost the morale of his troops and revive the revolutionary cause.

Washington planned a surprise attack on the Hessian forces in Trenton. He chose to cross the Delaware River on the night of December 25, 1776, during a severe winter storm, when the Hessians would least expect an attack. Washington's forces crossed the icy river at night and then marched toward Trenton in the early hours of December 26. The timing was carefully chosen to maintain the element of surprise and catch the enemy off guard.

Washington's well-timed attack took advantage of the Hessians' relaxed state. The Hessians had been celebrating Christmas and were not prepared for an attack. This surprise allowed Washington's forces to quickly gain the upper hand. Once Washington's troops reached Trenton, they launched a swift and coordinated assault. The Hessian forces, caught off guard and disorganised, were quickly overwhelmed.

The Battle of Trenton resulted in a significant victory for the Continental Army. Washington's timing and the element of surprise allowed his forces to defeat the Hessian troops with minimal losses. The victory boosted the morale of the Continental Army and reinvigorated the revolutionary cause.

The Battle of Trenton is a good example of how the importance of timing, as articulated by Sun Tzu, can usher in victory. Washington's decision to launch a surprise attack on the morning after Christmas, during adverse weather conditions, caught the enemy unprepared and delivered a crucial win for the American forces. This battle underscores the significance of choosing the right moment to strike and the impact that timing can have on the outcome of a conflict.

Winning Without Fighting. Sun Tzu stressed that the best victory is one achieved without resorting to direct confrontation. By using strategies such as alliances, diplomacy, and psychological warfare, a commander can avoid unnecessary bloodshed and achieve their objectives more efficiently. An example of a strategy that aligns with Sun Tzu's fundamental of winning without fighting is the *Fall of Constantinople* in 1453. This event marked the end of the Byzantine Empire and the rise of the Ottoman Empire. While there was significant fighting involved, the Ottoman Sultan Mehmed II successfully used non-combative strategies to achieve his objectives and win without unnecessary bloodshed in certain aspects of the siege.

The Byzantine Empire, also known as the Eastern Roman Empire, was in a weakened state by the mid-15th century. Its capital, Constantinople, was a valuable and strategic city due to its location and economic importance. The Ottoman Sultan Mehmed II saw the capture of Constantinople as crucial to expanding his empire and establishing a stronghold in the region.

Mehmed II worked to isolate the Byzantines diplomatically by making alliances with other neighbouring states. He ensured that they would not come to the aid of Constantinople during the siege. Mehmed II used psychological tactics to pressure the Byzantines. For example, he demanded the surrender of the city multiple times, offering lenient terms in exchange for their compliance. This approach sowed doubt and fear among the defenders. Mehmed II blockaded Constantinople's land and sea access, preventing any external aid from reaching the city. By cutting off supplies, he aimed to weaken the defenders and force them to surrender without a full-scale battle.

Mehmed II employed advanced siege engineering, such as building a large cannon to breach the city's formidable walls. This technological superiority placed additional pressure on the Byzantines. Mehmed II attempted to negotiate with the Byzantines, proposing terms of surrender that included allowing the citizens to leave the city unharmed. Though the Byzantines ultimately resisted, his willingness to negotiate demonstrated his preference for a peaceful resolution.

While the fall of Constantinople did involve significant fighting, Mehmed II's use of diplomatic isolation, psychological warfare, and blockades contributed to the Ottoman victory. His strategic approach aimed to minimise unnecessary bloodshed and achieve his objectives with minimal direct conflict.

The collapse of Constantinople demonstrates how Mehmed II employed tactics in line with Sun Tzu's fundamental of winning without fighting. By isolating the city, cutting off supplies, and employing psychological and technological advantages, Mehmed II put significant pressure on the Byzantines, aiming to achieve victory with minimal combat. Though the final outcome involved intense fighting, the strategies used illustrate Sun Tzu's principles of achieving victory without prolonged or excessive conflict.

Leadership and Discipline. Effective leadership and discipline are crucial for success in Sun Tzu's philosophy. Commanders must be able to inspire and direct their troops, while also maintaining order and cohesion within their ranks. An example of where Sun Tzu's fundamental of leadership and discipline delivered victory is the Battle of Gaugamela, also known as the Battle of Arbela, fought on October 1, 331 BCE. This battle was one of the most significant victories of Alexander the Great during his campaign against the Persian Empire.

Alexander the Great, the King of Macedonia, was on a mission to conquer the Persian Empire. In the lead-up to the Battle of Gaugamela, Alexander's forces faced a larger Persian army led by King Darius III. The battle took place on the plains of Gaugamela (near modern-day Iraq), and the outcome would determine the future of the Persian Empire.

Alexander exhibited strong leadership by personally leading his troops into battle. He was known for his charismatic presence and ability to inspire his soldiers with his courage and strategic vision. Alexander's army was highly disciplined and trained, with soldiers skilled in various combat techniques and formations. This discipline allowed them to execute complex manoeuvres on the battlefield.

Alexander's army utilised the phalanx formation, which was a tight infantry formation known for its strength and resilience. This formation provided a strong defensive and offensive advantage during the battle. Alexander's forces were trained to adapt to changing battlefield conditions. They could quickly respond to enemy movements and adjust their strategies accordingly. Alexander executed a strategic manoeuvre known as the *hammer and anvil* tactic. He led his cavalry on a diagonal charge against the Persian left flank, creating a gap in the enemy lines. This allowed his infantry to advance and exploit the opening.

The Battle of Gaugamela resulted in a decisive victory for Alexander the Great and his forces. His leadership and the discipline of his army played a crucial role in overcoming the larger Persian army. The victory marked a turning point in Alexander's campaign and led to the eventual fall of the Persian Empire.

The Battle of Gaugamela is a historic and classic example of how strong leadership and disciplined forces can deliver victory in battle. Alexander the Great's ability to lead his troops effectively, combined with the discipline and adaptability of his army, allowed him to achieve a significant win against a larger and more powerful opponent. This battle underscores the importance of Sun Tzu's principles of leadership and discipline in achieving strategic success.

THE FIVE FACTORS

Sun Tzu also outlines five key factors that influence success in warfare. These are as follows:

The Way. Sun Tzu's *The Way* refers to one of the key concepts in his famous military treatise, *The Art of War*. In the text, *The Way* (Dao in Chinese) is an essential element of successful military strategy and leadership. It encompasses the alignment of the ruler, the army, and the people with a shared purpose and moral code.

According to Sun Tzu, the ruler who follows *The Way,* can create harmony and unity within the state, leading to the full support of the people for the ruler's decisions and goals. *The Way* underlines the importance of clear communication, mutual trust, and a sense of duty between the ruler and their subordinates. This unity is crucial for maintaining an effective military force and achieving strategic objectives.

In broader terms, *The Way* can be understood as the guiding principles or philosophy that underpin a successful strategy, whether in warfare or other areas of life. It involves aligning one's actions with a higher purpose and maintaining integrity, discipline, and focus in pursuing goals.

Heaven. In Sun Tzu's treatise, The Art of War, Heaven (Tian in Chinese) is one of the five fundamental factors that determine the outcome of a battle or war. *Heaven* specifically refers to natural and environmental elements that can affect military strategy and operations. This includes factors like weather conditions (rain, wind, temperature), natural disasters, and the changing seasons. Understanding and accounting for these factors is crucial for making strategic decisions such as when to engage in battle, how to position troops, and which routes to take. By considering *Heaven*, a skilled strategist can use the natural environment to their advantage and gain an upper hand in battle.

Earth. In Sun Tzu's *The Art of War*, *Earth* (Di in Chinese) is one of the five fundamental factors that determine the outcome of a battle or war. *Earth* refers to the physical geography and terrain that can influence military strategy and tactics. This includes factors such as:

- **Distances**: The space between different locations and how they can impact movement and communication.
- **Topography**: The shape and features of the landscape, such as hills, mountains, valleys, and plains.
- **Natural obstacles**: Rivers, forests, and other features that can impede or aid troop movement.
- **Strategic positions**: Key locations that provide tactical advantages, such as high ground or choke points.

A skilled military leader takes these geographical factors into account when planning operations, positioning troops, and manoeuvring in battle. Understanding the *Earth* allows a commander to make strategic decisions that can optimise resources, avoid unnecessary conflicts, and gain advantages over the enemy. Sun Tzu described 'Nine Grounds' to help with understanding the 'Earth'.

The Nine Grounds. Sun Tzu categorises different types of terrain or situations into nine grounds, each with its own strategic implications. Understanding the terrain and adapting strategies accordingly is crucial for success. The grounds include:

- **Dispersive.** Dispersive Ground refers to terrain where an army is operating within its own territory, close to its base or home. In such areas, the soldiers naturally feel a strong connection to the land and people, and they may be more motivated to defend it. However, the soldiers might also be tempted to scatter and focus on personal matters rather than staying unified and disciplined. Sun Tzu advises commanders to keep the troops tightly controlled on dispersive ground to avoid having them stray too far or lose focus on the main objectives. By maintaining order and discipline, the commander can harness the soldiers' familiarity with the land and their motivation to protect it, turning these factors into strategic advantages.

- **Facile.** Each type of ground presents its own challenges and opportunities for a military commander. "Facile Ground" or "Light Ground" is often understood as easy terrain, where troops can move freely without significant obstacles. This type of ground may seem advantageous at first glance because it allows for quick movement and deployment, but it can also make the army vulnerable to surprise attacks if the commander is not cautious. On light ground, the strategy should focus on speed and flexibility while maintaining vigilance for enemy movements and potential traps. The open, easy-to-move terrain can be both an asset and a liability, depending on how well the commander adapts to the situation.
- **Contentious.** Contentious Ground refers to terrain that is favourable to either side in a battle and is, therefore, likely to be contested by both sides. This type of ground is strategically significant because control over it can provide advantage to the side that holds it. It may be a location that offers a tactical advantage, such as a key pass, a resource-rich area, or a position that can control access to other parts of the battlefield. Sun Tzu advises commanders to be cautious when operating on contentious ground. To gain the upper hand, a commander should be prepared for direct confrontation and should aim to assert dominance over the contested area. It's important to recognise the importance of controlling this ground and to use it to one's advantage while denying it to the enemy.
- **Open**. Open Ground refers to terrain that is free of obstacles and easily accessible from multiple directions. It is an area where troops can move freely without being hindered by natural barriers such as mountains, rivers, or forests. This type of ground allows for easy manoeuvrability and can be advantageous for both advancing and

retreating forces. In discussing open ground, Sun Tzu advises that the commander should ensure that the army uses the freedom of movement to its advantage, maintaining flexibility and preparedness for potential enemy attacks. At the same time, the commander should be cautious because the enemy may also take advantage of the open terrain for their own strategies. On open ground, it is essential to maintain a well-ordered formation and remain vigilant, as the enemy may approach from any direction. The army should also be prepared to adjust its strategy quickly, as open ground can make it challenging to predict the enemy's movements and intentions.

- **Intermediary Ground**. This refers to terrain that lies between the territories of opposing forces, making it a point of strategic importance because it allows access to multiple destinations and can connect different regions or armies. In modern terms, it can be thought of as territory that encompasses crossroads, highways, or other transit points crucial for movement and control. On intermediary ground, Sun Tzu advises commanders to carefully evaluate the strategic significance of the area and the potential risks and benefits of controlling it. The commander must decide whether to advance, retreat, or stay put based on the overall strategic situation and the movements of the enemy.
- **Serious Ground**. This points to a terrain where an army's survival or strategic advantage is at stake. It is ground where the army's position is so crucial that losing it could lead to serious consequences, such as being cut off from supplies or being surrounded by the enemy. This type of ground can be strategically important because it often plays a pivotal role in determining the outcome of a battle. On serious ground, Sun Tzu advises commanders to take decisive and bold actions to secure the position and maintain the army's advantage. This may involve positioning the troops in a defensive stance to hold the ground or launching an aggressive attack to capture or defend key points.
- **Difficult Ground**. Difficult Ground refers to terrain that is challenging to navigate due to its physical features such as

mountains, steep hills, dense forests, narrow passes, marshes, or other obstacles. Such terrain can impede the movement of troops and supplies, making it more difficult for an army to advance or manoeuvre effectively. When dealing with difficult ground, Sun Tzu advises commanders to be cautious and vigilant. The challenging terrain can be both an asset and a liability depending on how well it is managed. Difficult ground can provide natural defences and protection against enemy attacks. It may also allow a smaller force to hold off a larger one by using the terrain to their advantage. However, navigating difficult ground can be slow and laborious, potentially leaving troops vulnerable to ambushes or other threats. Supplies and communication may also be hindered. In order to effectively operate on difficult ground, a commander should adjust tactics to make use of the terrain for cover and protection. He ought to take careful, calculated steps to avoid being ambushed or outflanked. Identify and control strategic locations such as passes, heights, or crossings.

- **Hemmed-In Ground**. This refers to terrain that restricts the movement of an army because it is surrounded by obstacles or natural barriers such as mountains, rivers, or marshes. This type of ground can be challenging for an army because it can limit their options for manoeuvre and escape, potentially leaving them vulnerable to enemy attacks. When operating on hemmed-in ground, Sun Tzu advises commanders to take a proactive and decisive approach. The army must hold its position and defend against enemy attacks to avoid being overrun. Confined space must be utilised effectively, potentially taking advantage of natural barriers for defence. Troops must be motivated by highlighting the need to fight for survival and the importance of maintaining their position. Sun Tzu states that on hemmed-in ground, there may be little room for retreat or manoeuvre, so a strong, unified defence is essential. By holding their position and using the terrain to their advantage, an army can resist enemy attacks and potentially turn the situation in their favour.
- **Desperate Ground**. This refers to terrain where an army's survival

is at risk, often due to being surrounded or facing an immediate threat of annihilation. This type of ground is where the army has no choice but to fight for its survival because retreat or surrender is not an option. When operating on desperate ground, Sun Tzu advises commanders to take bold and resolute action while instilling a strong sense of urgency and fighting spirit among the soldiers by emphasising the critical nature of the war and battlefield scenario and the need to fight for survival. Time is of the essence on desperate ground, so decisions must be made swiftly and effectively. By eliminating any chance of escape, soldiers will fight more fiercely, knowing that their only option is to win or perish. Sun Tzu notes that when soldiers understand that they are fighting for their lives, they will display extraordinary bravery and tenacity. By acknowledging the gravity of the situation and motivating the troops accordingly, a skilled commander can harness the desperation of the situation to their advantage, potentially turning the tide of battle.

The Commander. The Commander refers to the military leader's abilities and qualities, which play a crucial role in determining the success of an army. Sun Tzu outlines several key characteristics that a successful commander should possess:

- **Wisdom**: The ability to understand situations, assess risks, and make sound decisions.
- **Sincerity**: Being honest and straightforward, which inspires trust and loyalty among subordinates.
- **Benevolence**: Showing kindness and concern for the well-being of soldiers.
- **Courage**: Demonstrating bravery and willingness to take calculated risks when necessary.
- **Strictness**: Maintaining discipline and enforcing rules to ensure order and effectiveness within the army.

A capable commander can lead the army effectively, inspire loyalty and respect, and make strategic decisions that lead to victory. Sun Tzu states that the quality of the commander can be a decisive factor in the outcome of a battle.

Method and Discipline. Method and Discipline refers to the internal organisation, structure, and discipline within the army. This includes the establishment and enforcement of rules, protocols, and procedures that ensure the effective functioning of the military force. Key aspects of Method and Discipline include:

- **Organisational structure**: The division of the army into units with clear hierarchies and roles, such as commanders, officers, and soldiers.
- **Training and preparation**: Ensuring that soldiers are well-trained and prepared for battle.
- **Rules and regulations**: The establishment of clear rules and guidelines for behaviour and conduct within the army.
- **Discipline and enforcement**: The enforcement of rules and discipline to maintain order and effectiveness.

A disciplined army is one that can execute strategies efficiently, follow orders precisely, and maintain cohesion even in the face of adversity. Sun Tzu underscores the importance of strict discipline and strong methods as essential for achieving victory in battle.

These factors encompass the moral, environmental, situational, leadership, and organisational aspects of strategy, providing a comprehensive framework. The strategic toolset below is drawn from Sun Tzu's teachings.

A Strategic Toolset Based on Sun Tzu's Art of War

Step 1: The Way. Define the Desired Strategic Outcome and Create a Compelling Narrative on Why the Organisation Must Prevail and How it Will Achieve Success

Defining the desired strategic outcome and creating a compelling narrative are critical components of a successful strategic plan for any organisation. This step helps align the organisation toward a common goal and motivate individuals to work together to achieve success. Here's how to approach this process:

Defining the Desired Strategic Outcome

- **Understand the Organisation's Vision and Mission**. Begin with a clear understanding of the organisation's vision (where it wants to be in the future) and mission (its purpose). This provides a foundation for setting strategic goals.
- **Identify Key Objectives**. Define specific, measurable, achievable, relevant, and time-bound (SMART) objectives that align with the organisation's mission and vision. These objectives should focus on areas such as growth, profitability, market share, or other critical aspects of the business.
- **Assess the Competitive Landscape**. Delve inside the market, industry trends, and competitors to understand the external environment. This helps to identify opportunities and challenges that the organisation may face.
- **Determine Key Performance Indicators (KPIs)**. One needs to select KPIs that will measure progress toward the desired outcome. These should be clear and quantifiable metrics that provide insights into the organisation's performance.
- **Set Priorities**. Prioritise objectives and initiatives based on their potential impact and feasibility. This helps focus resources on the most critical areas for achieving the desired outcome.

Creating a Compelling Narrative

- **Craft a Clear and Concise Message**. Create a message that clearly communicates the organisation's goals and strategic direction. The narrative should be easy to understand and resonate with all stakeholders.
- **Highlight the Importance of the Outcome**. Explain why the desired strategic outcome is essential for the organisation and its stakeholders. Emphasise the potential benefits and positive impact on the business and its people.
- **Connect to Values and Beliefs**. Align the narrative with the organisation's values and beliefs. This helps to create a sense of purpose and commitment among employees and other stakeholders.

- **Inspire and Motivate**. Utilise storytelling techniques in order to create an inspiring narrative. Share stories of past successes, challenges overcome, and lessons learned. Highlight examples of resilience, innovation, and teamwork.
- **Explain the Path to Success**. Provide a roadmap outlining the steps the organisation will take to achieve the desired outcome. Describe how the organisation will leverage its strengths and address challenges.
- **Encourage Participation and Collaboration**. Make it clear that achieving the desired outcome requires the collective effort of everyone in the organisation. Encourage open communication and collaboration to foster a sense of ownership and commitment.
- **Adapt the Narrative for Different Audiences**: Tailor the narrative to suit different audiences, such as employees, customers, investors, or partners. Focus on what is most relevant to each group and how they can contribute to the organisation's success.
- **Be Honest and Transparent**: A compelling narrative is built on honesty and transparency. Acknowledge challenges and potential obstacles while showcasing the organisation's ability to overcome them.

By defining the desired strategic outcome and creating a compelling narrative, one can guide the organisation toward success while inspiring and motivating stakeholders to work together toward common and shared goals.

Step 2: Know Yourself, Know Your Enemy. Compare Strengths, and Weaknesses to Identify Where You and the Enemy Hold a Critical Advantage

Understanding yourself, your enemy, and the comparative strengths and weaknesses between the two parties is crucial for effective strategy development. Here's how you can assess and compare these aspects to identify where you and your enemy hold critical advantages:

Know Yourself

- **Evaluate Your Capabilities**. Understand your organisation's capabilities, resources, and expertise. Assess your strengths and weaknesses across different areas such as operations, finances, human resources, technology, and market position.
- **Assess Your Strategic Goals**. Clarify your strategic objectives and evaluate how they align with your organisation's vision and mission. Determine which goals are most achievable given your current resources.
- **Review Past Performance**. Analyse your past performance, including successes and failures. Identify patterns and lessons learned to understand what works well and where improvements can be made.
- **Gather Feedback**. Seek input from employees, customers, and other stakeholders to gain a broader perspective on your organisation's performance and areas for improvement.

Know Your Enemy

- **Research Your Competitors**. Conduct a thorough and incisive analysis of your competitors, including their products, services, market share, customer base, and recent strategic moves.
- **Assess Their Capabilities**. Evaluate your competitors' strengths and weaknesses across different areas, such as technology, supply chain, marketing, and talent.
- **Analyse Their Strategies**. Comprehend your competitors' strategic goals and approaches. Study their past performance and behaviour to anticipate their potential future moves.
- **Identify Key Threats and Opportunities**. Determine the threats posed by competitors and the opportunities they may present. This could include market gaps they may be exploiting or areas where they are vulnerable.

Compare Strengths and Weaknesses

- **Create a SWOT Analysis**. Perform a SWOT analysis (Strengths, Weaknesses, Opportunities, Threats) to compare your organisation's strengths and weaknesses with those of your competitors.
- **Identify Critical Advantages**. Analyse areas where you have a competitive advantage over your enemies, such as superior products, services, technology, or customer relationships.
- **Recognise Areas of Vulnerability**. Identify areas where your enemies have an advantage over you, such as better market positioning, stronger financial resources, or a more extensive distribution network.
- **Determine Points of Leverage**. Find opportunities to leverage your strengths against your enemies' weaknesses or areas where you can neutralise their advantages.

Identify Critical Advantages

- **Highlight Unique Differentiators**. Focus on what makes your organisation unique compared to your competitors. This could be proprietary technology, brand reputation, or exceptional customer service.
- **Exploit Market Gaps**. Look for market niches or areas where competitors are underperforming and capitalise on these opportunities.
- **Plan Targeted Strategies**. Develop targeted strategies that utilise your strengths to exploit your competitors' weaknesses. For example, if you have a strong online presence and your competitors do not, focus on online marketing and sales.
- **Adapt to Changing Circumstances**. Continuously monitor your competitors' actions and adjust your strategies as needed to maintain your critical advantages.

By knowing yourself and your enemy, and comparing strengths and weaknesses, you can identify where you and your competitors hold critical advantages. This knowledge will guide your strategic decisions and help you achieve success in a competitive environment.

Step 3: Heaven and Earth. Determine the Type of Ground(s) on Which the Battles will Take Place

The key takeaway of this stage is to identify and analyse deeply the factors and elements of a problem that are beyond human control. Terrain and weather are obvious examples of these, but it can include many other areas such as time, distance, communications and consumable logistics. In this step, it is also essential to consider resources and assets available to both you and the adversary. To implement Sun Tzu's teachings on Heaven and Earth, lets delve inside the following actions:

- **Conduct a Thorough Assessment**. Analyse your environment to understand the factors of Heaven and Earth that affect your situation. Identify opportunities and risks based on these factors.
- **Plan Strategically**. Use your assessment to develop strategies that leverage your strengths and minimise weaknesses. Anticipate changes in your environment and adapt your plans accordingly.
- **Monitor and Adjust**. Continuously monitor the environment for changes and adjust your strategies as needed. Flexibility and adaptability are key to responding effectively to shifting circumstances.
- **Make Informed Decisions**. Base your decisions on a thorough understanding of Heaven and Earth. Consider the potential impact of external factors and choose the best course of action.

Step 4: The Commander

Sun Tzu articulates the importance of the commander as a crucial factor in successful strategy and operations in *The Art of War*. The commander's qualities and actions play a significant role in shaping the outcomes of engagements. Implementing Sun Tzu's teachings on the commander can help you lead effectively and achieve strategic goals. Here are key aspects of Sun Tzu's teachings on the commander and how you can implement them:

Virtues of the Commander

- **Wisdom**: Demonstrate sound judgment, knowledge, and understanding.

- **Sincerity**: Be honest, credible, and straightforward in your dealings.
- **Benevolence**: Show concern and care for your team and their well-being.
- **Courage**: Display bravery and resolve, especially in challenging situations.
- **Discipline**: Maintain order, enforce rules, and set clear expectations.

Know Your People

- Understand the strengths, weaknesses, and motivations of your team members.
- Leverage their individual skills and characteristics to maximise effectiveness.

Build Trust and Loyalty

- Foster trust through honesty, consistency, and reliability.
- Earn the loyalty of your team by demonstrating genuine care for their welfare and success.

Make Decisive and Informed Decisions

- Base one's decisions on a thorough understanding of the situation and available information.
- Act promptly, adroitly and confidently to guide your team effectively.

Communicate Clearly and Consistently

- Provide clear and concise instructions, expectations, and feedback.
- Keep your team informed about the overall strategy and their role in achieving it.

Lead by Example

- Embody the values and behaviours you expect from your team.
- Show resilience and determination, especially during challenging times.

Foster a Cohesive Team

- Encourage teamwork, cooperation, and mutual respect among team members.
- Create a supportive and inclusive environment that promotes collaboration.

Adaptability and Flexibility

- Be open to changing strategies and plans based on new information and circumstances.
- Guide your team through adjustments and transitions smoothly.

Monitor and Evaluate

- Continuously assess the performance of your team and the progress of your plans.
- Provide constructive feedback and adjust your strategies as needed.

Motivate and Inspire

- Encourage your team to achieve their best and work towards common goals.
- Recognise and reward achievements to boost morale and motivation.

By implementing Sun Tzu's teachings on the commander, you can lead your team more effectively and navigate challenges with greater confidence. A skilled commander can inspire trust, loyalty, and dedication from their team, ultimately contributing to the success of the mission.

Step 5: Method and Discipline

In *The Art of War*, Sun Tzu underlines the importance of method and discipline as key components of successful strategy and leadership. Method and discipline involve organising and managing resources effectively, maintaining control over your team, and ensuring consistent execution of your plans. Here are some ways to implement Sun Tzu's teachings on method and discipline in your own context:

Method

- **Organise Resources Efficiently**. Properly manage your available resources, including personnel, time, finances, and equipment. Create systems and processes to optimise their use and avoid waste.
- **Standardise Procedures**. Develop clear and standardised processes for your team to follow. This ensures consistency and reliability in your operations and helps streamline tasks.
- **Allocate Roles and Responsibilities**. Clearly define the roles and responsibilities of each team member. This helps establish accountability and ensures that everyone knows their specific duties.
- **Plan Logistically**. Anticipate the logistical needs of your projects and operations. Ensure smooth supply chains, transportation, and other logistical considerations to support your goals.
- **Monitor Performance**. Continuously track the performance of your team and operations. Use data and metrics to measure success and identify areas for improvement.

Discipline

- **Enforce Clear Expectations**. Set clear expectations for behaviour, performance, and outcomes. Communicate these expectations to your team and hold them accountable.
- **Lead by Example**. Demonstrate discipline in your own actions and behaviour. Show commitment to your goals and adherence to rules and standards.
- **Maintain Consistency**. Be consistent in your decision-making and enforcement of rules. Inconsistencies can lead to confusion and undermine trust.
- **Train and Develop Your Team**. Invest in the training and development of your team members. Well-trained individuals are more likely to adhere to procedures and contribute positively to your objectives.
- **Foster a Culture of Respect**. Promote a culture where team members respect one another and work together harmoniously.

Discipline should be balanced with empathy and understanding.

- **Adapt and Improve**. While discipline is important, be open to feedback and willing to adapt when necessary. Use lessons learned to refine your methods and improve your practices.

By implementing these teachings on method and discipline, you can create a well-structured and efficient environment that supports your strategic goals. Consistent execution, proper resource management, and a disciplined team contribute to achieving success in various contexts.

Step 6: Adaptability and Flexibility

Sun Tzu highlights the importance of adaptability and flexibility in *The Art of War*, as they are crucial for responding effectively to changing circumstances on the battlefield. In modern contexts such as business, leadership, or personal development, implementing these teachings can help you navigate dynamic environments and achieve success. Here are some ways to implement Sun Tzu's teachings on adaptability and flexibility:

Be Open to Change. Cultivate an open mindset and be willing to embrace change. Recognise that plans may need to be adjusted based on new information or shifting circumstances.

Stay Informed. Continuously monitor your environment and gather information about trends, events, and changes. Use data and insights to assess your situation and identify opportunities for adjustment.

Plan for Contingencies. Develop backup plans and alternative strategies in case your initial plans need to be altered. Identify potential risks and challenges, and prepare solutions to address them.

Be Proactive, Not Reactive. Anticipate changes and take proactive measures to address them. Avoid reacting impulsively to unexpected situations; instead, assess the situation and make informed decisions.

Adapt Your Strategies. Modify your strategies as needed based on changing circumstances. Be prepared to pivot your approach to achieve your goals more effectively.

Empower Your Team. Encourage your team to be flexible and open to new ideas and approaches. Provide them with the autonomy to make decisions and adjust their methods as needed.

Foster a Learning Culture. Promote continuous learning and improvement within your team or organisation. Encourage experimentation and innovation to discover more effective approaches.

Embrace Diversity. Leverage diverse perspectives and experiences to approach challenges in new ways. Foster an inclusive environment where different viewpoints are welcomed and considered.

Stay Calm Under Pressure. Maintain composure and resilience in the face of uncertainty or setbacks. Take the time to assess the situation and consider your options before making decisions.

Learn from Experience. Reflect on past successes and failures to identify lessons learned. Use these insights to refine your strategies and improve your adaptability.

By implementing these teachings, you can develop the ability to navigate complex and ever-changing environments effectively. Adaptability and flexibility allow you to seize opportunities and respond to challenges in a way that aligns with your goals.

Step 7: Deception and Misdirection

Sun Tzu's teachings on deception and misdirection are central to *The Art of War*. He emphasises the value of misleading and confusing opponents to gain a strategic advantage. While these tactics are often associated with military strategies, they can also be applied in various other contexts such as business, sports, and personal decision-making. Here are ways you can implement Sun Tzu's teachings on deception and misdirection:

Conceal Your Intentions. Keep your true objectives and plans hidden from your opponents. Avoid giving away your strategy through obvious actions or statements.

Create Diversions. Use false information, feints, or distractions to mislead your opponents about your actual plans. For example, in business, you might introduce a decoy product or service to distract competitors from your main focus.

Manipulate Perceptions. Shape your opponents' perceptions by providing selective or misleading information. Use ambiguity and vagueness to create uncertainty and confusion.

Use Surprise. Take actions that your opponents do not expect, catching them off guard. In competitive situations, this could involve sudden changes in strategy or unexpected moves.

Know When to Show Weakness. Sometimes it's advantageous to appear weaker or less capable than you are. This can lead opponents to underestimate you or make mistakes in their approach.

Leverage Timing. Execute your deceptive tactics at the right time to maximise their effectiveness. Timing is crucial for making your actions seem more natural and less suspicious.

Exploit Opponents' Biases. Understand your opponents' tendencies, assumptions, and biases, and use them to your advantage. For example, if an opponent is known to be aggressive, you might bait them into a rash decision.

Keep Your Options Open. Maintain flexibility in your plans so you can adapt your strategy based on how your opponents respond to your deception. This allows you to capitalise on opportunities as they arise.

Know When to Use Deception. Deception should be used judiciously and ethically, as excessive use can lead to mistrust and reputational damage. Choose your moments carefully and weigh the potential risks and benefits.

Monitor Outcomes. Observe the impact of your deceptive tactics and adjust your approach as needed. Learning from your successes and failures can help you improve your use of deception.

By implementing these teachings thoughtfully and strategically, you can gain an edge in competitive situations and navigate complex environments effectively. However, it's important to balance deception with integrity and ethical considerations to maintain trust and reputation in the long run.

Step 8: Winning Without Fighting

Sun Tzu's teachings on winning without fighting are a core aspect of his strategic philosophy in *The Art of War*. Sun Tzu champions achieving victory through strategy, intelligence, and manipulation rather than direct conflict. This approach can be applied in various contexts such as business, negotiation, or personal conflict resolution. Here are ways you can implement Sun Tzu's teachings on winning without fighting:

Know Yourself and Your Opponent. Gain a deep understanding of your strengths, weaknesses, and objectives, as well as those of your opponent. Use this knowledge to craft strategies that give you the upper hand without engaging in direct confrontation.

Choose Your Battles Wisely. Assess whether engaging in direct conflict is necessary or beneficial. If you can achieve your goals without fighting, avoid conflict and choose a different approach.

Leverage Intelligence and Information. Gather information about your opponent's plans, movements, and weaknesses. Use this intelligence to shape your strategies and create opportunities for victory without direct confrontation.

Use Diplomacy and Negotiation. Seek diplomatic solutions and negotiate terms that benefit you while avoiding direct conflict. Build relationships and alliances to create leverage and influence outcomes in your favour.

Manipulate Perceptions. Influence your opponent's perceptions by controlling the information they receive. Use misinformation, ambiguity, or selective communication to guide their decisions and actions.

Create Distractions and Diversions. Draw your opponent's attention away from your true objectives by creating diversions. This can involve feints, decoys, or misdirection to keep them off balance.

Exhaust Your Opponent. Force your opponent to expend resources and energy unnecessarily, weakening their position. This can be achieved through strategic manoeuvres, such as drawing them into unfavourable situations.

Use Non-Confrontational Means. Consider alternative strategies such as economic pressure, psychological tactics, or legal action. These methods can be effective in achieving your goals without direct combat.

Know When to Retreat. Sometimes avoiding confrontation or withdrawing from a situation can be a strategic move. This allows you to preserve your resources and avoid unnecessary losses.

Maximise Your Advantages. Use your strengths and advantages to the fullest while minimising risks. Capitalise on your position and assets to achieve your goals without resorting to fighting.

By implementing these teachings, you can achieve your objectives in a more efficient and less costly manner. Winning without fighting not only minimises damage but also preserves your resources for future opportunities and challenges.

Step 9: Speed and Timing.

Sun Tzu stresses the importance of speed and timing in *The Art of War* as key elements of successful strategy. Properly executed, speed and timing can help you seize opportunities, gain an advantage over opponents, and achieve your goals more efficiently. Here are some ways you can implement Sun Tzu's teachings on speed and timing in various contexts such as business, leadership, or personal development:

Plan and Prepare. Thorough planning and preparation allow you to act quickly when opportunities arise. Identify critical moments when speed and timing will be most effective and develop strategies to capitalise on them.

Be Decisive. Practice making decisions quickly and confidently based on available information. Avoid hesitating or over-analysing situations when fast action is needed.

Recognise the Right Moment. Train yourself to recognise the right moment to act based on changing circumstances. Monitor developments in your environment to identify windows of opportunity.

Streamline Processes. Optimise your operations to reduce delays and inefficiencies. Establish clear procedures and communication channels to facilitate swift action.

Maintain Flexibility. Stay agile and adaptable to respond effectively to unexpected changes. Adjust your plans and strategies as needed to take advantage of new opportunities.

Coordinate with Your Team. Ensure your team is on the same page and ready to act quickly when necessary. Establish a system for rapid communication and coordination to enable swift responses.

Leverage Surprise. Use the element of surprise to catch opponents off guard and gain an advantage. Plan actions that are unexpected but strategically sound.

Anticipate Opponents' Actions. Predict your opponents' movements and timing to position yourself advantageously. Use this foresight to strike first or avoid unfavourable situations.

Prioritise Key Objectives. Focus on your most important goals and objectives and prioritise actions that advance them. This ensures your speed and timing are directed towards impactful outcomes.

Monitor Outcomes. Continuously assess the results of your actions and adjust your approach as needed. Learning from experience helps you to improve your sense of timing and speed over time.

Step 10: Leadership and Morale

Sun Tzu's teachings on leadership and morale are central to the successful implementation of strategy and achieving victory in *The Art of War*. Effective leadership and strong morale are crucial for motivating and guiding your team, as well as fostering a cohesive and determined group. Here are ways you can implement Sun Tzu's teachings on leadership and morale in various contexts such as business, sports, or personal development:

Lead by Example. Demonstrate the qualities and behaviours you expect from your team. Show commitment, integrity, and resilience in your actions.

Communicate Clearly. Provide clear and concise instructions, goals, and expectations. Listen to your team's feedback and address their concerns.

Be Decisive. Make informed decisions confidently and promptly. Avoid indecision or frequent changes in direction.

Empower Your Team. Delegate authority and responsibility to capable team members. Trust your team to take ownership of their roles and tasks.

Recognise and Reward Achievements. Celebrate successes and acknowledge individual and team contributions. Positive reinforcement boosts morale and motivates your team.

Foster a Collaborative Culture. Encourage teamwork and open communication among team members. Promote a culture of mutual respect and cooperation.

Adapt to Changing Situations. Be flexible and willing to adjust your strategies based on new information. Guide your team through changes smoothly and confidently.

Create a Positive Work Environment. Foster a supportive and inclusive atmosphere for your team. Address conflicts and concerns promptly to maintain harmony.

Provide Clear Vision and Purpose. Communicate your vision and the purpose behind your goals. Help your team understand how their work contributes to the bigger picture.

Offer Training and Development. Provide opportunities for your team to grow and develop their skills. Investing in their development can boost confidence and morale.

Show Empathy and Support. Be attentive to your team's needs and well-being. Offer support during challenging times and help them navigate obstacles.

Encourage Open Communication. Allow team members to voice their opinions and concerns. Listen actively and address issues that may affect morale.

Set Achievable Goals. Break down larger goals into smaller, achievable milestones. This helps maintain motivation and a sense of progress.

Promote Work-Life Balance. Encourage a healthy balance between work and personal life. Overworked or stressed team members can experience a decline in morale.

By implementing Sun Tzu's teachings on leadership and morale, you can create a strong and motivated team that is more likely to achieve success. Effective leadership fosters a positive and cohesive environment, while high morale keeps your team engaged and committed to reaching your goals.

Sun Tzu – A Summary

The Art of War by Sun Tzu offers a wealth of strategic concepts that extend beyond the realm of military tactics. Its principles can be applied to various aspects of life where strategy and decision-making are crucial. The focus on knowledge, adaptability, deception, and holistic understanding of the factors influencing success continues to make *The Art of War* a timeless guide for strategic thinking.

The Fundamentals of Sun Tzu's Teachings:

- Preparation and Planning.
- Adaptability and Flexibility.
- Deception and Indirect Approach.
- Know Yourself and Know the Enemy.
- The Importance of Timing.
- Winning Without Fighting.
- Leadership and Discipline.

The Five Factors:

- The Way.
- Heaven.
- Earth.
- The Commander.
- Method and Discipline.

A Strategic Toolset Based on Sun Tzu's Art of War.

Step 1: The Way. Define the Desired Strategic Outcome and Create a Compelling Narrative on Why the Organisation Must Prevail and How it Will Achieve Success

- Understand the Organisation's Vision and Mission.
- Identify Key Objectives.
- Assess the Competitive Landscape.
- Determine Key Performance Indicators (KPIs).
- Set Priorities.
- Craft a Clear and Concise Message.
- Highlight the Importance of the Outcome.
- Connect to Values and Beliefs.
- Inspire and Motivate.
- Explain the Path to Success.
- Encourage Participation and Collaboration.
- Adapt the Narrative for Different Audiences.
- Be Honest and Transparent.

Step 2: Know Yourself, Know Your Enemy. Compare Strengths, and Weaknesses to Identify Where You and the Enemy Hold a Critical Advantage

- Evaluate Your Capabilities.
- Assess Your Strategic Goals.
- Review Past Performance.
- Gather Feedback.
- Research Your Competitors.
- Assess Their Capabilities.
- Analyse Their Strategies.
- Identify Key Threats and Opportunities.
- Create a SWOT Analysis.
- Identify Critical Advantages.
- Recognise Areas of Vulnerability.

- Determine Points of Leverage.
- Highlight Unique Differentiators.
- Exploit Market Gaps.
- Plan Targeted Strategies.
- Adapt to Changing Circumstances.

Step 3: Heaven and Earth. Determine the Type of Ground(s) on Which the Battles will Take Place

- Conduct a Thorough Assessment.
- Plan Strategically.
- Monitor and Adjust.
- Make Informed Decisions.

Step 4: The Commander

- Know Your People.
- Build Trust and Loyalty.
- Make Decisive and Informed Decisions.
- Communicate Clearly and Consistently.
- Lead by Example.
- Foster a Cohesive Team.
- Adaptability and Flexibility.
- Monitor and Evaluate.
- Motivate and Inspire.
- Recognise and reward.

Step 5: Method and Discipline

- Organise Resources Efficiently.
- Standardise Procedures.
- Allocate Roles and Responsibilities.
- Plan Logistically.
- Monitor Performance.

- Enforce Clear Expectations.
- Lead by Example.
- Maintain Consistency.
- Train and Develop Your Team.
- Foster a Culture of Respect.
- Adapt and Improve.

Step 6: Adaptability and Flexibility

- Be Open to Change.
- Stay Informed.
- Plan for Contingencies.
- Be Proactive, Not Reactive.
- Adapt Your Strategies.
- Empower Your Team.
- Foster a Learning Culture.
- Embrace Diversity.
- Stay Calm Under Pressure.
- Learn from Experience.

Step 7: Deception and Misdirection

- Conceal Your Intentions.
- Create Diversions.
- Manipulate Perceptions.
- Use Surprise.
- Know When to Show Weakness.
- Leverage Timing.
- Exploit Opponents' Biases.
- Keep Your Options Open.
- Know When to Use Deception.
- Monitor Outcomes.

Step 8: Winning Without Fighting

- Know Yourself and Your Opponent.
- Choose Your Battles Wisely.
- Leverage Intelligence and Information.
- Use Diplomacy and Negotiation.
- Manipulate Perceptions.
- Create Distractions and Diversions.
- Exhaust Your Opponent.
- Use Non-Confrontational Means.
- Know When to Retreat.
- Maximise Your Advantages.

Step 9: Speed and Timing

- Plan and Prepare.
- Be Decisive.
- Recognise the Right Moment.
- Streamline Processes.
- Maintain Flexibility.
- Coordinate with Your Team.
- Leverage Surprise.
- Anticipate Opponents' Actions.
- Prioritise Key Objectives.
- Monitor Outcomes.

Step 10: Leadership and Morale

- Lead by Example.
- Communicate Clearly.
- Be Decisive.
- Empower Your Team.
- Recognise and Reward Achievements.

- Foster a Collaborative Culture.
- Adapt to Changing Situations.
- Create a Positive Work Environment.
- Provide Clear Vision and Purpose.
- Offer Training and Development.
- Show Empathy and Support.
- Encourage Open Communication.
- Set Achievable Goals.
- Promote Work-Life Balance.

Chapter Six

Julius Caesar and his 'Commentaries on the Gallic War'

"Without training, they lacked knowledge. Without knowledge, they lacked confidence. Without confidence, they lacked victory."

—Julius Caesar

IN THIS CHAPTER

- About Julius Caesar and the Gallic War.
- The Key Strategic Lessons from the Campaigns of Julius Caesar:
  - Effective Leadership.
  - Preparation and Planning.
  - Divide and Conquer.
  - Psychological Warfare.

  * Diplomacy, Partnerships and Alliances.
  * Logistics and Supply Lines.
  * Speed and Mobility.
  * Calculated Risk Taking.
  * Decisive Actions.
  * Adaptability and Flexibility.
- Julius Caesar's Ten Step Strategic Toolset.
- Commentaries on the Gallic War – A Summary.

About Julius Caesar and the Gallic War

Julius Caesar's "Commentarii de Bello Gallico" (Commentaries on the Gallic War) is a classic and iconic first-hand account of his campaigns in Gaul between 58 and 50 BCE. The text provides detailed descriptions of his military strategies, tactics, and leadership style. His military campaigns in Gaul were pivotal in his rise to power and in the expansion of Roman influence in Western Europe. His campaigns, detailed in his commentaries, provide insight into his military strategies, leadership, and interactions with the local tribes. Lasting from 58 BC to 50 BC, these campaigns showcased Caesar's tactical genius, adaptability, and ability to maintain control over his troops and the region.

Gaul was a region that included modern-day France, Belgium, Switzerland, and parts of Germany and Italy. Prior to Caesar's campaigns, it was inhabited by a number of diverse tribes and peoples, many of whom were often in conflict with one another. The Roman Senate, increasingly concerned about the threat these tribes posed to Roman territories, granted Caesar proconsular command over Illyricum, Cisalpine Gaul, and Transalpine Gaul in 58 BC, giving him the authority to address these threats.

Caesar's campaigns began in earnest in 58 BC with the Helvetii migration. The Helvetii, a Gallic tribe from modern-day Switzerland, sought to migrate westward, which would have brought them into conflict with Roman territories. Caesar decisively defeated the Helvetii at the Battle of Bibracte, forcing them to return to their homeland.

Later that year, Caesar faced the Germanic Suebi tribe, led by Ariovistus.

In a swift campaign, Caesar defeated Ariovistus at the Battle of Vosges, solidifying his reputation as a military commander, and demonstrating the strength of the Roman army.

Over the following years, as time passed, Caesar continued his campaigns across Gaul, engaging various tribes in battle and forming alliances with others. In 57 BC, he fought the Belgae in northern Gaul, one of the most powerful and numerous tribal confederations. Caesar's victories in these campaigns allowed him to establish Roman dominance over the region. Caesar also campaigned in modern-day Brittany against the Veneti, who controlled the Atlantic trade routes. In a significant naval battle, Caesar's forces defeated the Veneti, gaining control of the region's strategic waterways.

In 52 BC, the most significant challenge to Roman authority in Gaul emerged in the form of Vercingetorix, a charismatic chieftain of the Arverni tribe. Vercingetorix united several tribes in a revolt against Roman rule. This uprising led to some of the most intense and brutal battles of the Gallic Wars. Caesar's siege of Alesia in 52 BC was a defining moment in the campaigns. Despite being outnumbered, Caesar's strategic prowess and the discipline of his troops led to a Roman victory. Vercingetorix surrendered, marking a significant turning point in Roman control over Gaul.

Caesar's campaigns in Gaul not only expanded Roman territory but also had significant economic and political benefits for Rome. The conquered lands provided resources and wealth that contributed to Rome's prosperity. Caesar's commentaries on the Gallic Wars helped to shape his public image, providing a narrative of his achievements and military successes.

Ultimately, Caesar's campaigns in Gaul played a key role in his rise to power within the Roman Republic. His success as a military leader and the wealth he gained through these campaigns enabled him to leverage his influence in Roman politics. His actions in Gaul laid the foundation for his later role in the transformation of the Roman Republic into the Roman Empire.

In summary, Julius Caesar's military campaigns in Gaul were instrumental in expanding Roman influence in Western Europe and solidifying Caesar's reputation as one of history's greatest military leaders. His strategic and tactical acumen allowed him to conquer and control the diverse and often hostile tribes of the region, securing a lasting legacy for both him and Rome. His campaigns offer several key strategic lessons.

The Key Strategic Lessons from the Campaigns of Julius Caesar

Effective Leadership. Caesar led from the front, setting an example for his soldiers, and earning their loyalty. Julius Caesar maintained morale and discipline in his armies through a combination of effective leadership, clear communication, and the implementation of strict discipline.

One key example of how Caesar managed this can be seen in his handling of the siege of Alesia in 52 BC. During the siege, Caesar's forces had surrounded the town of Alesia, which was under the control of the Gallic chieftain Vercingetorix. At the same time, Caesar's army found itself surrounded by a large relief force of Gallic tribes attempting to break the siege.

Caesar clearly communicated the strategic situation and the plan of action to his troops. He inspired them with a sense of purpose and outlined their roles in the battle, emphasising the importance of victory for the success of their campaign. Caesar divided his forces to deal with the Gallic relief army and the besieged forces within Alesia simultaneously. This allowed his army to remain organised and focused, even when faced with attacks from both sides. Caesar remained present on the battlefield throughout, often moving among his soldiers to provide encouragement and direction. His presence boosted morale and demonstrated his confidence in their ability to succeed.

Caesar's construction of two sets of fortifications, one facing the besieged town and another facing outward to defend against the relief force, was a bold and innovative tactic. This not only showcased his strategic genius but also instilled confidence in his troops' ability to defend themselves.

Caesar enforced strict discipline among his troops, ensuring that they followed his commands precisely and remained focused on the task at hand. His emphasis on discipline helped maintain order and cohesion in his army during the intense and prolonged siege.

By maintaining a strong leadership style, clear communication, and a disciplined approach, Caesar successfully sustained his army's morale and discipline during the siege of Alesia. This contributed significantly to his ultimate victory in the battle, which in turn played a crucial role in the overall success of his Gallic campaigns.

Preparation and Planning. Caesar meticulously planned his campaigns, gathering intelligence on his enemies and their terrain. This preparation allowed him to execute well-coordinated strategies. In 58 BC, the Helvetii, a Gallic tribe from modern-day Switzerland, began migrating westward, aiming to settle in Gaul. This migration posed a threat to Roman territories and could have destabilised the region. Caesar's response to the Helvetii's movement showcases his planning and preparation for military campaigns.

Caesar began by gathering intelligence about the Helvetii's intentions, movements, and numbers. This information allowed him to understand the scale of the threat and plan his strategy accordingly. Before engaging the Helvetii, Caesar sought alliances with nearby tribes, such as the Aedui, who could provide him with support and valuable knowledge of the region.

Caesar strategically positioned his forces along the Rhône River to block the Helvetii's migration route. This move demonstrated his foresight and understanding of the region's geography. Caesar was able to rapidly mobilise his forces, a testament to his organisational skills. He raised legions, equipped them, and moved them to the front lines in a timely manner.

Caesar planned and executed his battle strategies with precision. For example, during the Battle of Bibracte, he used his cavalry to scout the Helvetii's movements and positioned his legions on high ground, giving him a tactical advantage. Despite initial setbacks, Caesar was able to adapt his plans as the situation evolved. When the Helvetii changed their route, he followed and engaged them in battle at Bibracte, where he ultimately defeated them.

Caesar ensured his army had access to adequate supplies and established secure supply lines. This logistical planning allowed him to sustain his forces during the campaign. Caesar's careful planning and preparation for the campaign against the Helvetii enabled him to respond effectively to the threat and achieve a decisive victory.

Divide and Conquer. Caesar employed the strategy of dividing his enemies by exploiting existing divisions among the Gallic tribes. This prevented them from uniting against him and made it easier to defeat them separately. During his campaigns in Gaul, Caesar encountered numerous tribes that were often in conflict with one another. He capitalised on these divisions to strengthen his position and maintain control over the region. One instance that illustrates his divide-and-conquer strategy is his handling of the Belgae tribes in 57 BC.

The Belgae were a powerful confederation of tribes in northern Gaul. Caesar recognised that the Belgae were not a unified entity and were divided into different tribes with varying interests and allegiances. He exploited these divisions to weaken their collective resistance.

Caesar negotiated with some tribes within the Belgae confederation, offering them favourable terms to become allies or to remain neutral in his conflict with other tribes. By securing the support of certain tribes, he was able to isolate and focus his efforts on the more hostile ones. Caesar targeted key tribes within the Belgae confederation, such as the Nervii, and defeated them in battle. By taking down influential tribes, he weakened the overall strength of the Belgae and reduced the likelihood of a united front against him.

Caesar deftly utilised diplomacy to divide the Belgae tribes further. He offered terms to those who surrendered, which included protection from other tribes and the opportunity to retain their territories. This approach helped him gain valuable intelligence and support from within the confederation. By dealing with each tribe individually, Caesar could systematically conquer them and prevent them from forming a unified resistance. This approach allowed him to defeat the Belgae in a series of battles, rather than facing a large, coordinated force.

Through the use of divide-and-conquer strategies, Caesar was able to dismantle the Belgae confederation and expand Roman influence in the region. This approach was effective throughout his campaigns in Gaul and contributed significantly to his overall success.

Psychological Warfare. Caesar used psychological warfare to intimidate and divide his enemies. He demonstrated immaculate strength and decisiveness, which helped demoralise opposing forces and encouraged allies to remain loyal. One notable instance of this is his siege of the Gallic town of Avaricum in 52 BC.

Caesar's reputation as a formidable military commander preceded him in Gaul. He cultivated an image of invincibility and ruthlessness through his decisive victories and the destruction of enemy forces. This reputation instilled fear in many Gallic tribes, making them more likely to surrender or negotiate rather than face him in battle.

At Avaricum, Caesar ordered the destruction of the surrounding fields and crops to starve the town's inhabitants. This tactic not only weakened the town's ability to resist but also served as a warning to other Gallic tribes of the consequences of opposing Caesar.

Caesar made strategic use of public displays of Roman power and discipline to impress and intimidate his enemies. For instance, during sieges, he constructed formidable siege works and fortifications that showcased the strength and capabilities of his forces.

Caesar often targeted individual Gallic chieftains or factions within tribes, offering them favourable terms if they would surrender or turn against their own people. This strategy sowed discord among the tribes and weakened their ability to present a united front against him. This was the principle of 'divide and conquer'.

During the siege of Avaricum, Caesar's forces used catapults and other siege engines to bombard the town with projectiles. This constant pressure not only inflicted physical damage but also wore down the morale of the defenders, leading to their eventual defeat.

Caesar's swift and decisive actions in battle and his ability to adapt to changing circumstances demonstrated his military prowess. This made him a feared and respected opponent, influencing the decisions of Gallic tribes and leaders.

By employing psychological warfare tactics, Caesar was able to manipulate his enemies' perceptions, instil fear and doubt, and weaken their will to fight. These strategies played a key role in his success during the Gallic Wars and contributed to his ultimate victory in the region.

Diplomacy, Partnerships and Alliances. While military force was a key part of his strategy, Caesar also used diplomacy to forge alliances and secure support from local tribes. These alliances helped him maintain control over Gaul. One notable example of Caesar's use of diplomacy and alliances can be seen in his relationship with the Aedui tribe.

The Aedui were a powerful Gallic tribe located in what is now central France. Early in his campaigns, Caesar recognised the strategic importance of forming an alliance with the Aedui, as they were a significant regional power and had long-standing ties to Rome. This alliance provided several key benefits to Caesar.

The Aedui were one of the most influential tribes in Gaul, and their support gave Caesar a strategic advantage in the region. The alliance with the Aedui provided him with access to their resources, knowledge of the local terrain, and additional manpower. By securing the allegiance of the Aedui, Caesar was able to drive a wedge between the various Gallic tribes. This alliance disrupted any potential unity among the tribes and made it easier for Caesar to engage them individually.

Caesar used his relationship with the Aedui as leverage in negotiations with other tribes. By presenting himself as a protector of the Aedui, he positioned himself as a mediator and gained credibility in his dealings with other Gallic tribes. The alliance was mutually beneficial. The Aedui gained Roman support and protection against rival tribes, while Caesar secured a base of operations and reliable allies in his campaigns.

Caesar often involved the Aedui in his military campaigns, using their soldiers to supplement his own forces. This cooperation allowed him to maintain a strong military presence in Gaul and achieve his strategic goals. Caesar consistently protected the interests of the Aedui, further strengthening their alliance. For example, he intervened in disputes involving the Aedui and other tribes, helping to solidify his reputation as a reliable partner.

By forming alliances with powerful tribes like the Aedui, Caesar was able to secure his position in Gaul, gain valuable intelligence and support, and effectively divide and conquer his enemies. This diplomatic approach played a significant role in his overall success during the Gallic Wars.

Logistics and Supply Lines. Caesar paid close attention to logistics, ensuring his army was well-supplied and could maintain its strength in the field. Control of supply lines and resources was crucial for his success. One notable example of his use of logistics can be seen in his campaigns against the Belgae in 57 BC.

The campaign against the Belgae in 57 BC required Caesar to operate in northern Gaul, a region far from his base of operations in Cisalpine Gaul. The Belgae were a confederation of powerful tribes, and Caesar needed to maintain his army's strength and mobility while dealing with unfamiliar territory and hostile tribes.

Caesar established secure and efficient supply lines to provide his army with necessary provisions such as food, equipment, and other essentials. This involved coordinating the transportation of supplies from his base of operations to his army in the field. Caesar organised the use of local resources by procuring supplies from allied or neutral tribes in the region. This minimised the distance supplies had to travel and allowed him to maintain his army's operational efficiency.

To secure his positions and protect his supply lines, Caesar built fortified camps during his campaigns. These camps served as bases of operations and storage areas for his supplies, ensuring his army's safety and readiness for battle.

Caesar utilised rivers for transportation, allowing him to move supplies quickly and efficiently. By navigating rivers such as the Rhône, he was able to transport large quantities of provisions and reinforcements to support his campaigns.

Caesar's flexibility in logistics allowed him to adapt to changing circumstances. For instance, if his supply lines were threatened, he could quickly adjust his routes or rely more heavily on local resources to sustain his army.

Caesar maintained strict discipline and organisation in his army, ensuring that supplies were distributed efficiently and that soldiers followed procedures for maintaining and securing provisions.

By effectively and pristinely managing logistics and supply chains during the campaign against the Belgae, Caesar was able to keep his army well-provisioned and mobile, which was essential for his success in the region. His ability to adapt and organise his resources in a challenging environment showcased his logistical expertise and contributed significantly to his victories.

Speed and Mobility. Caesar's campaigns were marked by his ability to move his legions quickly across various terrains. His rapid movement allowed him to outmanoeuvre his enemies and gain a strategic advantage. Julius Caesar used speed and mobility as crucial components of his strategy during his campaigns in Gaul. His ability to move his forces quickly and decisively often caught his enemies off guard and allowed him to secure strategic victories. One notable example of this can be seen in his campaign against the Nervii tribe in 57 BC.

In 57 BC, Caesar faced the Nervii, a powerful and warlike tribe located in the modern-day region of Belgium. The Nervii were known for their fierce fighting ability and their strong fortifications. Caesar's strategy against them showcased his use of speed and mobility.

Caesar moved his legions rapidly through the territory to confront the Nervii. His ability to march his troops quickly allowed him to reach the battlefield before the Nervii could fully prepare. The Nervii expected Caesar to follow the main road along the Sambre River, but Caesar chose a different route, crossing the river at a different point. This manoeuvre surprised the Nervii and allowed him to catch them off guard.

Once on the battlefield, Caesar deployed his troops quickly and efficiently. His use of scouts and reconnaissance allowed him to position his forces effectively, giving him an advantage over the Nervii. Caesar capitalised on the Nervii's lack of preparation by launching a swift and decisive attack. His rapid movements prevented the Nervii from organising a strong defence, leading to a Roman victory.

After defeating the Nervii, Caesar did not allow his forces to rest on their laurels. Instead, he maintained momentum by quickly advancing against other nearby tribes, further securing Roman control over the region. Caesar's adaptability allowed him to adjust his plans as needed. When his cavalry suffered a surprise attack from the Nervii, he quickly reoriented his legions to counter the threat and regain the initiative.

By using speed and mobility as part of his strategy, Caesar was able to outmanoeuvre and outfight his enemies, gaining significant advantages on the battlefield. His ability to move his forces quickly and decisively often proved to be a decisive factor in his successes during the Gallic Wars.

Calculated Risk-taking. Caesar was willing to take calculated risks when the potential rewards outweighed the dangers. His boldness often caught his enemies off-guard and led to significant victories. One example of Caesar taking a calculated risk during his campaigns in Gaul was the Battle of the Sabis (also known as the Battle of the Sambre) also against the Nervii in 57 BC.

Caesar engaged the Nervii near the Sambre River, but he knew the Nervii were already preparing for his approach. To surprise them, he decided to cross the river quickly and engage the Nervii directly, risking a battle in an unfamiliar and potentially unfavourable location. Caesar initially underestimated the strength and readiness of the Nervii. Despite this, he decided to press forward, risking a confrontation with a formidable and potentially larger enemy force.

The Nervii launched a surprise attack on Caesar's forces as they were building a camp. This caught Caesar off guard, but he quickly adapted and took control of the situation. He took the risk of not having fully prepared his legions for battle, relying on their training and discipline to respond effectively.

Caesar took a calculated risk by rapidly deploying his legions to counter the Nervii's attack, despite being in the middle of building a camp. His ability to quickly organise his forces and launch a counterattack turned the tide of the battle in his favour. Caesar personally led his troops in the battle, taking the risk of exposing himself to direct combat. His presence on the battlefield motivated his soldiers and helped maintain their resolve.

Despite the initial setback, Caesar's strategic risks paid off, resulting in a decisive victory against the Nervii. This victory not only secured Roman dominance in the region but also showcased Caesar's ability to adapt to unexpected challenges. By taking calculated risks during the Battle of the Sabis, Caesar demonstrated his confidence in his army's capabilities and his ability to adapt quickly to changing circumstances. His willingness to take risks and make bold decisions contributed significantly to his success during the Gallic Wars

Decisive Actions. When opportunities presented themselves, Caesar took decisive actions to capitalise on them. He knew when to engage in battle and when to retreat strategically. In 56 BC, the Veneti, a maritime tribe from the north-western coast of Gaul (modern-day Brittany), rebelled against Roman authority. This posed a significant challenge to Caesar because the Veneti controlled a crucial coastal region and had a powerful navy. Caesar's decisive action in dealing with the Veneti is a prime example of his leadership.

Upon learning of the Veneti's rebellion and their capture of Roman envoys, Caesar immediately took decisive action. He gathered a fleet and prepared his legions for a naval campaign against the Veneti. Recognising the Veneti's naval strength, Caesar quickly built a fleet of ships suited for the coastal waters. He adapted Roman ship designs for the rough Atlantic waters, enabling his forces to engage the Veneti on their terms.

Caesar's fleet, commanded by experienced officers, met the Veneti's ships in a decisive naval battle. Despite the Veneti's advantage in familiarity with the waters, Caesar's fleet managed to outmanoeuvre and defeat the Veneti. After defeating the Veneti fleet, Caesar took decisive action by punishing the tribe harshly for their rebellion. He executed their leaders and sold the rest of the population into slavery. This served as a strong warning to other tribes against rebelling.

By quickly suppressing the Veneti rebellion, Caesar secured control of the important coastal region. This allowed him to maintain his supply lines and communication with Rome, which were vital to his overall campaign strategy. Caesar's swift and decisive action in the campaign against the Veneti demonstrated his ability to adapt to different types of warfare (land and sea) and his willingness to take immediate and forceful measures to maintain control. This approach played a key role in his success during the Gallic Wars.

Adaptability and Flexibility. Caesar often faced new and unexpected challenges in his campaigns, including diverse tribes and shifting alliances. He was able to adapt quickly to changing circumstances, adjusting his tactics and strategies as needed. Julius Caesar's adaptability and flexibility in his military strategies, were key factors in his success during the Gallic Wars. One notable example of this can be seen in his campaign against the Germans led by Ariovistus in 58 BC.

In 58 BC, Caesar faced Ariovistus, a Germanic king who had established himself in Gaul. The campaign demonstrates Caesar's adaptability and flexibility in dealing with a formidable enemy. Initially, Caesar attempted to negotiate with Ariovistus to persuade him to leave Gaul peacefully. However, Ariovistus rejected Caesar's terms, forcing Caesar to prepare for a military confrontation. Upon realising that negotiations would not be fruitful, Caesar quickly mobilised his legions and marched to confront Ariovistus. His ability to move his forces rapidly demonstrated his flexibility in shifting from diplomacy to military action.

Ariovistus was known for his cavalry and the ferocity of his warriors. Caesar adapted his tactics to counter this threat, using his infantry's discipline and formation to hold off the Germanic forces. Caesar's adaptability extended to his choice of battlefield. He positioned his forces on higher ground, which provided a tactical advantage and limited Ariovistus's ability to use his cavalry effectively.

Caesar took the initiative by launching a surprise attack on Ariovistus's camp. This move disrupted Ariovistus's plans and forced him into a battle on Caesar's terms. Caesar made efficient use of intelligence gathered from scouts and local allies. This allowed him to anticipate Ariovistus's movements and adjust his strategy accordingly.

Caesar's adaptability and flexibility in strategy ultimately led to a decisive victory against Ariovistus. This victory not only eliminated a major threat but also solidified Roman control in the region. Caesar's campaign against Ariovistus showcases his ability to adapt to changing circumstances and modify his strategies as needed. His quick transition from diplomacy to military action, coupled with his use of intelligence and choice of battlefield, exemplify his strategic flexibility during the Gallic Wars.

Julius Caesar's campaigns in Gaul demonstrate the importance of strategic planning, adaptability, and strong leadership in achieving military success. His lessons continue to be studied for their relevance in modern strategic thinking.

It is possible to derive a strategic toolset from Julius Caesar's work. The ten-step toolset below is drawn from key lessons identified in the Gallic War.

Julius Caesar's Ten Step Strategic Toolset

Step 1: Appoint a Charismatic Leader

Developing and implementing effective and functioning strategy requires a charismatic leader. The first step of any strategy development must therefore be about selecting a suitable person for the most senior leadership role. Selecting and appointing a charismatic leader involves identifying individuals who possess qualities such as vision, emotional intelligence, communication skills, and a strong ability to inspire and motivate others. Here are some steps you can take to select and appoint a charismatic leader:

Define the Role and Expectations: Clearly define the role you are appointing the leader to and outline the expectations and responsibilities associated with it. This will help you identify the key qualities and skills needed in a candidate.

Identify Key Qualities. Look for candidates who exhibit charisma, which includes traits such as:

- Vision and the ability to articulate a compelling and inspiring narrative for the future.

- Strong communication skills, including the ability to speak persuasively and listen actively.
- Emotional intelligence, such as empathy and the ability to connect with others on a personal level.
- Confidence and the ability to take decisive action when needed.
- Integrity and authenticity in their actions and decisions.

Evaluate Past Performance. Review the candidates' past performance and achievements. Look for evidence of their ability to lead and inspire others, particularly in challenging situations.

Conduct Interviews. During the interview process, assess the candidates' communication skills and their ability to connect with and influence others. Ask them about their experiences leading teams and how they motivate and inspire others.

Gather Feedback. Seek feedback from colleagues, subordinates, and other stakeholders who have worked with the candidates. This can provide insights into their leadership style and how they are perceived by others.

Look for Alignment with Organisational Values. Choose a candidate whose values align with the organisation's culture and mission. A leader who embodies the organisation's values is more likely to inspire loyalty and trust.

Consider a Trial Period. Depending on the context, you may consider appointing the candidate in an acting or interim capacity to observe their leadership in practice before making a final decision.

Assess Charismatic Leadership Potential. Evaluate the candidates' potential for charismatic leadership through behavioural assessments, situational role-playing, or psychological evaluations.

Offer Support and Development. Once a leader is appointed, provide ongoing support and opportunities for development to help them grow and succeed in their role.

Monitor Performance and Impact. After appointing the leader, monitor their performance and the impact they have on the organisation and their team. Adjust your decision, if necessary, based on their effectiveness.

By adhering to these slew of selective steps, one can increase the likelihood of selecting and appointing a charismatic leader who will have a positive impact on the organisation and its people.

Step 2: Maintain Morale and Discipline

Ensuring good morale and discipline within your organisation requires a comprehensive approach that encompasses leadership, communication, and organisational culture. Here are several suggestions to help maintain good morale and discipline:

Provide Strong Leadership. Leaders set the tone for the organisation. Display integrity, consistency, and fairness in your decisions and actions. Be approachable and willing to listen to employees' concerns.

Create a Positive Work Environment. Foster a culture of respect, trust, and inclusivity. Encourage collaboration and teamwork and recognise and reward employees for their contributions.

Communicate Effectively. Maintain open lines of communication with employees. Share information transparently and provide regular updates on organisational goals and performance. Listen actively to employees' feedback and concerns.

Set Clear Expectations. Define and communicate clear expectations regarding job performance, behaviour, and responsibilities. Provide employees with the resources and training they need to meet these expectations.

Offer Opportunities for Growth. Provide opportunities for professional development and career advancement. Invest in training and mentoring programs to help employees grow and feel valued within the organisation.

Recognise and Reward Achievement. Recognise and reward employees for their hard work and achievements. This can boost morale and motivate employees to continue performing well.

Provide Work-Life Balance. Support employees in achieving a healthy work-life balance by offering flexible work arrangements and respecting personal time. This can lead to higher job satisfaction and reduced burnout.

Address Issues Promptly. Address any issues or conflicts promptly and fairly. This includes dealing with underperformance, misconduct, or interpersonal conflicts in a constructive and respectful manner.

Promote Team Building. Encourage team-building activities and opportunities for employees to build relationships outside of work tasks. This can strengthen team cohesion and improve collaboration.

Lead by Example. Demonstrate the values and behaviours you expect from employees. Lead by example in terms of work ethic, professionalism, and adherence to organisational policies.

Encourage Employee Engagement. Involve employees in decision-making processes and solicit their input on important matters. Engaged employees are more likely to feel invested in the organisation's success.

Monitor and Evaluate. Regularly monitor employee morale and discipline through surveys, feedback sessions, and performance evaluations. Use the data collected to identify areas for improvement.

By implementing these methods, one can create an environment where employees feel motivated, supported, and engaged, which can lead to good morale and discipline within your organisation.

Step 3: Gather Timely and Accurate Intelligence

Gathering strategic intelligence on an adversary is a critical component of successful strategic planning. It involves collecting, analysing, and interpreting information about the adversary's capabilities, intentions, and potential actions. Here are some key steps and methods for gathering strategic intelligence on an adversary:

Define Intelligence Objectives. Start by identifying the specific questions you need to answer about the adversary. These could include their capabilities, intentions, suppliers, or financial strength.

Use Multiple Sources. Gather intelligence from a variety of sources to get a comprehensive view of the adversary and to ensure rigour has been applied. Contradictory information should be analysed further. Sources can include:

- **Open-source intelligence (OSINT)**. Publicly available information such as news articles, reports, and online content.
- **Human intelligence (HUMINT)**. Information gathered from human sources, such as informants or agents.
- **Signals intelligence (SIGINT)**. Intercepted communications or electronic signals.
- **Imagery intelligence (IMINT)**. Aerial or satellite images that provide visual information about the adversary's activities.
- **Measurement and signature intelligence (MASINT)**. Scientific and technical data collected from various sources.

Monitor Key Indicators. Track specific indicators that can provide insight into the adversary's capabilities and intentions, such as troop movements, equipment deployments, or economic activity.

Analyse Patterns and Trends. Look for patterns and trends in the data collected to identify potential strategies or tactics the adversary may employ. This can help you anticipate their actions.

Utilise Intelligence Analysis Techniques. Employ techniques such as trend analysis, scenario analysis, and red teaming to evaluate the intelligence collected and identify potential threats or opportunities.

Collaborate with Allies. Share intelligence and insights with allies to gain a broader perspective on the adversary and strengthen your strategic position.

Stay Updated. Continuously monitor and update intelligence to account for changes in the adversary's behaviour or capabilities. Timeliness is crucial in strategic intelligence.

Verify and Cross-Check Information. Validating the accuracy of the intelligence gathered by cross-checking information from different sources. This helps avoid acting on incorrect or misleading intelligence.

Protect Your Own Intelligence Sources. Ensuring the security of your intelligence operations and sources to prevent compromise. This includes protecting data and maintaining operational secrecy.

Integrate Intelligence with Strategic Planning. Use the intelligence gathered to inform strategic decision-making and planning. This can help you anticipate the adversary's moves and formulate effective counterstrategies.

By adhering to these steps and methods, you can gather strategic intelligence on an adversary that can provide valuable insights for making informed decisions and developing effective strategies.

Step 4: Identify Fault Lines in the Adversaries' Organisation and then Divide and Conquer

Identifying weaknesses in a competitor can provide valuable insights for formulating a divide-and-conquer strategy. This approach involves exploiting the competitor's vulnerabilities to gain a strategic advantage. Here are steps to identify weaknesses in a competitor and implement a divide-and-conquer strategy.

Conduct a Comprehensive Analysis. Begin with a thorough analysis of the competitor's organisation, including its structure, operations, market presence, and performance. Examine various aspects such as financials, market share, product lines, customer base, and reputation.

Identify Key Areas of Vulnerability. One can search for specific areas where the competitor may be weak or vulnerable. These can include:

- **Market share**. A competitor with declining market share or limited presence in certain markets may be vulnerable.
- **Product quality or range**. Weaknesses in product quality or a limited product range can be exploited.
- **Customer satisfaction**. Low customer satisfaction or loyalty can indicate a vulnerability.
- **Financial stability**. A competitor with financial difficulties may struggle to sustain operations or invest in new opportunities.
- **Organisational structure**. A rigid or inefficient structure can hinder a competitor's ability to adapt or respond quickly.
- **Leadership issues**. Weak or unstable leadership can create internal divisions or hinder strategic decision-making.

Monitor Competitor Behaviour. Observe how the competitor behaves in response to market changes or competitive pressures. Look for signs of internal conflict, indecision, or erratic behaviour that may indicate underlying weaknesses.

Leverage Competitive Intelligence. Gather intelligence on the competitor's activities, plans, and strategies. This can provide insights into areas where they may be struggling or overextending themselves.

Assess Relationships and Alliances. Examine the competitor's relationships with suppliers, partners, and allies. Weaknesses in these relationships can create opportunities to divide and conquer.

Evaluate Customer Perception. Analyse customer feedback and reviews of the competitor's products or services. Negative perceptions can be an indication of weaknesses that can be exploited.

Formulate a Divide-and-Conquer Strategy. Based on the identified weaknesses, develop a strategy to exploit them. This could include:

- **Targeting specific market segments**. Focus on areas where the competitor is weak or has limited presence.
- **Offering superior products or services**. Address customer dissatisfaction with the competitor by offering better alternatives.
- **Building alliances with their partners or customers**. Attracting key partners or customers away from the competitor can weaken their position.
- **Exploiting internal divisions**. If the competitor has internal conflicts, use them to your advantage.
- **Execute with Caution**. Be cautious in executing the divide-and-conquer approach. Avoid being too aggressive or overt, as this could provoke a strong response from the competitor.

By carefully analysing the competitor's weaknesses and formulating a targeted strategy, you can effectively divide and conquer to gain a competitive advantage.

Step 5: Intimidate the Adversary

Intimidating an adversary organisation involves creating a perception of strength and control while instilling fear or doubt about their ability to succeed as a prelude to a battle. However, it's significant and important to approach this strategy with caution and ethics, as overly aggressive or unethical intimidation tactics can backfire and harm your reputation. Here are some methods to intimidate an adversary organisation.

Project Strength and Confidence. Demonstrate your organisation's strength through visible successes, strategic alliances, and strong leadership. Confidence can be a powerful tool in intimidating an adversary.

Display Superior Capabilities. Showcase your organisation's superior capabilities, whether in terms of technology, resources, or expertise. This can make the adversary think twice about engaging in direct competition.

Control the Narrative. Manage the public perception of the competition by highlighting your achievements and strengths. Use effective communication to shape the narrative in your favour.

Demonstrate Preparedness. Show that your organisation is prepared for any eventuality. This includes having contingency plans, strong security measures, and a well-coordinated team.

Leverage Intelligence. Use intelligence to anticipate the adversary's moves and stay ahead of them. Being able to predict their actions can give you a strategic advantage.

Exploit Psychological Warfare. Engage in psychological warfare by creating uncertainty and doubt in the adversary's mind. This can be done through subtle but impactful messaging, disinformation, or displays of unexpected strength.

Show Determination and Persistence. Demonstrate your resolve and willingness to fight for your interests. This can discourage the adversary from pursuing aggressive tactics against you.

Utilise Legal and Ethical Means. Use legal and ethical means to challenge the adversary's actions. Legal challenges, regulatory scrutiny, or public exposure of unethical behaviour can intimidate an adversary.

Strengthen Your Position. Solidify your position in the market by securing key partnerships, customers, or supply chains. This can make it more difficult for the adversary to challenge you.

Control Access and Resources. Limit the adversary's access to critical resources, such as suppliers, distribution channels, or information. This can weaken their ability to compete effectively.

Engage in Strategic Signalling. Send strategic signals through public statements, announcements, or demonstrations of power. This can communicate your intentions and capabilities to the adversary.

Focus on Reputation Management. Protect your organisation's reputation and ensure it remains strong. A solid reputation can instil fear in the adversary and deter them from engaging in conflict.

Remember that while intimidating an adversary can provide a strategic advantage, it should be done ethically and with consideration for potential consequences. Overly aggressive tactics can damage relationships, provoke retaliation, and harm your reputation in the long run. It's important to strike a balance between assertiveness and diplomacy.

Step 6: Identify Partners and Allies

Identifying good business partners and allies is essential for building strong relationships that can provide mutual benefits, enhance your business capabilities, and contribute to your strategic goals. Here are some key steps to identify and evaluate potential business partners and allies.

Define Your Objectives. Start by clearly defining your business objectives and what you hope to achieve through a partnership or alliance. This will guide your search for partners whose goals align with yours.

Research Potential Partners. Look for organisations that complement your business and share similar values and goals. Consider their reputation, market presence, financial stability, and track record of successful partnerships.

Assess Compatibility. Evaluate potential partners for compatibility in terms of culture, values, and communication styles. Compatibility ensures that both parties can work effectively together and avoid conflicts.

Review Capabilities and Strengths. Assess the potential partner's capabilities, resources, and strengths. Consider how their expertise or assets can complement and enhance your business.

Evaluate Past Performance. Review the potential partner's past performance in similar partnerships or collaborations. Look for evidence of successful outcomes and a strong commitment to collaboration.

Check References. Ask for references from previous partners or clients and seek feedback on their experiences. This can provide insights into the potential partner's reliability and integrity.

Analyse Strategic Fit. Determine how the potential partner's business aligns with your strategic goals and objectives. Consider whether the partnership can create synergies and provide opportunities for growth.

Consider Long-Term Potential. Evaluate the potential for a long-term relationship with the partner. A strong, enduring partnership can yield more benefits over time than a short-term one.

Review Legal and Ethical Considerations. Ensure the potential partner operates within legal and ethical boundaries. This helps protect your business from potential risks and reputational damage.

Assess Communication and Trust. Evaluate the potential partner's communication style and their willingness to share information openly. Trust is a critical component of successful partnerships.

Negotiate Terms and Expectations. Clearly define and negotiate the terms of the partnership, including roles, responsibilities, and expectations. This helps avoid misunderstandings and conflicts down the line.

Look for Complementary Networks. Consider how the potential partner's networks and connections can benefit your business. Access to new markets, customers, or suppliers can be a valuable asset.

Pilot the Partnership. If possible, start with a pilot project or a smaller-scale collaboration to test the relationship and assess how well you work together.

By following these steps, you can identify potential business partners and allies that align with your goals and offer the potential for a mutually beneficial relationship. Establishing strong partnerships can help your business grow and thrive.

Step 7: Ensure Adequate Resources and Logistics

Ensuring adequate resources and logistics for your strategy is critical for successful implementation and achieving your goals. Effective planning and management can help you allocate resources efficiently and maintain a smooth supply chain. Here are some key steps to ensure you have the resources and logistics needed for your strategy.

Identify Resource Requirements. Determine the resources needed to execute your strategy, including human resources, financial resources, equipment, technology, and materials.

Assess Availability and Accessibility. Evaluate the availability and accessibility of the resources you need. Consider factors such as current inventory, supplier reliability, and potential lead times.

Create a Detailed Budget. Develop a comprehensive budget that outlines the costs associated with your strategy. This includes expenses for procurement, production, logistics, and other related costs.

Establish Relationships with Suppliers. Build strong relationships with reliable suppliers who can consistently provide the quality and quantity of resources you need. Negotiate favourable terms and maintain open lines of communication.

Plan for Contingencies. Prepare for unexpected disruptions by creating contingency plans. This could involve maintaining buffer stock, diversifying suppliers, or having backup plans for critical resources.

Optimise Supply Chain and Logistics. Streamline your supply chain and logistics to ensure efficient movement of resources. This includes optimising transportation routes, warehousing, and inventory management.

Monitor and Track Resources. Implement systems to monitor and track resource usage and availability in real time. This helps you identify potential shortages and adjust your plans as needed.

Allocate Resources Strategically. Distribute resources according to the priorities and needs of your strategy. Avoid over-allocating to one area at the expense of others.

Review and Adjust Regularly. Regularly review your resource allocation and logistics plans to ensure they remain aligned with your strategy and any changes in the operating environment.

Leverage Technology. Utilise technology solutions such as inventory management software, demand forecasting, and supply chain analytics to enhance efficiency and visibility.

Engage in Risk Management. Identify and assess potential risks that could impact your resource availability or logistics. Develop risk management strategies to mitigate or respond to these risks.

Collaborate with Stakeholders. Involve key stakeholders, including team members, suppliers, and partners, in planning and decision-making processes. Their input can provide valuable insights into resource and logistics challenges.

Ensure Regulatory Compliance. Stay informed of relevant regulations and standards that may impact your resources and logistics. Ensure your plans comply with all legal and ethical requirements.

By following these steps and maintaining a proactive approach to resource and logistics management, you can ensure that your strategy is well-supported and has the best chance of success.

Step 8: Act More Quickly Than the Adversary

Acting more quickly and decisively than your adversary can provide you with a significant strategic advantage. It allows you to capitalise on opportunities, pre-empt potential threats, and dictate the pace and direction of engagement. Here are some strategies to ensure that you act quickly and decisively.

Streamline Decision-Making. Simplify your decision-making processes to reduce delays. Define clear decision-making authority and protocols and empower leaders to make decisions efficiently.

Prepare in Advance. Anticipate potential scenarios and prepare responses in advance. This includes creating contingency plans and decision trees for likely situations.

Develop Situational Awareness. Maintain up-to-date intelligence and information about your adversary and the environment. This allows you to recognise opportunities and threats quickly.

Leverage Technology. Utilise technology such as real-time data analytics, monitoring systems, and communication tools to stay informed and make decisions faster.

Empower Your Team. Delegate authority and empower your team members to act autonomously within defined boundaries. This can speed up decision-making and execution at different levels of your organisation.

Practice and Train. Conduct regular training and exercises to build your team's ability to react quickly and decisively. Scenarios and simulations can help you practice decision-making under pressure.

Foster a Proactive Mindset. Encourage a culture of proactivity and innovation within your organisation. Being proactive allows you to anticipate and address challenges before they arise.

Maintain Flexibility. Design your strategy and operations to be flexible and adaptable to changing circumstances. This allows you to pivot quickly when needed.

Focus on Key Priorities. Prioritise tasks and objectives to focus your resources on what matters most. This ensures that you can act quickly on high-priority issues.

Cultivate Strong Communication. Maintain clear and efficient communication channels within your team. This allows for rapid information sharing and decision-making.

Monitor and Evaluate Continuously. Continuously monitor your performance and evaluate outcomes to identify areas for improvement. This can help you act more quickly in future situations.

Stay Informed. Keep abreast of industry trends, market changes, and emerging threats. Being well-informed helps you anticipate and respond more effectively.

Leverage Relationships and Networks: Utilise your networks and alliances to gain insights and support for quick decision-making and action.

By streamlining your decision-making processes, staying informed, and empowering your team, you can act more quickly and decisively than your adversary. This agility can give you a competitive edge and increase your chances of success.

Step 9: Determine the Decisive Actions Required for Success

Determining the decisive actions required for strategic success involves a combination of strategic planning, analysis, and evaluation. It requires identifying the critical levers that will have the most significant impact on achieving your goals and focusing your efforts accordingly. Here are some key steps to determine the decisive actions required for strategic success.

Set Clear Objectives. Start by defining clear, measurable objectives that align with your overall strategic goals. This will help you identify the actions needed to achieve these targets.

Conduct a SWOT Analysis. Perform a Strengths, Weaknesses, Opportunities, and Threats (SWOT) analysis to assess your internal and external environment. This can help you identify potential opportunities to capitalise on and challenges to address.

Prioritise Initiatives. Identify and prioritise initiatives that will have the most significant impact on achieving your objectives. Consider factors such as potential Return on Investment (ROI), risk, and alignment with your goals.

Identify Key Performance Indicators (KPIs). Define KPIs that will help you measure progress towards your objectives. These metrics will guide your decision-making and help you track the effectiveness of your actions.

Analyse Competitive Landscape. Study the competitive landscape to understand your position relative to your competitors. Identify their strengths and weaknesses and determine how your actions can give you a competitive edge.

Consider Resource Allocation. Evaluate your available resources and allocate them strategically to support your key initiatives. Ensure that you have the right people, technology, and capital to execute your actions effectively.

Develop Action Plans. Create detailed action plans for each initiative, outlining the specific steps, timelines, and responsibilities involved. This provides a roadmap for execution and helps ensure accountability.

Leverage Data and Insights. Utilise data and insights to inform your decision-making. This includes market research, customer feedback, and performance data to guide your actions.

Plan for Contingencies. Anticipate potential challenges and develop contingency plans to address them. This allows you to stay flexible and adapt your actions as needed.

Collaborate and Communicate. Foster collaboration and communication within your team and with stakeholders. This ensures everyone is aligned and working towards the same goals.

Monitor and Adjust. Continuously monitor progress towards your objectives and evaluate the effectiveness of your actions. Be prepared to adjust your plans based on new information or changing circumstances.

Focus on Execution. While planning is important, execution is where real impact is made. Focus on efficient and effective execution of your decisive actions to drive success.

By following these steps and regularly reassessing your strategic approach, you can determine the decisive actions required for strategic success and maximise your chances of achieving your goals.

Step 10: Prepare and Resource for the Unexpected

Strategically preparing and resourcing for the unexpected involves building resilience into your organisation so that you can respond effectively to unforeseen events and disruptions. Here are key steps to prepare and resource for the unexpected.

Conduct Risk Assessments. Identify potential risks and threats that could impact your business. This includes internal and external risks such as supply chain disruptions, economic downturns, regulatory changes, or natural disasters.

Develop Contingency Plans. Create contingency plans for the most likely risks. These plans outline steps to take in response to different scenarios, ensuring you can act quickly and efficiently when unexpected events occur.

Maintain Emergency Reserves. Keep emergency reserves of critical resources such as cash, inventory, and raw materials. This buffer can help you navigate disruptions without major interruptions to operations.

Diversify Supply Chains. Reduce dependency on single suppliers or sources of resources. Diversification helps mitigate risks associated with supply chain disruptions and provides alternative options.

Build Redundancy. Create redundancy in key systems and processes, such as IT infrastructure and communication channels. Redundancy ensures continuity even if one system fails.

Foster a Culture of Adaptability. Encourage a culture of flexibility and adaptability within your organisation. This empowers your team to respond quickly to changing circumstances.

Invest in Training and Preparedness. Conduct regular training and drills to prepare your team for emergency situations. Familiarity with emergency protocols can help reduce response times.

Implement Robust Communication Channels. Ensure clear and efficient communication channels are in place for disseminating information and coordinating responses during unexpected events.

Monitor and Evaluate Continuously. Continuously monitor your business environment for signs of change and potential risks. This allows you to anticipate disruptions and adjust your plans accordingly.

Leverage Technology and Data. Use technology and data analytics to gain real-time insights into your operations and market trends. This can help you detect anomalies early and respond proactively.

Collaborate with Partners and Allies. Strengthen relationships with partners and allies who can provide support during times of crisis. This includes suppliers, customers, and industry associations.

Stay Informed on Regulations and Compliance. Keep up with changes in regulations and compliance requirements that may impact your business. Being prepared for regulatory changes can help you avoid disruptions.

Document Processes and Knowledge. Maintain clear documentation of key processes and institutional knowledge. This can help ensure continuity even if key personnel are unavailable.

Create a Crisis Management Team. Establish a crisis management team responsible for coordinating responses to unexpected events. This team should have clear roles and responsibilities.

Conduct Regular Reviews and Updates. Regularly review and update your contingency plans and risk assessments. As your business evolves, new risks may arise that need to be addressed.

By taking these proactive measures, you can strategically prepare and resource for the unexpected, allowing your organisation to respond effectively to challenges and maintain resilience in the face of disruptions.

Commentaries on the Gallic War – A Summary

Julius Caesar's "Commentarii de Bello Gallico" (Commentaries on the Gallic War) is a first-hand account of his campaigns in Gaul between 58 and 50 BCE. The text provides detailed descriptions of his military strategies, tactics, and leadership style.

The Key Strategic Lessons from the Campaigns of Julius Caesar are:

- Effective Leadership.
- Preparation and Planning.
- Divide and Conquer.
- Psychological Warfare.
- Diplomacy, Partnerships and Alliances.
- Logistics and Supply Lines.
- Speed and Mobility.
- Calculated Risk Taking.
- Decisive Actions.
- Adaptability and Flexibility.

Julius Caesar's Ten Step Strategic Toolset:

Step 1: Appoint a Charismatic Leader

- Define the Role and Expectations.
- Identify Key Qualities.
- Evaluate Past Performance.
- Conduct Interviews.
- Gather Feedback.
- Look for Alignment with Organisational Values.
- Consider a Trial Period.
- Assess Charismatic Leadership Potential.
- Offer Support and Development.
- Monitor Performance and Impact.

Step 2: Maintain Morale and Discipline

- Provide Strong Leadership.
- Create a Positive Work Environment.
- Communicate Effectively.
- Set Clear Expectations.
- Offer Opportunities for Growth.
- Recognise and Reward Achievement.
- Provide Work-Life Balance.
- Address Issues Promptly.
- Promote Team Building.
- Lead by Example.
- Encourage Employee Engagement.
- Monitor and Evaluate.

Step 3: Gather Timely and Accurate Intelligence

- Define Intelligence Objectives.

- Use Multiple Sources.
- Monitor Key Indicators.
- Analyse Patterns and Trends.
- Utilise Intelligence Analysis Techniques.
- Collaborate with Allies.
- Stay Updated.
- Verify and Cross-Check Information.
- Protect Your Own Intelligence Sources.
- Integrate Intelligence with Strategic Planning.

Step 4: Identify Fault Lines in the Adversaries' Organisation and then Divide and Conquer

- Conduct a Comprehensive Analysis.
- Identify Key Areas of Vulnerability.
- Monitor Competitor Behaviour.
- Leverage Competitive Intelligence.
- Assess Relationships and Alliances.
- Evaluate Customer Perception.
- Formulate a Divide-and-Conquer Strategy.
- Targeting specific market segments.
- Offering superior products or services.
- Building alliances with their partners or customers.
- Exploiting internal divisions.
- Execute with Caution.

Step 5: Intimidate the Adversary

- Project Strength and Confidence.
- Display Superior Capabilities.
- Control the Narrative.
- Demonstrate Preparedness.

- Leverage Intelligence.
- Exploit Psychological Warfare.
- Show Determination and Persistence.
- Utilise Legal and Ethical Means.
- Strengthen Your Position.
- Control Access and Resources.
- Engage in Strategic Signalling.
- Focus on Reputation Management.

Step 6: Identify Partners and Allies

- Define Your Objectives.
- Research Potential Partners.
- Assess Compatibility.
- Review Capabilities and Strengths.
- Evaluate Past Performance.
- Check References.
- Analyse Strategic Fit.
- Consider Long-Term Potential.
- Review Legal and Ethical Considerations.
- Assess Communication and Trust.
- Negotiate Terms and Expectations.
- Look for Complementary Networks.
- Pilot the Partnership.

Step 7: Ensure Adequate Resources and Logistics

- Identify Resource Requirements.
- Assess Availability and Accessibility.
- Create a Detailed Budget.
- Establish Relationships with Suppliers.
- Plan for Contingencies.

- Optimise Supply Chain and Logistics.
- Monitor and Track Resources.
- Allocate Resources Strategically.
- Review and Adjust Regularly.
- Leverage Technology.
- Engage in Risk Management.
- Collaborate with Stakeholders.
- Ensure Regulatory Compliance.

Step 8: Act More Quickly Than the Adversary

- Streamline Decision-Making.
- Prepare in Advance.
- Develop Situational Awareness.
- Leverage Technology.
- Empower Your Team.
- Practice and Train.
- Foster a Proactive Mindset.
- Maintain Flexibility.
- Focus on Key Priorities.
- Cultivate Strong Communication.
- Monitor and Evaluate Continuously.
- Stay Informed.
- Leverage Relationships and Networks.

Step 9: Determine the Decisive Actions Required for Success

- Set Clear Objectives.
- Conduct a SWOT Analysis.
- Prioritise Initiatives.
- Identify Key Performance Indicators (KPIs).
- Analyse Competitive Landscape.

- Consider Resource Allocation.
- Develop Action Plans.
- Leverage Data and Insights.
- Plan for Contingencies.
- Collaborate and Communicate.
- Monitor and Adjust.
- Focus on Execution.

Step 10: Prepare and Resource for the Unexpected

- Conduct Risk Assessments.
- Develop Contingency Plans.
- Maintain Emergency Reserves.
- Diversify Supply Chains.
- Build Redundancy.
- Foster a Culture of Adaptability.
- Invest in Training and Preparedness.
- Implement Robust Communication Channels.
- Monitor and Evaluate Continuously.
- Leverage Technology and Data.
- Collaborate with Partners and Allies.
- Stay Informed on Regulations and Compliance.
- Document Processes and Knowledge.
- Create a Crisis Management Team.
- Conduct Regular Reviews and Updates.

Conclusion

The astute reader will have already noted common themes from across the various texts. This suggests that while strategic philosophies have a strong cultural component, there are clearly critical elements that transcend national identity, geographical location and historical period and could be considered as core components of all successful strategy. The table below compares the different fundamentals from the six ancient texts in an attempt to pull out common themes. I have changed the order of the fundamentals described by the various texts in order to make it easier to compare similar philosophies. Those common to all texts are listed first. Some fundamentals appear more than once as they sit in multiple categories. (See table on next page)

Adaptability, Flexibility and Continual Learning

The most critical of fundamental elements that appear in all the ancient texts, and modern ones for that matter, are the overriding requirement for adaptability, flexibility and continual learning. This is such an essential part of strategy that it merits deeper discussion. The geopolitical, informational, military and economic environment in which strategy operates is constantly changing due to political shifts, the perceptions of populations, technological advancements, climate change, unexpected events, economic fluctuations, fickle consumer preferences and the like. Actions taken as part of a strategy also force change in the system and cause adversaries and allies to react, often in unintended ways. Antagonists are also attempting to impose their strategy upon you and seek competitive advantage by targeting weakness and exploiting opportunities. Organisations must adapt to these dynamic changes to remain competitive and relevant. Adaptable strategies also enable organisations to identify, assess, and

	Musashi	*Mahabharata*	*Kautilya*	*Sangam Poems*	*Sun Tzu*	*Julius Caesar*
Fundamental 1 (Adaptability, Flexibility & Continual Learning)	Never stop developing and improving your strategic mindset.	Adaptability and Flexibility. Role of Wisdom and Counsel.	Test and Adjust the Action.	Adaptability and Resilience.	Adaptability and Flexibility.	Adaptability and Flexibility.
Fundamental 2 (Leadership)	X	Leadership and Decision-Making.	Select an Effective Strategic Leader (*Vijigishu*).	Leadership and Governance.	Leadership and Discipline.	Effective Leadership.
Fundamental 3 (Preparation and Planning)	Clearly Define What Counts as a Gain and What Counts as a Loss. Take note of details.	Strategic Planning and Vision.	Define the Spiritual End-State (*Yogakshema*) Develop Options.	X	Preparation and Planning.	Preparation and Planning.
Fundamental 4 (Deception and Psychology)	Perceptions and Feelings are as Important as Movement and Objects. Develop intuitive judgement ability.	Deception and Diplomacy	Consider the Tools and Levers that can be Applied Against Entity Weak Points.	X	Deception and Indirect Approach. Winning Without Fighting.	Psychological Warfare. Divide and Conquer.
Fundamental 5 (Knowledge)	Know a lot about many things.	Understanding the Enemy	Understand the Strategic Context Conduct an Analysis of the Entities (*Mandala*). Identify Entity Weak Points.	Environmental Awareness.	Know Yourself and Know Your enemy.	X

	Musashi	*Mahabharata*	*Kautilya*	*Sangam Poems*	*Sun Tzu*	*Julius Caesar*
Fundamental 6 (Logistics)	Do nothing that is unnecessary. Doing nothing is as important as activity.	X	Determine the Resources Available.	Economic Strategies.	X	Logistics and Supply Lines.
Fundamental 7 (Ethics, Values and Standards)	Adopt a strategic mindset at all times.	*Dharma* – Righteousness. War Ethics and Conduct.	Determine the Strategic Approaches to be Used.	Ethics and Virtue	X	X
Fundamental 8 (Decisive Action, Courage, Bravery)	X	X	Decide on an Option, Refine it and Take Action.	Courage and Bravery	The Importance of Timing	Decisive Actions Speed and Mobility
Fundamental 9 (Diplomacy, Partner-ships and Alliances)	X	Alliance Building Deception and Diplomacy	X	Diplomacy and Alliances Social Cohesion and Unity Cultural Soft Power.	X	Diplomacy, Partner-ships and Alliances. Divide and Conquer.
Fundamental 10 (Understand Risk)	X	The Influence of Fate and Destiny.	Consider Calamities (Risks).	X	X	Calculated Risk Taking.
Fundamental 11 (Self Awareness)	Be Self Aware.	X	X	X	Know Yourself and Know Your enemy.	X
Fundamental 12 (Innovation and Creativity)	X	X	X	Innovation and Creativity.	X	X

respond to risks more effectively as they anticipate that unexpected and unforeseen events will occur, often at the worst possible moment. Once strategists accept the inevitability of this, it is easier to adopt adaptability, flexibility and continual learning as a core process.

Economics, industrial might, trading power and logistics are essential ingredients to good strategy. Unfortunately, in the contemporary geopolitically unstable world, modern markets and economic systems are characterised by high levels of uncertainty and complexity. Flexible strategies allow organisations to respond quickly to unforeseen challenges and opportunities, rather than being locked into a rigid plan that may become obsolete. When plans fail or deliver sub-optimal results, lessons must be learned so the same mistakes are not made again. However, it is important to accept that failure is inevitable at some stage and must be seen as a focussed learning experience that can be exploited. Organisations that punish, ignore or hide failure, or attempt to apportion blame without analysis, are doomed to disaster and perdition. Flexibility in strategy permits better allocation and reallocation of resources in response to changing conditions, ensuring that resources are used efficiently and effectively.

Continual and persistent learning enables organisations to stay ahead of competitors by fostering innovation and improving processes. Adaptable and flexible strategies help in capitalising on new trends and technologies before competitors can gain advantage. Continual learning fosters a culture of innovation, encouraging employees to acquire new skills and knowledge. This, in turn, leads to the development of new products, services, and business models that address deficiencies, exploit new opportunities and drive growth. A culture of continual learning and adaptability also helps in attracting and retaining talent. Employees are more likely to be engaged and motivated in an environment that supports their growth and adapts to their needs.

Organisations that are adaptable and flexible are better equipped to handle setbacks, crises and disruptions. As strategy is a clash of wills and systems, the adversary will always be attempting to deliver devasting blows and some will succeed. It is essential that organisations can handle these unexpected and horrific setbacks. This resilience is crucial for long-term sustainability and success. Strategic leadership is essential as there will be internal dissent and factions that will seek easy exit strategies rather than face the ordeal of another hammer blow from a determined adversary. On the other side of the same coin, organisations must remain poised to grasp fleeting opportunities such as an adversary making a mistake or an activity delivering far more success than anticipated.

In summary, adaptability, flexibility, and continual learning are essential components of a robust strategy as they enable organisations to navigate a complex and ever-changing environment, maintain competitive advantage, foster innovation, and ensure long-term sustainability and success.

Leadership, Preparation and Planning, Deception, Psychology, Knowledge

The next most important fundamental elements happen to be leadership, preparation and planning, deception, psychology, and knowledge. These are also very common themes in modern military doctrine and contemporary strategic philosophies. This suggests that like adaptability, flexibility and continual learning, they are a critical core component of all strategy. Leadership, preparation and planning, deception and psychology and knowledge could be described as cerebral fundamentals as they flow from the brain and character of the strategic leader. A strategic leader deficient in any of these areas will likely be a failure. Let's look at each in turn.

Leadership

Strategic leadership is such a vast and complex subject that it deserves a separate book, so I won't dwell on it too much here. Sound leadership is critical to good strategy for several reasons, as effective leaders provide the vision, guidance, motivation, and decision-making capabilities necessary to formulate, implement, and adapt strategies. Here's why sound leadership is so essential:

Vision and Direction. Leaders set the strategic vision and direction for the organisation. They articulate a clear and compelling future state that aligns with the organisation's values and objectives, ensuring that everyone understands the long-term goals and their role in achieving them.

Decision-Making. Effective leaders are decisive and make informed decisions that shape the strategic direction of the organisation. They analyse information, assess risks, weigh alternatives, and choose the best course of action, which is crucial for navigating complex and uncertain environments.

Resource Allocation. Sound leadership involves judicious allocation of resources, including finances, personnel, and time. Leaders prioritise initiatives that align with strategic objectives and ensure that resources are deployed efficiently to maximise impact and return on investment.

Motivation and Inspiration. Leaders inspire and motivate their teams to pursue strategic goals with enthusiasm and commitment. By fostering a sense of purpose and passion, leaders can drive higher levels of performance and engagement, which are essential for executing strategic initiatives effectively.

Change Management. Strategic shifts often require significant organisational changes. Effective leaders manage these transitions smoothly by communicating the need for change, addressing resistance, and guiding the organisation through the transformation process, ensuring that strategic objectives are met.

Crisis Management. In times of crisis, strong leadership is indispensable. Leaders must remain calm, provide direction, make quick decisions, and communicate effectively to steer the organisation through challenges and minimise disruptions to strategic plans.

Culture and Values. Leaders shape the organisational culture and uphold its values. A positive culture that promotes collaboration, innovation, and ethical behaviour supports strategic success. Leaders reinforce these values through their actions and decisions, setting the tone for the entire organisation.

Adaptability and Agility. The ability to adapt to changing circumstances is a hallmark of sound leadership. Leaders must be agile, willing to pivot strategies when necessary, and able to seize new opportunities or respond to threats effectively, ensuring that the organisation remains competitive and resilient.

Stakeholder Management. Leaders engage with various stakeholders, including employees, customers, investors, and partners. By maintaining strong relationships and understanding stakeholder needs and expectations, leaders ensure alignment and support for strategic initiatives.

Accountability and Performance Monitoring. Effective leaders establish clear accountability and performance metrics to track progress towards strategic goals. They hold themselves and their teams accountable for results, ensuring that strategic plans are executed effectively and that any deviations are addressed promptly.

Key Components of Sound Leadership for Strategy

- **Clear Communication**: Leaders must communicate the strategic vision, goals, and plans effectively to ensure that everyone in the organisation understands and is aligned with the strategy.
- **Empowerment and Delegation**: Effective leaders empower their teams by delegating authority and responsibility, fostering a sense of ownership and accountability for strategic initiatives.
- **Continuous Learning**: Leaders must be committed to continuous learning and development, staying informed about industry trends, emerging technologies, and best practices to inform strategic decisions.
- **Emotional Intelligence**: High emotional intelligence helps leaders to connect with their teams, understand their needs, and manage relationships effectively, which is crucial for fostering collaboration and commitment to strategic goals.
- **Ethical Leadership**: Upholding ethical standards and integrity are essential for building trust and credibility, both internally and externally, ensuring that strategies are not only effective but also socially responsible and sustainable.

In conclusion, sound leadership is foundational to good strategy. It leads to the development of the vision, decisiveness, motivation, and adaptability needed to formulate and execute strategies effectively. By fostering a positive culture, managing change, and engaging stakeholders, effective leaders ensure that strategic initiatives are successful, and that the organisation can navigate challenges and seize opportunities in a dynamic environment.

Preparation and Planning

Preparation and planning are essential for good and opportune strategy, because, they provide the foundation for informed decision-making, effective resource allocation, risk management, and successful execution. Here are several key reasons why preparation and planning are so crucial:

Informed Decision-Making. Effective strategy requires a deep understanding of the environment in which an organisation operates. Preparation and planning involve gathering and analysing relevant data, market trends, competitor activities, and internal capabilities. This comprehensive information base enables leaders to make informed decisions that are grounded in reality.

Clear Objectives and Goals. Preparation and planning help to define clear objectives and goals. By setting specific, measurable, achievable, relevant, and time-bound (SMART) goals, organisations can focus their efforts and resources on what matters most. Clear goals also provide a benchmark against which progress can be measured.

Resource Allocation. Strategic planning ensures that resources—financial, human, and technological—are allocated efficiently and effectively. By understanding priorities and potential constraints, organisations can direct their resources to areas that will have the greatest impact, avoiding waste and optimising outcomes.

Risk Management. Every strategy involves risks. Preparation and planning enable organisations to identify potential risks and develop mitigation strategies. By anticipating challenges and creating contingency plans, organisations can reduce the likelihood of disruptions and minimise their impact if they occur.

Coordination and Alignment. Strategic planning ensures that all parts of an organisation are working towards the same goals. It aligns the efforts of different departments and teams, ensuring coordination and synergy. This alignment enhances overall efficiency and effectiveness.

Flexibility and Adaptability. While planning is essential, it also needs to account for the fact that change is inevitable. Good strategic planning includes flexibility and adaptability, allowing organisations to pivot and adjust their strategies in response to new information or changing circumstances.

Performance Measurement. Preparation and planning establish benchmarks and key performance indicators (KPIs) that allow organisations to track progress and measure success. Regular performance reviews based on these metrics help in adjusting strategies and improving outcomes over time.

Improved Execution. A well-prepared and well-planned strategy is easier to execute because it provides a clear roadmap. Everyone involved understands their roles, responsibilities, and timelines, reducing confusion and increasing the likelihood of successful implementation.

Building Consensus and Buy-In. Strategic planning processes often involve input from various stakeholders, which helps build consensus and buy-in. When people are involved in the planning process, they are more likely to support the strategy and work towards its success.

Key Components of Effective Preparation and Planning

- **Environmental Scanning**: Analysing external and internal environments to identify opportunities, threats, strengths, and weaknesses.
- **Goal Setting**: Defining clear, actionable goals that align with the organisation's vision and mission.
- **Resource Assessment**: Evaluating the availability and capabilities of resources necessary to implement the strategy.
- **Risk Analysis**: Identifying potential risks and developing mitigation plans.
- **Stakeholder Engagement**: Involving key stakeholders in the planning process to ensure alignment and support.
- **Action Plans**: Developing detailed action plans that outline the steps required to achieve strategic goals.

- **Performance Metrics**: Establishing KPIs and benchmarks to measure progress and success.
- **Review and Adaptation**: Regularly reviewing progress and making necessary adjustments to stay on course.

In conclusion, preparation and planning are the bedrock of good strategy. They provide the clarity, direction, and framework needed to navigate complexities, allocate resources wisely, manage risks, and achieve organisational goals. Without thorough preparation and planning, strategies are likely to be poorly executed, leading to suboptimal results and missed opportunities

Deception

Deception is a crucial element in strategy for several reasons. First of all, it creates an element of surprise, which can give the deceiver a significant advantage. By misleading the opponent about one's true intentions, capabilities, or plans, the deceiver can catch the opponent off guard, making it more difficult for them to respond effectively. When an opponent is deceived, they may allocate their resources inefficiently. For example, in a military context, if an enemy is led to believe that an attack will occur at a specific location, they may concentrate their forces there, leaving other areas vulnerable. In business, a rival company might misallocate marketing funds or product development efforts based on false information about a competitor's strategy.

Deception can have a profound psychological impact on the opponent or the arch antagonist. It can spawn confusion, doubt, and uncertainty, which can impair decision-making. An opponent who is unsure of what to believe or expect is more likely to make mistakes. By misleading an opponent, a smaller or weaker force can appear stronger or more formidable than it actually is. This can deter an opponent and antagonist from taking aggressive actions or can be used to amplify the impact of an actual attack. Deception can be used to achieve broader strategic objectives without direct confrontation. For instance, in diplomacy, a country might use deception to create alliances or drive wedges between opponents without resorting to open conflict.

Principles of Effective Deception

- **Credibility**: The deceptive information must be believable and fit within the context of what the opponent knows or expects. The best deception plans show the enemy something they are expecting to see.
- **Plausibility**: The deception should be plausible enough that the opponent doesn't easily detect it as a ruse. This can take considerable resource. For example, Soviet doctrine advised commanders to commit 25% of the real force to deception.
- **Consistency**: Consistent false information is more likely to be believed than contradictory or erratic messages.
- **Patience**: Effective deception often requires patience and careful planning to ensure that the false narrative is accepted and acted upon by the opponent.
- **Assessment**. It is critical to assess whether the adversary has accepted the deception as real.

Psychology

Understanding human psychology is essential when formulating strategy because human behaviour and decision-making processes are influenced by a range of psychological factors. Here's why an understanding of psychology is crucial:

Predicting Behaviour. A deep understanding of human psychology allows strategists to predict how individuals and groups are likely to behave in certain situations. This includes anticipating reactions to different stimuli, stress responses, and decision-making patterns.

Influencing and Persuading. Strategies often aim to influence or persuade people, whether they are competitors, allies, customers, or employees. Knowledge of psychology helps in crafting messages, incentives, and environments that effectively motivate and persuade these audiences.

Exploiting Cognitive Biases. Humans are subject to various cognitive biases that can affect their judgments and decisions. By understanding these biases, strategists can design tactics that exploit them. For instance, framing effects can influence choices by presenting options in a way that highlights potential gains or losses.

Enhancing Communication. Effective communication is a cornerstone of any strategy. Understanding psychology helps in tailoring communication to resonate with different audiences, ensuring messages are clear, compelling, and motivating.

Managing Emotions. Emotions play a significant role in decision-making. Strategies that account for emotional responses can be more effective in managing conflicts, fostering cooperation, and maintaining morale. For instance, recognising the importance of pride, fear, or anger can help in designing strategies that address these emotions constructively.

Building Trust and Relationships. Trust is fundamental in any strategic interaction. Psychological insights help in understanding how trust is built, maintained, and repaired. This is crucial for forming alliances, negotiating deals, and maintaining long-term relationships.

Adapting to Cultural Differences. Cultural psychology helps in understanding how cultural backgrounds influence behaviour and decision-making. This is essential in global strategies where cultural sensitivity can mean the difference between success and failure.

Improving Decision-Making Processes. An understanding of psychology helps in designing decision-making processes that mitigate the effects of biases and enhance rational thinking. This includes structured decision-making frameworks and promoting a culture that values critical thinking and diverse perspectives.

In conclusion one may contend that, understanding human psychology is crucial for formulating effective strategies because it provides insights into how people think, feel, and act. This knowledge enables strategists to craft more effective, persuasive, and adaptive strategies across various domains.

Knowledge

A good knowledge base is essential for formulating strategy for several key reasons:

Informed Decision-Making. A comprehensive knowledge base provides the necessary information to make well-informed decisions. This includes understanding market conditions, competitive landscapes, technological trends, regulatory environments, and internal capabilities. Accurate and current information ensures that strategic choices are grounded in reality.

Identifying Opportunities and Threats. A well-maintained knowledge base helps in identifying opportunities for growth and innovation as well as potential threats. By continually gathering and analysing data, organisations can anticipate changes and respond proactively, rather than reactively.

Benchmarking and Best Practices. Knowledge of industry benchmarks and best practices allows an organisation to measure its performance against competitors and industry standards. This insight helps in setting realistic goals and adopting proven strategies to enhance efficiency and effectiveness.

Risk Management. Strategic decisions often involve significant risks. A solid knowledge base helps in identifying and assessing these risks accurately. Understanding historical data, market volatility, and previous outcomes enables better risk mitigation strategies.

Enhancing Innovation. Knowledge fosters innovation by providing insights into new technologies, market needs, and emerging trends. An organisation with a strong knowledge base can more effectively innovate, develop new products or services, and improve existing ones.

Efficient Resource Allocation. A deep understanding of internal and external environments enables better allocation of resources. This includes financial resources, human capital, and technological assets. Efficient resource allocation ensures that strategic initiatives are well-supported and more likely to succeed.

Building Competitive Advantage. A robust knowledge base can be a source of competitive advantage. It allows organisations to understand their unique strengths and weaknesses relative to competitors. Leveraging this understanding helps in crafting strategies that capitalise on strengths and address weaknesses.

Stakeholder Alignment. A well-informed strategy aligns the interests and expectations of various stakeholders, including employees, customers, investors, and partners. Clear and accurate information helps in communicating the strategy effectively and securing buy-in from all relevant parties.

Adaptability and Flexibility. In a rapidly changing environment, the ability to adapt is crucial. A comprehensive knowledge base enables continuous learning and flexibility in strategy formulation. Organisations can pivot quickly when new information or changes in the market occur.

In conclusion, a good knowledge base is the foundation upon which effective strategies are built. It ensures that decisions are informed, risks are managed, opportunities are seized, and resources are allocated efficiently. This comprehensive understanding enables organisations to develop and implement strategies that are realistic, innovative, and aligned with their overall goals and objectives.

Logistics, Ethics, Values and Standards

Analysis of the six ancient texts shows that the next most important grouping of fundamentals are logistics, ethics, values and standards. Let's look at each of these in turn.

Logistics

Sound logistics are essential for good strategy because they ensure the efficient and effective execution of plans. Here are several reasons why logistics play a critical role in the success of a strategy:

Resource Optimisation. Logistics involves the management of resources such as materials, personnel, and equipment. Efficient logistics ensure that these resources are utilised optimally, reducing waste and cost. This allows organisations to achieve their strategic objectives without overspending.

Timely Execution. Good logistics ensure that goods and services are delivered on time and in an opportune manner. In many strategic initiatives, timing is crucial. Delays can lead to missed opportunities, increased costs, and dissatisfaction among customers or stakeholders. Effective logistics help maintain schedules and meet deadlines.

Customer Satisfaction. Logistics directly impact customer satisfaction.

Reliable and timely delivery of products and services enhances customer experience and loyalty. A strategic focus on logistics ensures that customer needs are met consistently, supporting overall strategic goals.

Competitive Advantage. Superior logistics can provide a competitive edge. Companies that can deliver products faster, more reliably, and at lower costs than their competitors can dominate their markets. Effective logistics strategies can differentiate a company and make it more attractive to customers.

Risk Management. Logistics planning includes risk assessment and mitigation strategies. By identifying potential disruptions in the supply chain (such as natural disasters, political instability, or supplier issues), organisations can develop contingency plans to maintain operations. This resilience is critical for the successful implementation of any strategy.

Cost Efficiency. Sound logistics reduce operational costs through efficient transportation, warehousing, and inventory management. Cost savings from improved logistics can be redirected to other strategic initiatives, enhancing overall organisational effectiveness.

Scalability. Good logistics systems are scalable, allowing organisations to expand operations smoothly. Whether entering new markets or increasing production capacity, efficient logistics ensure that growth can be managed without compromising quality or delivery times.

Supply Chain Integration. Effective logistics integrate all sage segments of the supply chain, from the suppliers to the end customers and clientele. This integration improves communication, coordination, and collaboration among all parties involved, leading to a more cohesive and efficient strategic implementation.

Adaptability and Flexibility. Logistics systems that are well-designed are adaptable and flexible, allowing organisations to respond quickly to changing market conditions, customer demands, or unforeseen events. This agility is vital for maintaining strategic momentum and competitive positioning.

In conclusion one may contend that sound logistics are a cornerstone of good strategy because they enable the practical implementation of plans, ensuring resources are used efficiently, timelines are met, and customer satisfaction is achieved. By optimising logistics, organisations can reduce costs, mitigate risks, enhance flexibility, and maintain a competitive edge, all of which are critical for strategic success

Ethics, Values and Standards

Ethics, values, and standards are crucial for formulating good strategy for several reasons:

Building Trust and Reputation. Adhering to strong ethics and values builds trust among stakeholders, including customers, employees, investors, and partners. A reputation for integrity and ethical behaviour enhances the credibility of an organisation and fosters loyalty and long-term relationships.

Sustainable Success. Strategies grounded in ethical principles are more likely to be sustainable over the long term. Unethical practices might offer short-term gains but often lead to long-term damage, including legal penalties, financial losses, and reputational harm.

Employee Alignment and Motivation. When strategies align with the organisation's values and ethical standards, employees are more likely to feel engaged and motivated. A clear sense of purpose and shared values can enhance morale, productivity, and retention.

Risk Mitigation. Ethical behaviour and adherence to standards help in mitigating risks, particularly those related to legal compliance and regulatory requirements. By operating within legal and ethical boundaries, organisations avoid fines, sanctions, and other legal repercussions.

Customer Loyalty and Brand Strength. Customers are increasingly valuing corporate social responsibility and ethical behaviour in the contemporary context. Companies that demonstrate a commitment to ethical practices can differentiate themselves in the market, attracting and retaining customers who prioritise values and ethics.

Guidance in Decision-Making. Values and ethical standards provide a framework for decision-making, especially in complex or ambiguous situations. They help leaders and employees navigate difficult choices and ensure that actions are consistent with the organisation's principles.

Social Responsibility and Impact. Organisations have a responsibility to contribute positively to society. Strategies that incorporate ethical considerations and social values can have a significant impact on community well-being, environmental sustainability, and social justice.

Compliance and Governance. Adherence to ethical standards and values ensures compliance with laws and regulations. Good governance practices, rooted in strong ethical principles, help in maintaining transparency, accountability, and integrity within the organisation.

In conclusion, integrating ethics, values, and standards into strategy formulation is not only the right thing to do but also makes good business sense. It leads to sustainable success, builds trust, enhances reputation, and ensures that the organisation operates within legal and moral boundaries. Ultimately, ethical strategies create a solid foundation for enduring success and positive impact.

DIPLOMACY, ALLIANCES, PARTNERSHIPS, UNDERSTANDING RISK, DECISIVE ACTION, SPEED AND MOBILITY, COURAGE AND BRAVERY

The next grouping of fundamentals is deeply interconnected with a focus on defence and security. However, they are equally applicable to business and other sectors. They could be considered as 'aggressive' and 'proactive' fundamentals:

Diplomacy, Alliances and Partnerships

Alliances, diplomacy, and partnerships are crucial components of a good strategy because they enable organisations to achieve objectives that might be difficult or impossible to accomplish alone. Here's why they are so important:

Resource and Capability Enhancement. Alliances and partnerships allow organisations to pool resources, knowledge, and expertise. This collaboration can lead to enhanced capabilities that no single entity might possess. For instance, companies can share R&D costs, access new technologies, and leverage each other's strengths to innovate and improve products or services.

Market Access and Expansion. Strategic alliances and partnerships can provide access to new markets and customer bases. By partnering with local firms or entering into joint ventures, organisations can navigate regulatory environments more effectively, understand local consumer behaviour, and establish a presence in new regions more quickly and efficiently.

Risk Sharing. Collaborations can help distribute risks associated with large projects or market entry. By sharing the financial, operational, and market risks, organisations can undertake more ambitious projects than they might be able to on their own. This risk-sharing can also lead to more resilient strategic initiatives.

Competitive Advantage. Forming strategic alliances can provide a competitive edge. Partnerships can lead to better supply chain management, cost reductions, improved product offerings, and enhanced customer service. In industries where technological advancements are rapid, alliances can keep companies at the forefront of innovation.

Innovation and Learning. Alliances and partnerships foster innovation by combining different perspectives and expertise. Collaborative efforts often lead to creative solutions and advancements that individual organisations might not achieve independently. Additionally, organisations can learn best practices from their partners, enhancing their own operations.

Influence and Negotiation Power. In diplomacy, both in business and international relations, partnerships and alliances increase negotiation power. By aligning with others, organisations or nations can exert more influence over industry standards, regulations, or international policies. This collective bargaining can lead to more favourable outcomes.

Cultural and Social Synergies. Partnerships can provide cultural and social insights that enhance strategic initiatives. Understanding local customs, traditions, and social norms is critical for success in international markets. Local partners can bridge cultural gaps, ensuring that strategies are culturally sensitive and well-received.

Operational Efficiency. Operational efficiencies can be achieved through strategic partnerships. By collaborating on logistics, production, and distribution, organisations can streamline operations, reduce costs, and improve service delivery. Efficient supply chains and shared infrastructure contribute to overall strategic success.

Adaptability and Resilience. Alliances and partnerships can augment organisational adaptability and resilience. In times of crisis or rapid change, having strong relationships with partners can provide the necessary support and flexibility to adapt quickly. This network of alliances can help organisations navigate uncertainties and emerge stronger.

Key Components of Successful Alliances and Partnerships

- **Aligned Objectives**: Ensuring that all parties have shared goals and mutually beneficial outcomes.
- **Trust and Communication**: Building and maintaining trust through open, transparent communication.
- **Complementary Strengths**: Partnering with entities that offer complementary strengths and capabilities.
- **Clear Agreements**: Establishing clear, well-defined agreements regarding roles, responsibilities, and expectations.
- **Conflict Resolution Mechanisms**: Having mechanisms in place to resolve conflicts and disagreements efficiently.
- **Regular Evaluation**: Continuously evaluating the partnership to ensure it meets strategic goals and making adjustments as needed.

In conclusion, alliances, diplomacy, and partnerships are integral to formulating and executing successful strategies. They provide access to resources, markets, and expertise, enhance competitive advantage, and enable risk sharing. By leveraging these collaborative relationships, organisations can achieve greater innovation, operational efficiency, and adaptability, ultimately driving strategic success

Understanding Risk

Understanding risk is crucial while formulating strategy because it enables organisations to anticipate, prepare for, and mitigate potential negative impacts on their objectives. Here's why comprehending risk is so important a task:

Informed Decision-Making. Risk assessment provides a clearer picture of the potential outcomes of strategic decisions. By understanding the risks involved, leaders can make informed choices, balancing potential rewards against possible downsides.

Proactive Problem Solving. Identifying risks early in the strategic planning process allows organisations to address potential problems before they materialise. This proactive approach can prevent minor issues from escalating into major crises.

Resource Allocation. Understanding risks helps in prioritising resource allocation. Organisations can direct resources towards high-risk areas that need more attention and investment in mitigation strategies, ensuring better protection and more efficient use of assets.

Competitive Advantage. Effective risk management can provide a competitive edge. Organisations that can anticipate and navigate risks better than their competitors are more likely to seize opportunities and avoid pitfalls, positioning themselves favourably in the market.

Financial Stability. Comprehensive risk assessment is vital for financial planning and stability. By understanding potential financial risks, organisations can create buffers, such as contingency funds, insurance, and diversified investments, to safeguard against financial instability.

Stakeholder Confidence. Transparent risk management builds confidence among stakeholders, including investors, employees, customers, and partners. When stakeholders see that an organisation understands and manages risks effectively, they are more likely to trust and support it.

Legal and Regulatory Compliance. Understanding and managing risks related to legal and regulatory requirements is crucial for compliance. Non-compliance can result in fines, sanctions, and damage to reputation. Risk assessment ensures that strategies are aligned with legal standards.

Operational Continuity. Identifying operational risks helps in developing contingency plans to ensure business continuity. This is especially important in scenarios like natural disasters, cyberattacks, or supply chain disruptions. Effective risk management ensures that operations can continue or quickly resume after a disruption.

Strategic Flexibility and Adaptability. Understanding risk allows organisations to build flexibility and adaptability into their strategies. They can develop alternative plans and responses for different risk scenarios, ensuring that they can adapt swiftly to changing circumstances.

Innovation and Growth. While risk is often associated with negative outcomes, it also encompasses the uncertainties involved in pursuing new opportunities. Understanding these risks can help organisations take calculated risks, fostering innovation and growth while minimising potential downsides.

Key Components of Risk Management in Strategy Formulation

- **Risk Identification**: Systematically delineating potential risks that could impact the strategy.
- **Risk Assessment**: Evaluating the likelihood and potential impact of identified risks.
- **Risk Prioritisation**: Ranking risks based on their severity and the organisation's capacity to manage them.
- **Risk Mitigation**: Developing strategies and actions to minimise the impact of high-priority risks.
- **Monitoring and Review**: Continuously monitoring risks and the effectiveness of mitigation strategies and adjusting a necessary element.

Practical Approaches to Risk Management

- **SWOT Analysis**: Identifying strengths, weaknesses, opportunities, and threats to understand internal and external risks.
- **Scenario Planning**: Creating different scenarios to anticipate and plan for potential future risks.
- **Risk Matrices**: Using tools to visually assess and prioritise risks based on their impact and likelihood.
- **Contingency Planning**: Developing backup plans for critical operations in case primary strategies fail due to unforeseen risks.

In conclusion, understanding risk is integral to formulating robust and resilient strategies. It allows organisations to anticipate challenges, allocate resources effectively, ensure operational continuity, and foster innovation. By comprehensively assessing and managing risks, organisations can enhance their strategic planning, safeguard their interests, and achieve long-term success

Decisive Action, Speed and Mobility

Decisive action, speed, and mobility are critical components of successful strategy because they enable organisations to effectively respond to opportunities and threats in dynamic environments. Here's why these elements are so important:

Exploiting Opportunities. In fast-moving situations, opportunities often arise suddenly and may be fleeting. Decisive action allows organisations to capitalise on these opportunities before competitors do. Speed ensures that initiatives can be launched quickly to gain first-mover advantages or respond to emerging trends.

Competitive Advantage. Speed and mobility can provide a significant competitive edge. Organisations that can quickly adapt to changes, innovate, and bring products or services to market faster than competitors are more likely to dominate their industries. This agility helps in staying ahead of the competition and meeting customer demands promptly.

Crisis Management. In times of crisis, such as natural disasters, economic downturns, or public relations issues, the ability to act decisively and swiftly is crucial. Quick and effective responses can mitigate damage, maintain operations, and protect the organisation's reputation.

Resource Efficiency. Decisive action minimises the time and resources spent on decision-making processes. By reducing delays and bureaucracy, organisations can allocate resources more effectively and maintain momentum in their strategic initiatives.

Adaptability to Change. In a constantly evolving environment, the ability to move quickly and adapt to new circumstances is vital. Mobility allows organisations to pivot their strategies, reallocate resources, and implement new plans efficiently, ensuring they remain relevant and resilient.

Maintaining Morale and Confidence. Decisive leadership instils confidence in employees, investors, and other stakeholders. When leaders act quickly and decisively, it demonstrates control and foresight, boosting morale and trust within the organisation.

Market Responsiveness. Speed and mobility enable organisations to respond effectively to customer feedback and market demands. Rapid iteration and improvement of products or services based on real-time data can enhance customer satisfaction and loyalty.

Innovation and Development. In industries driven by innovation, such as technology, pharmaceuticals, and consumer electronics, speed to market is crucial. The ability to quickly develop, test, and launch new products can determine success or failure. Decisive action facilitates rapid innovation cycles and continuous improvement.

Key Components of Decisive Action, Speed, and Mobility:

- **Clear Vision and Objectives**: Having a well-defined vision and clear strategic objectives ensures that actions are aligned with the overall goals of the organisation.
- **Empowered Decision-Making**: Decentralising decision-making and empowering frontline managers and employees to act swiftly reduces bottlenecks and accelerates response times.
- **Agile Processes**: Implementing agile methodologies, such as iterative development and continuous feedback loops, allows for rapid adaptation and continuous improvement.
- **Efficient Communication**: Fast and effective communication channels enable quick dissemination of information and coordination across the organisation.
- **Flexible Resources**: Maintaining flexible resource allocations and having contingency plans in place ensures that the organisation can quickly shift focus and resources as needed.

Practical Approaches to Enhance Decisive Action, Speed, and Mobility

- **Lean Management**: Adopting lean principles to streamline processes, eliminate waste, and enhance operational efficiency.
- **Scenario Planning**: Preparing for various scenarios to enable quick decision-making when unexpected events occur.
- **Technology Adoption**: Leveraging advanced technologies for real-time data analysis, automation, and communication to accelerate decision-making and execution.
- **Cross-Functional Teams**: Creating cross-functional teams to enhance collaboration and speed up project execution.

In conclusion, one may advance the notion that, decisive action, speed, and mobility are essential for executing effective strategies in today's fast-paced and ever-changing environment. These elements enable organisations to seize opportunities, respond to threats, innovate continuously, and maintain a competitive edge. By fostering a culture of agility and empowerment, organisations can ensure they are well-positioned to achieve their strategic goals and thrive in the face of uncertainty

Courage and Bravery

Courage and bravery are essential for good strategy, though they might not be mentioned as often as other strategic principles. These qualities are crucial for several reasons:

Decision-Making Under Uncertainty. Strategic decisions often involve uncertainty and risk. Courage allows leaders to make bold decisions despite the unknowns. Bravery in decision-making is essential for seizing opportunities that others might shy away from due to fear of failure or uncertainty.

Implementing Change. Strategic shifts often require significant changes, which can be met with resistance from within the organisation. It takes courage to lead through such changes, confronting opposition, and staying committed to the vision despite obstacles and pushback.

Risk-Taking. Innovation and growth often require taking calculated risks.

Leaders must be brave and courageous enough to pursue new ventures, enter untested markets, or invest in cutting-edge technologies. Without courage, organisations may stagnate, missing out on potential breakthroughs and opportunities for advancement.

Facing Adversity. During crises or challenging times, courageous leadership is critical. Bravery helps leaders to remain calm, focused, and decisive under pressure, guiding their teams through adversity and making tough calls that are necessary for survival and recovery.

Ethical Integrity. Maintaining ethical integrity can sometimes require bravery, especially when it involves standing up against unethical practices, making unpopular decisions, or speaking out in the face of wrongdoing. Courage ensures that strategies are not only effective but also ethically sound.

Inspiring and Motivating Teams. Courageous leaders inspire and motivate their teams. When employees see their leaders displaying bravery in the face of challenges, they are more likely to feel empowered and motivated to contribute their best efforts. This can lead to greater overall commitment and performance.

Long-Term Vision. Pursuing a long-term vision often involves enduring short-term sacrifices and setbacks. Bravery is necessary to stay the course and continue working towards the strategic goals, even when immediate results are not favourable.

Key Components of Courage and Bravery in Strategy

- **Visionary Leadership**: Having a clear, bold vision that may not be immediately achievable but drives long-term strategic direction.
- **Resilience**: The ability to persevere and maintain strategic focus despite setbacks, criticism, or failures.
- **Integrity**: Upholding ethical standards and making tough, principled decisions, even when it's difficult or unpopular.
- **Decisiveness**: The ability to make firm decisions promptly, even in the face of incomplete information or uncertainty.

- **Risk Management**: Understanding and managing risks effectively, balancing bold initiatives with strategic foresight and preparation.

Practical Ways to Foster Courage and Bravery in Strategy

- **Encourage a Culture of Innovation**: Promote an organisational culture that values creativity and innovation, where taking calculated risks is encouraged and supported.
- **Provide Support and Resources**: Equip leaders and teams with the necessary tools, resources, and training to make courageous decisions and take bold actions.
- **Lead by Example**: Demonstrate bravery and courage in leadership roles, setting a standard for others to follow.
- **Celebrate Bold Moves**: Recognise and reward initiatives that demonstrate courage, whether they succeed or fail, to reinforce the value of bravery in strategic pursuits.

In conclusion, courage and bravery are integral to good strategy. They empower leaders to make bold decisions, inspire their teams, uphold ethical standards, and navigate through uncertainties and challenges. By fostering these qualities, organisations can pursue innovative and transformative strategies that drive long-term success and resilience

SELF-AWARENESS

Self-awareness at the individual and organisational level is a fundamental requirement for the duo of Musashi and Sun Tzu. Others hint at its importance within different fundamentals, but none are as explicit as the Eastern strategic philosophers. I believe part of this is cultural in that 'face' and 'honour' were so important in these cultures that it was essential to mask and hide one's weaknesses. This might explain why Musashi and Sun Tzu implored their followers to be honest with themselves, even if they had to portray a different image to others. But we all wear a mask for others to a certain extent, so an analysis of why self-awareness is crucial for good strategy, is still very useful.

Self-awareness also helps organisations recognise their internal strengths and weaknesses. This understanding allows them to leverage strengths to gain a competitive advantage and address weaknesses to avoid potential pitfalls. Self-aware organisations are also able to set realistic and achievable goals based on a clear understanding of their capabilities and limitations. This ensures that strategic objectives are attainable and aligned with the organisation's true potential and not some pipedream, glorified image or narcissistic goal out of touch with reality. Brutally honest acknowledgement of strengths and weaknesses also helps organisations allocate resources more effectively. They can then engage in areas, where, they have a competitive advantage and can improve or mitigate the areas of weakness.

Self-awareness leads to more informed and objective decision-making. Organisations that understand their internal dynamics and external environment, can usher in strategic choices that are better suited to their scenario. Self-aware organisations are more adaptable because they are better equipped to recognise when the changes are needed. They can pivot strategies more effectively in response to internal and external changes.

Organisations that demonstrate self-awareness build trust and confidence among stakeholders, including employees, investors, and customers. Transparency about strengths and areas for improvement fosters credibility and reliability. Self-awareness ignites alignment and cohesion within the organisation itself. When everyone understands the organisation's true capabilities and challenges, it creates a unified direction and purpose. Self-awareness helps organisations identify opportunities that align with their strengths and avoid threats that exploit their weaknesses. This strategic alignment with the external environment is critical for success.

Self-aware organisations are committed to continuous improvement and enhancement of function and standards. They regularly assess and reflect on their performance, learn from mistakes, and make necessary adjustments to their strategy. Understanding the organisational culture and its impact on strategy execution is crucial. Self-aware organisations ensure that their strategies are compatible with their cultural values and practices, enhancing the likelihood of successful implementation.

In summation, self-awareness is essential as a component for good strategy, as it enables organisations to comprehend their internal and external environment comprehensively, make informed decisions, allocate resources effectively, and remain adaptable and aligned with their goals. This leads to more realistic, achievable, and sustainable strategic outcomes

INNOVATION AND CREATIVITY

While only the Sangam Poems list innovation and creativity as fundamental criteria in their own right, it is important to note that all the other texts incorporate innovation and creativity as an integral part of other fundamentals. Innovation and creativity are essential for strategy because they enable organisations to differentiate themselves, adapt to changing environments, solve complex problems, and drive long-term growth and success. Here's why these elements are so crucial:

Differentiation and Competitive Advantage. Innovation and creativity allow organisations to develop unique products, services, and business models that set them apart from competitors. Differentiation through creative solutions can lead to a significant competitive advantage, attracting customers and increasing market share.

Adaptation to Change. The business environment is constantly evolving due to technological advancements, market dynamics, and consumer preferences. Creativity enables organisations to anticipate and adapt to these changes by developing innovative strategies that address emerging trends and challenges.

Problem-Solving. Complex problems often require novel and apt solutions. Creativity fosters out-of-the-box thinking, allowing organisations to tackle issues in unique and effective ways. Innovative problem-solving can lead to breakthroughs that improve efficiency, reduce costs, and enhance overall performance.

Driving Growth and Expansion. Innovation is a key driver of growth. By continuously creating new products, services, and processes, organisations can open up new revenue streams, enter new markets, and expand their customer base. Creativity fuels this continuous cycle of development and expansion.

Enhancing Customer Experience. Creative strategies can prominently enhance and augment customer experience by addressing their needs and desires in innovative and creative ways. This can lead to increased customer satisfaction, loyalty, and advocacy, which are crucial for long-term success.

Sustaining Long-Term Success. In a highly competitive and fast-changing market, sustained innovation is necessary to remain relevant. Organisations that consistently invest in creativity and innovation are better positioned to navigate uncertainties and maintain their leadership position over the long term.

Cultural Transformation. A culture of innovation and creativity encourages employees to think differently, take risks, and collaborate. This cultural shift can lead to a more dynamic, engaged, and motivated workforce, driving overall organisational performance and resilience.

Key Components of Innovation and Creativity in Strategy:

- **Visionary Leadership**: Leaders who champion creativity and innovation set a clear vision that encourages and inspires their teams to think differently.
- **Organisational Culture**: A culture that values and rewards creative thinking, risk-taking, and continuous learning fosters an environment where innovation can thrive.
- **Cross-Functional Collaboration**: Encouraging collaboration across different departments and disciplines can lead to the exchange of diverse ideas and perspectives, sparking creativity.
- **Investment in R&D**: Allocating resources to research and development is essential for exploring new ideas, technologies, and processes that drive innovation.
- **Customer-Centric Approach**: Understanding, comprehending and anticipating customer needs through innovative solutions ensures that the organisation remains relevant and competitive.

Practical Approaches to Foster Innovation and Creativity

- **Encourage Brainstorming Sessions**: Regular brainstorming sessions can generate a wealth of creative ideas and solutions.
- **Adopt Agile Methodologies**: Agile practices promote iterative

development and continuous improvement, fostering an environment of innovation.

- **Provide Innovation Incentives**: Offering incentives and recognition for innovative ideas and successful implementations can motivate employees to contribute creatively.
- **Embrace Failure as a Learning Opportunity**: Creating a safe space where failure is viewed as a step toward innovation encourages experimentation and risk-taking.
- **Stay Informed About Trends**: Keeping up with industry trends, technological advancements, and market shifts helps identify opportunities for innovation.

In sum, innovation and creativity are the inseparable vitals for formulating and executing effective strategies. They drive differentiation, adaptation, growth, and customer satisfaction, ensuring that organisations can thrive in competitive and ever-changing environments. By fostering a culture that values and nurtures these qualities, organisations can achieve sustained success and resilience.

SUMMARY

It is striking just how similar strategic fundamentals appear to be across multiple philosophies. In fact, there are just twelve fundamentals that strategic leaders need to achieve for successful strategy. Practitioners would be very wise to use these as a checklist or handrail when tackling a complex problem or situation that requires a strategy. But a word of caution is required. While there may only be twelve fundamentals that need to be achieved, there are an infinite number of ways to deliver each of those fundamentals. Developing and adapting these ways are where the skill, art and science of strategy lies.

The fact that the six ancient strategic texts are still relevant today says much about the insights and wisdom of these ancient philosophers. Some of the selected writings and chosen literature on strategy are over 3000 years old and are just being developed into doctrine and guides for modern defence forces in various regions of the world. There is still much to learn from ancient strategies that is of relevance to the contemporary world.

Quick Reference Guide

It could take a lifetime to study the detail of the six great strategic philosophies analysed in this book. Most leaders in the modern world have not got the time to do this. This quick reference guide is designed to help strategists who understand the basic tenets of the ancient wisdom and just need a handy check list as a reminder of the most important elements.

Musashi – A Summary

Musashi's "*The Book of Five Rings*" provides advice and insights on how to create a strategic mindset. Musashi's key tenets are below.

- Musashi advocated for a strategic mindset rather than a defined methodology for tackling complex problems.
- He was of the view that every complex problem was completely unique and therefore could not be solved with templates, rules, toolsets, or procedures.
- Musashi stated that rigid approaches stifle innovation, creativity, and initiative but also give adversaries ample opportunity to guess what is coming next and take appropriate pre-emptive action or enable effective countermeasures.
- Earth (*Chi*). Musashi associates Earth with the foundation of strategy. This involves understanding the terrain, the environment, the politics, potential adversaries, allies, neutrals, and the wider situation. It is about knowing your own strengths and weaknesses and adapting your approach accordingly.
- Water (*Sui*). Water symbolises adaptability and fluidity. Musashi urges practitioners to be flexible in their strategies, capable of flowing around or over obstacles rather than confronting them

directly. Water teaches the importance of being receptive to change and adjusting tactics based on the evolving circumstances.

- Fire (*Ka*). Fire represents the intensity and decisiveness required in strategic actions. Musashi underlines the need to seize opportunities and act with commitment. The strategic concept of Fire involves exploiting weaknesses in the opponent's position and maintaining relentless pressure when the time is right.
- Wind (*Fu*). Wind signifies the ability to read and respond to the intentions of the opponent. Musashi encourages a deep understanding of human nature and the capacity to anticipate and counteract the strategies of others. The strategic concept of Wind involves psychological warfare and deception. To achieve Wind (*Fu*), the strategist must build a comprehensive understanding of human personality types and how they act under different pressures and in different situations.
- Void (*Ku*). Musashi described this as a state of emptiness where the mind is clear, allowing for intuitive and spontaneous action. The concept of the Void emphasises the importance of mastering oneself to achieve strategic excellence. Musashi encourages the practitioner to find this void, where there is no fixed form or limitation. It is a state of emptiness that allows for limitless possibilities. In the today's world, it means seeking innovative new ideas and ways of doing business and not being constrained by convention, narrow mindedness, or a lack of imagination and innovation.

From these tenets, a 5-step process can be applied to improve one's strategic mindset:

Step 1: Continually Improve Your Knowledge and Understanding of the Earth (Chi)

- Cultivate Curiosity.
- Read Widely.
- Stay Informed.
- Engage in Critical Thinking.

- Travel and Explore.
- Connect with People.
- Learn from History.
- Educate Yourself.
- Be Open-Minded.
- Engage in Discussions and Debates
- Seek Different Perspectives.
- Reflect on Your Own Beliefs.
- Stay Humble.

Step 2: Embrace the Void (Ku) at Least Once per Day to Improve Ingenuity and Innovation

- Diversify Your Experiences.
- Encourage a Growth Mindset.
- Challenge Assumptions.
- Embrace Failure as a Learning Opportunity.
- Develop a Creative Environment.
- Practice Mindfulness and Reflection.
- Collaborate and Brainstorm.
- Set Aside Dedicated Time for Creativity.
- Use Creative Techniques.
- Seek Inspiration from Different Disciplines.
- Read and Consume Creatively.
- Develop a Creative Ritual.
- Continuous Learning.
- Experiment and Iterate.

Step 3: Improve Your Understanding of People to Achieve Expertise in Wind (Fu)

- Practice Active Listening.
- Observe Non-Verbal Cues.

- Ask Open-Ended Questions.
- Cultivate Empathy.
- Be Mindful of Cultural Differences.
- Read Books on Psychology and Human Behaviour.
- Take Courses or Attend Workshops.
- Build Self-Awareness.
- Seek Diverse Experiences.
- Practice Patience.
- Consider Individual Differences.
- Reflect on Your Interactions.

Step 4: Develop Techniques for Dealing with Immovable Obstacles so Your Strategy can Flow Like Water (Sui)

- Assess the Situation.
- Seek Understanding.
- Build Relationships.
- Find Common Ground.
- Present Alternatives.
- Highlight Consequences.
- Engage Leadership Support.
- Leverage Data and Evidence.
- Build a Coalition.
- Negotiate and Compromise.
- Develop Patience and Persistence.
- Adapt to the Environment.
- Seek External Support.
- Know When to Let Go.

Step 5: Learn When to Strike with Fire (Ka) to Gain and Maintain the Initiative

- Define Clear Objectives.
- Gather Information.
- Set Priorities.
- Develop a Plan.
- Take Swift and Decisive Action.
- Anticipate and Mitigate Risks.
- Engage Stakeholders.
- Be Assertive in Communication.
- Leverage Resources Effectively.
- Monitor Progress Actively.
- Adaptability and Flexibility.
- Demonstrate Tenacity.
- Celebrate Small Wins.
- Seek Feedback and Continuous Improvement.
- Reflect and Learn.

THE *MAHABHARATA* – A SUMMARY

The *Mahabharata* is a multifaceted epic that weaves together mythology, philosophy, and history to create a rich tapestry of human experience. It includes several strategic concepts:

- *Dharma* (Righteousness).
- Strategic Planning and Vision.
- Alliance Building.
- Understanding the Enemy
- Adaptability and Flexibility.
- Deception and Diplomacy.
- Leadership and Decision-Making.
- The Role of Wisdom and Counsel.

- The Influence of Fate and Destiny.
- War Ethics and Conduct.

From these concepts a 10-step process to assist with developing a strategic mindset can be developed:

Step 1: Determine Your Personal Values

- Self-Reflection.
- Identify Core Values.
- Assess Priorities.
- Seek Feedback.
- Re-evaluate Over Time.

Step 2: Practice Describing End States in Terms of Feelings and Perceptions

- Identify Desired Emotions.
- Visualise the Impact.
- Use Descriptive Language.
- Connect to Values and Purpose.
- Engage Stakeholders.

Step 3: Determine the Types of People and Organisations You Will Work With

- Values Alignment.
- Reputation and Track Record.
- Communication.
- Expertise and Experience.
- Integrity and Trustworthiness.
- Collaborative Approach.
- Cultural Fit.
- Growth and Development.

- Responsiveness and Adaptability.
- Conflict Resolution Skills.
- Financial Stability.
- Shared Vision and Goals.

Step 4: Learn How to Read People and Situations

- Observe Nonverbal Cues.
- Listen Actively.
- Watch for Patterns.
- Consider Context.
- Pay Attention to Tone.
- Empathise.
- Ask Open-Ended Questions.
- Stay Curious.

Step 5: Demonstrate Cerebral Flexibility

- Expose Yourself to New Experiences.
- Challenge Your Beliefs.
- Practice Mindfulness.
- Engage in Critical Thinking.
- Read Widely.
- Learn a New Language.
- Collaborate with Others.
- Embrace Uncertainty.
- Practice Perspective-Taking.

Step 6: Practice Deception and Diplomacy

- Use Deception Sparingly.
- Maintain Ethical Boundaries.
- Consider Alternative Strategies.
- Uphold Transparency.

- Reflect on Long-Term Impact.

Step 7: Show Strong Leadership and Decision-Making Skills.

- Critical Thinking.
- Emotional Intelligence.
- Decisiveness.
- Adaptability.
- Communication Skills.
- Ethical Judgment.

Step 8: Seek Out Wisdom and Counsel

- Seek Diverse Experiences.
- Reflect on Life Lessons.
- Cultivate Self-Awareness.
- Practice Empathy.
- Embrace Lifelong Learning.
- Practice Patience and Thoughtfulness.
- Develop Critical Thinking Skills.
- Observe and Learn from Others.
- Listen Actively.
- Ask Open-Ended Questions.
- Offer Thoughtful Advice.
- Be Honest and Constructive.
- Respect Autonomy.
- Encourage Reflection.
- Be Humble.

Step 9: Prepare for the Unexpected

- Assess Risks.
- Create Contingency Plans.
- Build a Support Network.

- Stay Informed.
- Develop a Flexible Mindset.
- Hone Problem-Solving Skills.
- Maintain Physical and Mental Well-Being.
- Practice Financial Preparedness.

Step 10: Learn How to Act with Moral Courage.

- Clarify Your Values.
- Practice Self-Reflection.
- Educate Yourself.
- Cultivate Empathy.
- Surround Yourself with Support.
- Start with Small Acts.
- Take Calculated Risks.
- Prepare for Opposition.

KAUTILYA – A SUMMARY

Kautilya was an ancient Indian scholar, strategist, and philosopher who is best known for his seminal work on statecraft and political strategy, the *Arthashastra*. He one of the most influential figures in Indian political thought. His philosophy on adopting a strategic approach consisted of:

- The Strategic Leader – *Vijigishu*.
- Strategic Leadership Characteristics – *Svamisampad*.
- The Spiritual End State or *Yogakshema*.
- Diplomatic, Silent, Covert and Open Warfare.
- The Four Approaches – *Upayas*.
- The Tools of Foreign Policy – *Sadgunya*.
- Understanding the Enemy – The *Mandala* Analysis.

From his teachings in the Arthashastra, it is possible to develop a Kautilyan guide for adopting a strategic approach:

Step 1: Understand The Strategic Context. Ask the following questions:

- What is at stake and why does it matter?
- How does it affect our national interests?
- Who is opposed to our national interests and why?
- Is it a priority for us to change the situation, if so where does it sit?
- What are the government's current policy objectives over this issue?
- Is there a critical timeline associated with the issue?
- What needs to change?
- What does 'good enough' look like?
- What is the general sense of direction on this issue? Will it get worse if we do nothing? Will it negatively affect other areas? Will inaction damage our reputation or future options?
- Where are our knowledge gaps? What don't we know about the issue?

Step 2: Select the Vijigishu and Supporting Officials to Build the Strategy Team. Look for the following:

- Qualities that Inspire Confidence in Others.
- Approachability.
- Piety.
- Truthfulness.
- Ability to Understand Complex Issues.
- Ability to Think.
- Bravery and Moral Courage.
- Quickness of Decision.
- Strength of Mind.
- Eloquence and Charisma.
- Boldness.
- Good Memory.

Step 3: Define the Yogakshema. Consider feelings and perceptions such as:

- Material Prosperity.
- Security and Safety.
- Access to Resources.
- Social Welfare.
- Harmony and Justice.
- Quality of Life.
- Community Well-Being.
- Long-Term Sustainability.
- Contentment and Happiness.
- Resilience and Adaptability.
- Trust and Confidence.
- Satisfaction and Loyalty.
- Respect and Reputation.
- Empowerment and Engagement.
- Safety and Well-being.
- Optimism and Enthusiasm.
- Recognition and Value.
- Alignment with Values and Purpose.
- Clarity and Transparency.

Step 4: The Mandala Analysis. Identify and analyse stakeholders and entities:

- *Ari*. These are external 'hostile' states closest to the crisis or issue.
- *Mitra*. These are external 'friendly' states closest to the crisis or issue.
- *Arimitra*. Allies of external hostile states.
- *Mitramitra*. Non-state friendly supporters.
- *Arimitramitra*. Non-state supporters of hostile states.

- *Parashanigraha*. Overt internal opposition.
- *Aakranda*. Overt internal champions.
- *Parashanigrahasara*. Covert internal opposition.
- *Akrandasara*. Covert supporters of overt internal champions.

Step 5: ***Identify Entity Weak Points.*** Some areas to analyse.

- Internal divisions.
- Financial position.
- Capability gaps.
- Unfavourable terrain.
- Poor logistics.
- Inexperience and poor training.
- Toxic leadership.
- Over-centralised decision making.
- Low morale.
- Intelligence gathering and analytical deficiencies.
- Inferior equipment.

Step 6: ***Determine the Approaches.*** Consider the four warfare methodologies:

- Diplomatic.
- Silent.
- Covert.
- Open.

Step 7: ***Consider the Upayas and Sadgunyas and How They Could be Applied Against the Weak Points of the Mandala.***

- *Sama* (conciliation).
- *Dana* (gifts).
- *Bheda* (disruption or dissension).

- *Danda* (force).
- *Samdhi* (peace).
- *Vigraha* (war).
- *Asana* (staying quiet or neutrality).
- *Yana* (marching or preparing for war).
- *Samsraya* (seeking shelter or alliances).
- *Dvaidhibhava* (dual policy).

Step 8: Determine the Resources Available. Some common considerations.

- Money.
- Personnel.
- Equipment.
- Time.
- Supplies.
- Infrastructure.
- Communication systems.
- Industrial capacity.

Step 9: Develop Options.

- High risk.
- Medium risk.
- Low risk.
- Cheap.
- Expensive.

Step 10: Consider Calamities (Risks). Some points to consider:

- Weather and natural disasters.
- Political instability.
- Loss of key personnel.
- Cyber-attack.

- Scandal or PR disaster.
- Supply chain disruption.
- Market collapse or economic downturn.
- Unexpected legal action.
- Public disorder or insecurity.

Step 11: Decide on an Option, Refine and Take Action.

- Wargame.
- Scenario planning.
- Simulation.
- Pilot schemes and small-scale tests.
- Issue clear direction and commit.

Step 12: Test and Adjust. Adaptation will be essential.

THE *PURANANURU* – A SUMMARY

The *Purananuru* is a remarkable work that offers a unique glimpse into the lives, values, and beliefs of ancient Tamil society. It covers key subjects such as:

- Leadership and Governance.
- Diplomacy and Alliances.
- Ethics and Virtue.
- Adaptability and Resilience.
- Cultural Soft Power.
- Social Cohesion and Unity.
- Environmental Awareness.
- Innovation and Creativity.
- Courage and Bravery.

It is possible to derive a 10-step process from the *Purananuru* that can assist with adopting a strategic approach within one's personal life or an organisation. The steps are:

Step 1: Ensure Your Strategy Focuses on People.

- Understand the Needs and Goals of People.
- Promote Inclusivity and Diversity.
- Align Strategy with Values and Culture.
- Encourage Collaboration and Participation.
- Focus on Employee and Stakeholder Well-being.
- Create Clear Communication Channels.
- Adaptability and Flexibility.
- Empowerment and Autonomy.
- Consider Ethical and Social Responsibility.
- Measure Success and Impact.

Step 2: Always Attempt Diplomacy First and Reach Out to Potential Partners or Allies.

- Effective Communication.
- Negotiation and Mediation.
- Cultural Awareness and Sensitivity.
- Conflict Resolution and Peacebuilding.
- Confidentiality and Discretion.
- Strategic Thinking and Analysis.
- Relationship Building.
- Adherence to International Law and Norms.
- Patience and Persistence.
- Adaptability and Resilience.
- Ethical Conduct.
- Public Diplomacy.

Step 3: Power and Strength Flow from Prosperity. Prioritise Economic Issues in your Strategy.

- Assess the Economic Landscape.

- Identify Key Economic Objectives.
- Allocate Resources Effectively.
- Monitor Cash Flow and Profit Margins.
- Optimise Operational Efficiency.
- Invest in Innovation and Growth.
- Mitigate Economic Risks.
- Establish Partnerships and Collaborations.
- Stay Informed and Adapt.
- Measure Economic Impact and Outcomes.

Step 4: Ensure your Strategy Aligns with your Values.

- Identify Core Values.
- Assess Current Practices.
- Set Clear Objectives.
- Incorporate Values into Decision-Making.
- Communicate and Collaborate.
- Evaluate and Adjust.
- Lead by Example.
- Seek Feedback and Reflection.
- Stay Informed and Adaptable.
- Be Consistent.

Step 5: Stay Flexible and be Prepared to Adapt and Improvise.

- Cultivate a Flexible Mindset.
- Stay Calm and Focused.
- Gather Information and Assess the Situation.
- Leverage Previous Experience.
- Break Down the Problem.
- Be Resourceful and Creative.
- Communicate Effectively.

- Embrace Collaboration and Teamwork.
- Be Willing to Experiment.
- Stay Positive and Resilient.
- Reassess and Adjust as Needed.
- Learn from the Experience.

Step 6: Make your Vision or Offer Attractive to Stakeholders. Carrots Work Better than Sticks.

- Craft a Compelling Narrative.
- Align with Stakeholders' Interests.
- Involve Stakeholders in the Development Process.
- Set Clear, Achievable Goals.
- Demonstrate a Path to Success.
- Showcase Tangible Benefits and Impact.
- Communicate Regularly and Transparently.
- Demonstrate Leadership Commitment.
- Be Adaptive and Responsive.
- Celebrate Milestones and Achievements.

Step 7: Ensure Solidarity and Cohesion at Home.

- Establish a Clear Vision and Shared Goals.
- Promote Open Communication.
- Foster a Positive Organisational Culture.
- Encourage Collaboration and Teamwork.
- Provide Opportunities for Professional Growth.
- Set Clear Expectations and Accountability.
- Celebrate Achievements and Milestones.
- Address Conflicts Promptly and Fairly.
- Encourage Employee Involvement in Decision-Making.
- Lead by Example.

Step 8: Protect the Environment.

- Understand the Environmental Impact.
- Set Clear Environmental Goals.
- Incorporate Sustainable Practices.
- Follow Environmental Regulations and Standards.
- Promote a Culture of Environmental Awareness.
- Engage Stakeholders.
- Monitor and Measure Progress.
- Adopt Green Innovation and Technology.
- Communicate and Report.
- Be Adaptable and Open to Change.

Step 9: Be Innovative and Creative.

- Encourage Open-Mindedness.
- Create a Safe Environment for Experimentation.
- Promote Cross-Disciplinary Collaboration.
- Provide Time and Resources for Exploration.
- Encourage Continuous Learning.
- Foster a Culture of Feedback and Reflection.
- Embrace Iterative Processes.
- Provide Opportunities for Networking.
- Set Clear Goals and Challenges.
- Lead by Example.

Step 10: Be Prepared for Extreme Hardship and Sacrifice.

- Cultivate a Resilient Mindset.
- Establish a Support Network.
- Create a Contingency Plan.
- Develop Financial Reserves.
- Build Skills and Knowledge.

- Prioritise Health and Well-being.
- Set Realistic Expectations.
- Embrace Change and Uncertainty.
- Stay Committed to Your Values.
- Seek Professional Help if Needed.

SUN TZU – A SUMMARY

"The Art of War" by Sun Tzu offers a wealth of strategic concepts that extend beyond the realm of military tactics. Its principles can be applied to various aspects of life where strategy and decision-making are crucial. The focus on knowledge, adaptability, deception, and holistic understanding of the factors influencing success continues to make "The Art of War" a timeless guide for strategic thinking.

The Fundamentals of Sun Tzu's Teachings are:

- Preparation and Planning.
- Adaptability and Flexibility.
- Deception and Indirect Approach.
- Know Yourself and Know the Enemy.
- The Importance of Timing.
- Winning Without Fighting.
- Leadership and Discipline.

The Five Factors:

- The Way.
- Heaven.
- Earth.
- The Commander.
- Method and Discipline.

From these fundamentals, a strategic toolset based on Sun Tzu's Art of War can be formulated:

Step 1: ***The Way. Define the Desired Strategic Outcome and Create a Compelling Narrative on Why the Organisation Must Prevail and How it Will Achieve Success.***

- Understand the Organisation's Vision and Mission.
- Identify Key Objectives.
- Assess the Competitive Landscape.
- Determine Key Performance Indicators (KPIs).
- Set Priorities.
- Craft a Clear and Concise Message.
- Highlight the Importance of the Outcome.
- Connect to Values and Beliefs.
- Inspire and Motivate.
- Explain the Path to Success.
- Encourage Participation and Collaboration.
- Adapt the Narrative for Different Audiences.
- Be Honest and Transparent.

Step 2: ***Know Yourself, Know Your Enemy. Compare Strengths, and Weaknesses to Identify Where You and the Enemy Hold a Critical Advantage.***

- Evaluate Your Capabilities.
- Assess Your Strategic Goals.
- Review Past Performance.
- Gather Feedback.
- Research Your Competitors.
- Assess Their Capabilities.
- Analyse Their Strategies.
- Identify Key Threats and Opportunities.
- Create a SWOT Analysis.
- Identify Critical Advantages.

- Recognise Areas of Vulnerability.
- Determine Points of Leverage.
- Highlight Unique Differentiators.
- Exploit Market Gaps.
- Plan Targeted Strategies.
- Adapt to Changing Circumstances.

Step 3: Heaven and Earth. Determine the Type of Ground(s) on Which the Battles will Take Place.

- Conduct a Thorough Assessment.
- Plan Strategically.
- Monitor and Adjust.
- Make Informed Decisions.

Step 4: The Commander.

- Know Your People.
- Build Trust and Loyalty.
- Make Decisive and Informed Decisions.
- Communicate Clearly and Consistently.
- Lead by Example.
- Foster a Cohesive Team.
- Adaptability and Flexibility.
- Monitor and Evaluate.
- Motivate and Inspire.
- Recognise and reward.

Step 5: Method and Discipline.

- Organise Resources Efficiently.
- Standardise Procedures.
- Allocate Roles and Responsibilities.
- Plan Logistically.

- Monitor Performance.
- Enforce Clear Expectations.
- Lead by Example.
- Maintain Consistency.
- Train and Develop Your Team.
- Foster a Culture of Respect.
- Adapt and Improve.

Step 6: Adaptability and Flexibility.

- Be Open to Change.
- Stay Informed.
- Plan for Contingencies.
- Be Proactive, Not Reactive.
- Adapt Your Strategies.
- Empower Your Team.
- Foster a Learning Culture.
- Embrace Diversity.
- Stay Calm Under Pressure.
- Learn from Experience.

Step 7: Deception and Misdirection.

- Conceal Your Intentions.
- Create Diversions.
- Manipulate Perceptions:
- Use Surprise.
- Know When to Show Weakness.
- Leverage Timing.
- Exploit Opponents' Biases.
- Keep Your Options Open.
- Know When to Use Deception.

- Monitor Outcomes.

Step 8: Winning Without Fighting.

- Know Yourself and Your Opponent.
- Choose Your Battles Wisely.
- Leverage Intelligence and Information.
- Use Diplomacy and Negotiation.
- Manipulate Perceptions.
- Create Distractions and Diversions.
- Exhaust Your Opponent.
- Use Non-Confrontational Means.
- Know When to Retreat.
- Maximise Your Advantages.

Step 9: Speed and Timing.

- Plan and Prepare.
- Be Decisive.
- Recognise the Right Moment.
- Streamline Processes.
- Maintain Flexibility.
- Coordinate with Your Team.
- Leverage Surprise.
- Anticipate Opponents' Actions.
- Prioritise Key Objectives.
- Monitor Outcomes.

Step 10: Leadership and Morale.

- Lead by Example.
- Communicate Clearly.
- Be Decisive.
- Empower Your Team.

- Recognise and Reward Achievements.
- Foster a Collaborative Culture.
- Adapt to Changing Situations.
- Create a Positive Work Environment.
- Provide Clear Vision and Purpose.
- Offer Training and Development.
- Show Empathy and Support.
- Encourage Open Communication.
- Set Achievable Goals.
- Promote Work-Life Balance.

Commentaries on the Gallic War – A Summary

Julius Caesar's "Commentarii de Bello Gallico" (Commentaries on the Gallic War) is a first-hand account of his campaigns in Gaul between 58 and 50 BCE. The text provides detailed descriptions of his military strategies, tactics, and leadership style.

The Key Strategic Lessons from the Campaigns of Julius Caesar are:

- Effective Leadership.
- Preparation and Planning.
- Divide and Conquer.
- Psychological Warfare.
- Diplomacy, Partnerships and Alliances.
- Logistics and Supply Lines.
- Speed and Mobility.
- Calculated Risk Taking.
- Decisive Actions.
- Adaptability and Flexibility.

From these key strategic lessons, it is possible to produce a ten-step strategic toolset:

Step 1: Appoint a Charismatic Leader.

- Define the Role and Expectations.
- Identify Key Qualities.
- Evaluate Past Performance.
- Conduct Interviews.
- Gather Feedback.
- Look for Alignment with Organisational Values.
- Consider a Trial Period.
- Assess Charismatic Leadership Potential.
- Offer Support and Development.
- Monitor Performance and Impact.

Step 2: Maintain Morale and Discipline.

- Provide Strong Leadership.
- Create a Positive Work Environment.
- Communicate Effectively.
- Set Clear Expectations.
- Offer Opportunities for Growth.
- Recognise and Reward Achievement.
- Provide Work-Life Balance.
- Address Issues Promptly.
- Promote Team Building.
- Lead by Example.
- Encourage Employee Engagement.
- Monitor and Evaluate.

Step 3: Gather Timely and Accurate Intelligence.

- Define Intelligence Objectives.
- Use Multiple Sources.
- Monitor Key Indicators.

- Analyse Patterns and Trends.
- Utilise Intelligence Analysis Techniques.
- Collaborate with Allies.
- Stay Updated.
- Verify and Cross-Check Information.
- Protect Your Own Intelligence Sources.
- Integrate Intelligence with Strategic Planning.

Step 4: Identify Fault Lines in the Adversaries' Organisation and then Divide and Conquer.

- Conduct a Comprehensive Analysis.
- Identify Key Areas of Vulnerability.
- Monitor Competitor Behaviour.
- Leverage Competitive Intelligence.
- Assess Relationships and Alliances.
- Evaluate Customer Perception.
- Formulate a Divide-and-Conquer Strategy.
- Targeting specific market segments.
- Offering superior products or services.
- Building alliances with their partners or customers.
- Exploiting internal divisions.
- Execute with Caution.

Step 5: Intimidate the Adversary.

- Project Strength and Confidence.
- Display Superior Capabilities.
- Control the Narrative.
- Demonstrate Preparedness.
- Leverage Intelligence.
- Exploit Psychological Warfare.

- Show Determination and Persistence.
- Utilise Legal and Ethical Means.
- Strengthen Your Position.
- Control Access and Resources.
- Engage in Strategic Signalling.
- Focus on Reputation Management.

Step 6: Identify Partners and Allies.

- Define Your Objectives.
- Research Potential Partners.
- Assess Compatibility.
- Review Capabilities and Strengths.
- Evaluate Past Performance.
- Check References.
- Analyse Strategic Fit.
- Consider Long-Term Potential.
- Review Legal and Ethical Considerations.
- Assess Communication and Trust.
- Negotiate Terms and Expectations.
- Look for Complementary Networks.
- Pilot the Partnership.

Step 7: Ensure Adequate Resources and Logistics.

- Identify Resource Requirements.
- Assess Availability and Accessibility.
- Create a Detailed Budget.
- Establish Relationships with Suppliers.
- Plan for Contingencies.
- Optimise Supply Chain and Logistics.
- Monitor and Track Resources.

- Allocate Resources Strategically.
- Review and Adjust Regularly.
- Leverage Technology.
- Engage in Risk Management.
- Collaborate with Stakeholders.
- Ensure Regulatory Compliance.

Step 8: Act More Quickly Than the Adversary.

- Streamline Decision-Making.
- Prepare in Advance.
- Develop Situational Awareness.
- Leverage Technology.
- Empower Your Team.
- Practice and Train.
- Foster a Proactive Mindset.
- Maintain Flexibility.
- Focus on Key Priorities.
- Cultivate Strong Communication.
- Monitor and Evaluate Continuously.
- Stay Informed.
- Leverage Relationships and Networks.

Step 9: Determine the Decisive Actions Required for Success.

- Set Clear Objectives.
- Conduct a SWOT Analysis.
- Prioritise Initiatives.
- Identify Key Performance Indicators (KPIs).
- Analyse Competitive Landscape.
- Consider Resource Allocation.
- Develop Action Plans.

- Leverage Data and Insights.
- Plan for Contingencies.
- Collaborate and Communicate.
- Monitor and Adjust.
- Focus on Execution.

Step 10: Prepare and Resource for the Unexpected.

- Conduct Risk Assessments.
- Develop Contingency Plans.
- Maintain Emergency Reserves.
- Diversify Supply Chains.
- Build Redundancy.
- Foster a Culture of Adaptability.
- Invest in Training and Preparedness.
- Implement Robust Communication Channels.
- Monitor and Evaluate Continuously.
- Leverage Technology and Data.
- Collaborate with Partners and Allies.
- Stay Informed on Regulations and Compliance.
- Document Processes and Knowledge.
- Create a Crisis Management Team.
- Conduct Regular Reviews and Updates.

Bibliography

Betts, Richard K. "The Illusion of Strategy." *International Security*, Vol. 25, No. 2 (Fall 2000), 5–50.

Boesche, Roger. *The First Great Political Realist: Kautilya and His Arthashastra*. London, Lexington Books, 2002.

Caesar, Julius. (Translated by Carolyn Hammond). *The Gallic War.* Oxford: Oxford University Press, 1996.

Clausewitz, Carl von. *On War*, ed. and trans. Michael Howard and Peter Paret, ind. ed. Princeton: Princeton University Press, 1984.

Defence Academy of the United Kingdom. *Royal College of Defence Studies. Getting Strategy Right (Enough)*. London: RCDS, 2017./

Dixon, Norman F. *On the Psychology of Military Incompetence*. London: Futura Publications, 1985.

Dobelli R. *The Art of Thinking Clearly*. London: Sceptre, 2013.

Furnham, Adrian. *The Psychology of Behaviour at Work: The Individual in the Organisation*. Hove: Psychology Press, 2011.

Gray, Colin S. "Why Strategy is Difficult." *Joint Forces Quarterly,* (Summer 1999).

Harvard Business Review. "Execution is a People Problem, Not a Strategy Problem." Accessed 30 Mar 18. https://hbr.org/2017/01/execution-is-a-people-problem-not-a-strategy-problem.

Harvard Business Review. "Why Strategy Execution Unravels and What to do About it." Accessed 30 Mar 18.https://hbr.org/2015/03/why-strategy-execution-unravelsand-what-to-do-about-it.

Herbert, Vaidehi. *Purunanuru.* Digital Maxim LLC, 2015.

Hoffman, Frank. "Grand Strategy: The Fundamental Considerations," *Orbis* (Fall 2014).

Hrebiniak, Lawrence G. *Making Strategy Work: Leading Effective Execution and Change*. New Jersey: FT Press, 2013.

Janis, Irving Lester. *Groupthink*. Michigan: Houghton Mifflin, 1982.

Johnson, Dominic P. *Overconfidence and War*. Cambridge, MA: Harvard University Press, 2009.

Kahneman, Daniel. *Thinking, Fast and Slow*. London: Macmillan, 2011.

Kautilya's Arthashastra, Arthashastra_of_Chaṇakya_-_English.pdf (csboa.com) translated into English by R. Shamasastry, accessed 18 Feb 20.

Kautilya's Arthashastra, translated by R P Kangle, (Delhi: Motilal Banarsidass, 2014).

Kissinger, Henry. *World Order: Reflections on the Character of Nations and the Course of History,* USA: Penguin, 2015.

Matlary, Janne Haaland and Johnson, Rob (Eds), *Military Strategy in the Twenty-First Century: The Challenge for NATO*. (London: Hurst & Company, 2020).

Mlodinow, Leonard. *Elastic: Flexible Thinking in a Constantly Changing World*. London: Allen Lane, 2018.

Musashi, Miyamato. (Edited by Kane. L, Wilder.K, Burrese. A, Smedley. W.) *Musashi's Dokkodo (The Way of Walking Alone)*. Stickman Publications, Inc, 2015.

Musashi, Miyamoto. (Translated by D.E. Tarver). *The Book of Five Rings*. Lincoln: iUniverse Star, 2002.

Owen, David. *The Hubris Syndrome: Bush, Blair and the Intoxication of Power*. London: Politico's Publishing, 2007.

Paranjpe, Shrikant, *India's Strategic Culture: The Making of National Security Policy* (India: Routledge, 2020).

Petraeus, David and Roberts, Andrew. *Conflict. The Evolution of Warfare from 1945 to Ukraine*. London: William Collins, 2023.

Porter, Patrick. "Why Britain Doesn't Do Grand Strategy." *The RUSI Journal 155*, No. 4 (2010).

Rumelt, Richard. *Good Strategy/Bad Strategy: The Difference and Why it Matters*. London: Profile Books, 2011.

Sloan, Julia. *Learning to Think Strategically 4th Edition*. Abingdon: Routledge, 2020.

Smith, John D. (Translator). *The Mahabharata*. London: Penguin Classics, 2009.

Starzl, Timothy W., and Krishna S. Dhir. "Strategic Planning 2300 Years Ago: The Strategy of Kautilya. "*Management International Review* 26, No. 4 (1986): 70-77. Accessed February 18, 2021. http://www.jstor.org/stable/40227819.

Sullivan, Gordon R. and Michael V. Harper. *Hope is not a Method*. New York: Broadway Books, 1998.

Sun, Tzu. Translated by Lionel Giles. *The Art of War*. New Delhi: Fingerprint Classics, 2024.

Taleb, Nassim Nicholas. *Skin in the Game: Hidden Asymmetries in Daily Life*. London: Penguin UK, 2018.

Tetlock, Philip E., and Dan Gardner. *Superforecasting: The Art and Science of Prediction*. London: Random House, 2016.

Walker, S.M., & Watkins, D. (2022). Toxic Leadership: Research and Cases (1st ed.). Routledge. https://doi.org/10.4324/9781003202462

Wolor CW, Ardiansyah A, Rofaida R, Nurkhin A, Rababah MA. Impact of Toxic Leadership on Employee Performance. Health Psychol Res. 2022 Dec 17; 10(4): 57551.